VOODOO
AND POWER

THE POLITICS
OF RELIGION IN
NEW ORLEANS
1881–1940

VOODOO

AND

POWER

KODI A. ROBERTS

LOUISIANA STATE UNIVERSITY PRESS   BATON ROUGE

Published by Louisiana State University Press
lsupress.org

Louisiana Paperback Edition, 2023

Designer: Michelle A. Neustrom
Typeface: Whitman

Library of Congress Cataloging-in-Publication Data
Roberts, Kodi A., 1979–
    Voodoo and power : the politics of religion in New Orleans,
1881–1940 / Kodi A. Roberts.
        pages cm
    Includes bibliographical references and index.
    ISBN 978-0-8071-6050-3 (cloth : alk. paper) — ISBN 978-0-
8071-6051-0 (pdf) — ISBN 978-0-8071-6052-7 (epub) — ISBN
978-0-8071-8172-0 (paperback)
    1. Vodou—Louisiana—New Orleans—History—19th century.
2. Vodou—Louisiana—New Orleans—History—20th century. 3.
African Americans—Religion. 4. New Orleans (La.)—Religious life
and customs. I. Title.
    BL2490.R585 2015
    299.6'750976335—dc23

                                                    2015019894

Dedicated to Erika and Gabriel

CONTENTS

ACKNOWLEDGMENTS

I would like to thank my advisor, Julie Saville, for taking me on as a student and making it possible for me to continue my graduate studies at the University of Chicago. I have little doubt that her meticulous reading of my material and no-nonsense advice has made this project possible. Without Dr. Saville's generosity and patience I don't know where I would be today. I would also like to thank Stephan Palmié, whose enthusiasm about this subject matter, unmitigated support for my research, and encyclopedic knowledge of religious practices throughout the African diaspora have changed the way I look at African American culture and inspired me to add something to the field that I hope is worthwhile. I would also like to thank Thomas Holt, whose early critiques of my writing and analysis changed the way I approached all potential subjects and who was kind enough to share his great experience in the field of African American history with me as I prepared my examination fields. A huge thank you also goes to Dr. Amy Dru Stanley, who allowed me to audit her class and eventually oversaw my study of American legal history. That work plays a small but extremely significant role in this book and has guided the projects I continue to work on today. Thank you to the research librarians at New Orleans Public Library, Northwestern State University in Louisiana, University of New Orleans, and Tulane University. Any historian knows that without these experts we would be lost in the sea of materials we find, if we were able to find relevant material at all. Thank you also to Dr. Dain Borges, who was good enough to read some of my work and gave me invaluable advice and comparative perspective to broaden my thinking about African American religious traditions. Thank you to Jim Grossman, who helped me add material from urban studies to my examination materials, and Dwight Hopkins and Curtis Evans from the University of Chicago Divinity School, both of whom also helped me think through various aspects of my work. Thank you to Carolyn Morrow Long, who was kind enough to read and critique some of the earliest work that went into this book, as well as Martha Ward and Ina Fandrich for meeting with me and offering advice on the subject matter. Thank you to D. Ryan Gray, who pointed me to integral secondary literature in anthropology that really changed the way I contextualized much of the conversation I hope to contribute to here. Thank you Thomas Adams and Steve Striffler, who gave me one of the first opportunities to showcase my work on this project. Thomas continues to introduce me to amazing scholars and opportunities that have enhanced the work in this book. Thank you to the entire staff at the Center for the Study of Race Politics and Culture at the University of Chicago: Trayce Matthews, Waldo Johnson, Ramon Gutiérrez, and Michael Dawson. The Race Center provided an environment that made it possible for me to present my ideas and talk them over with scholars in fields who may have never seen my work under normal circumstances. The Center's Dissertation Fellowship, as well as research dollars I was guided to by Dr. Gutiérrez, also provided the funding I needed to complete this project. Doctors Johnson and Dawson were also generous with their time in conversations that helped me to navigate the often confusing terrain of graduate study. Thank you to Trayce Matthews, who took a chance on a brash young graduate student by hiring me on at the Race Center and gave me advice and moral support for eight years that allowed me to make the most of the opportunities presented to me at CSRPC. Thank you to all my colleagues: Elizabeth Todd, Janette Gail, David Ferguson, Marcelle Medford Lee, Kafi Moragne, Nell Gabiam, SaunJuhi Verma, all of whom sat through workshops, commented on chapters, and listened to the presentations and mock job talks that helped me finally get this project to this phase. Thank you to editor Rand Dotson for his patience with me during the publication process as well as all the staff at LSU Press that worked with me on this book. Thank you also to William Cooper, who recommended this manuscript to LSU Press for publication.

VOODOO
AND POWER

VOODOO AS AMERICAN CULTURE

On February 3, 2013, the Mercedes-Benz Superdome, formerly the Louisiana Superdome, located in downtown New Orleans, played host to the National Football League's Super Bowl XLVII. The NFL's annual championship game has become a cultural phenomenon and a testament to American capitalism. Because the game is often the most watched television broadcast of the year, commercial time during the contest is frequently the most expensive of the year. Thus, watching not just the game but the commercials has become something of a pop-culture tradition on Super Bowl Sunday. In 2013 Anheuser-Busch, the largest brewing company in the United States, purchased commercial time during the game to run a pair of ads for its Bud Light brand highlighting the unique culture of the host city. The star of the ads was Voodoo and its promise of power.

The first of the two ads depicts two young men carrying a rather bulky reclining chair out of a large white house. The men then take the chair on a journey through the city of New Orleans. They load the seat onto one of the iconic streetcars that shuttle tourists through the historic Garden District. One of the game-day enthusiasts is then shown seated in the chair outside what we can infer is a convenience store on what the very distinct street sign tells us is Ursulines Avenue, where they pick up a six-pack of Bud Light and place it in the chair. The unmistakable stucco walls, green French doors, and low balconies place the store in the Vieux Carré, or French Quarter, the city's oldest neighborhood and tourist center. After the pit stop our would-be movers carry the chair past a train depot and a power plant to the wrought-iron gates of a mansion, where they give their recently purchased beer to a large gentleman in a dark sport coat and a Kangol hat in exchange for admittance. In a dark hall lit by candles the men bring their seat before a regal figure seated on what can only be described as a throne. The figure, adorned in dark sunglasses and an immaculate white suit and top hat, is the rhythm-and-blues icon Stevie Wonder.

With his trademark ear-to-ear smile, Stevie asks his visitors, "What do we have here?" In response they ask the rather ominous Wonder, "Do you do lucky chairs?" Stevie replies, "Son that's really not my thang." But with a dramatic snap of his fingers Stevie creates a spark and a flash. A lithe, manicured young woman played by the popular Dominican American film star Zoe Saldana is whisked via time-lapse footage down the winding staircase behind Wonder to his side. Zoe takes Stevie's hand, bends over, and seductively whispers into his ear, "I'll do it." With a snap of her fingers this time, Saldana disappears, only to reappear across the hall, sprawled sensuously across the "lucky chair." She asks graciously, "How much you guys need?" Zoe snaps her fingers again, and we are transported back to the home where this adventure began.

In the living room a new gentleman enters the scene in front of the conspicuous recliner, which is flanked by the two men who have been hauling it through the Crescent City. The new figure taps the young man closest to him on the shoulder and warns, "Back up guys, that's my lucky chair," and he plops down with a beer to watch the game. The young movers, standing over the recliner and their unsuspecting victim, grin at each other with squinted eyes. As they toast each other by clanging the necks of their Bud Light bottles together, one replies, "It *was* your lucky chair." On the screen a tag line proclaims "It's Only Weird if It Doesn't Work" across the face of the unsuspecting football fan, who reacts with an expression of distress to what must be a tragic play for his team, as a frantic football announcer can be heard yelling in the background. Simultaneously, the theme to Stevie Wonders hit "Superstition" begins to play over the sounds of the room full of partygoers. The ad closes with a fade to an extreme close-up of Wonder's smile as he cackles ominously over his own hit song, while what one can only assume is lightning illuminates his face.

The second ad opens with a shot of the aforementioned Superdome, into which walks a dark-haired young man. The ads apparent star strolls past a security guard through the back halls of the stadium into the locker room, where he lifts a striped white gym sock from a huge cloth bin of socks. A cut to a close-up shows his eyes as he peers from behind a hairbrush, from which he pulls a single hair. Afterward, making his way to the center of the abandoned football field, he collects a handful of the Dome's green turf from the fifty-yard line. Leaving the stadium, he jogs past the same uptown streetcar featured in the previous ad. If you look carefully, you can see the two young men from the prior ad alighting with their "lucky chair."

The industrious young man then trots through a large wrought-iron gate into one of the city's unique aboveground cemeteries. Passing through the rows of vaults holding generations of the city's deceased, the collector encounters what looks like a party. Celebrants, gathered around a tub of ice conspicuously filled with Bud Light, mingle under strings of lights. Some of the most noticeable of the partygoers are masked in the traditional style of New Orleans's Mardi Gras. Making his way out of the cemetery, the young protagonist passes a local brass band on one of the stone-paved alleys that survive in the Vieux Carré, winding around St. Louis Cathedral and the old Cabildo, the seat of government in eighteenth-century Louisiana. Having apparently reached his destination, the dark-haired youth strolls off the street up onto the brick sidewalk and through the French doors of a Vieux Carré bar.

The bartender, making long strokes across the surface of the bar with a white towel, greets the young man and offers him a pair of blue-labeled bottles of Anheuser-Busch's featured beverage. The young man conspicuously slides one of the bottles back to the bartender, whereupon they simultaneously lift them and tap their bases. The bartender nods his head toward a passage, and the young man strides stylistically into it, the camera backing past a bevy of lit white candles. A door opens, and the collector strolls into a familiar large hall, where at the bottom of a winding staircase sits the white-suit-and-top-hat adorned Stevie Wonder. Rhythmically snapping his fingers, Stevie smiles a wide smile, his snaps accompanied by flames that rise from the extraordinary number of candles in the room and flash in accord with the gesture. Nodding his head in time with the music from "Superstition," which has begun to play in the background, Stevie gleefully asks his patron, "You lookin' for a little mojo?" The young man we have been following sets his turf and sock down next to what appears to be a shoestring, some pins, and a pair of unidentified red circles. Stevie exclaims, "Lets get lucky!" He snaps his fingers, and we are magically transported to seats in the now crowded and raucous Superdome, filled with screaming football fans. Over the loudspeakers an announcer's booming voice welcomes fans to Super Bowl XLVII!

Our apparent Voodoo client now appears centered in the shot. His dark varsity jacket is unbuttoned, revealing a red t-shirt bearing the emblem of the San

Francisco Forty-Niners, one of the championship's competing franchises. On his left sits another fan in a Forty-Niners football jersey. But to his right sits a thin, large-eyed fan of the Forty-Niners' opponents, the Baltimore Ravens. His clapping hands draw the viewer's attention to the purple-collared sweatshirt emblazoned with the Ravens logo just to the left of the zipper. From inside his now opened jacket our protagonist and apparent Forty-Niners fan pulls a Voodoo doll made of the Dome's turf, held together like a scarecrow by the accoutrement from Stevie Wonder's abode: a shoestring and red button eyes staring out over the familiar "SF" emblem on its makeshift chest. Apparently disturbed, the bearer of the Voodoo doll turns his eyes away from his prize to the hands of the Baltimore fan seated next to him, who holds a nearly identical Voodoo doll, its purple button eyes and "B" emblazoned bird head contrasting with the San Francisco doll of the now visibly irritated Forty-Niners fan. Centered between the two fans and their dolls, the tag line "It's Only Weird If It Doesn't Work" appears before the camera cuts to an outside wide shot of the colorfully lit stadium over a dark New Orleans sky erupting with fireworks. The face of Stevie Wonder, chuckling sinisterly, appears over the Superdome, his head leaning back with laughter and glee. An announcer then says, "Bud Light: for fans who do whatever it takes. Here we Go!"

To New Orleans natives or frequent visitors, some of the sites featured in the commercial may have been familiar. But to the millions of viewers with no personal experience with the city, it was the presence of Voodoo that signaled Anheuser-Busch's nod to the 2013 Super Bowl's host city. With only thirty to sixty seconds to visually represent the city of New Orleans, the creators of these ads chose Voodoo as the most recognizable aspect of Crescent City culture to highlight. Without even using the word *Voodoo*, the director and actors were able to successfully communicate to a national audience of millions that they were celebrating the big game in the Big Easy. The ads' focus suggests that the creators believed that for a broad audience Voodoo was synonymous with New Orleans.

Images associated with Voodoo have been ingrained into the American cultural imagination. The African-descended cultural icons Stevie Wonder and Zoe Saldana by their dress are able to signal to viewers that they are practitioners of Voodoo. The candlelit room in which they appear, as well as the cemetery, signal occult practices. This kind of ad is only effective when the viewing audience is familiar with these kinds of visual cues. With less than a minute to capture the attention of viewers and push the desired product, advertisers cannot include long verbal explanations. They count on viewers' familiarity with certain images to get their message across. In this case the message, aside from "Buy Bud Light," is "This is New Orleans!"

Some of the images used to invoke a previous knowledge of Voodoo and make it recognizable may be less apparent than the Voodoo dolls and cemetery featured in these Super Bowl ads. The creators of these ads have a great deal at stake. In 2013, thirty seconds of airtime during the Super Bowl went for an average of $3.5 million. Advertisers need consumers to get the point. So how do they get us to associate Stevie Wonder, an R&B artist, and Zoe Saldana, an actor, with Voodoo? Do lit candles say New Orleans? Do cemeteries scream Voodoo? Or do we commonly equate certain cultural and religious practices with certain groups of people? We have archetypes for many religious groups. Muslims, Jews, and Hindus all subscribe to belief systems that have frequently been tied to racial types, thus begging the question, Is the race of the artists featured in this ad relevant to our recognition of them as Voodoo practitioners? Do we assume that Voodoo practitioners are Black? Neither Wonder nor Saldana has any publicized connection to New Orleans or to Voodoo. Why would the ads' creators use them?

This book began with a simple question with an unbelievably complex answer: What is African American culture? What it means to be Black in America has shifted with the historical context and material realities surrounding the United States' African American population. I sought to gain insight into this question by studying what I believed was a decidedly African American cultural production, Voodoo in New Orleans. Among the most distinctive components of almost any culture are the religious beliefs and institutions constructed by the community to explain and order the physical, social, and spiritual universes in which they live. At their best, religious institutions and communities order those spheres in accord with the material reality of practitioners. While most African Americans in New Orleans and throughout the United States belong to one of the many Christian denominations that serve the overwhelming majority of the U.S. population, the Crescent City is also home to a distinct set of spiritual practices commonly termed *Voodoo*. Popular perception, literature, and scholarly work on Voodoo in New Orleans have treated these practices as a distinctly African American phenomenon. The term *Voodoo* has even been used to negatively categorize, however inaccurately, the Christian beliefs and practices of African Americans, demonstrating one of the most extreme examples of the racialization of the term.[1] Religious beliefs are frequently among the most telling expressions of the culture of any group, especially to the extent that those beliefs are created in reaction to and indicative of "the material and psychological realities of their daily existence."[2] Thus, research on the religion of a group stands to improve our comprehension of that group's culture more generally. I was surprised to find that primary sources seemed to suggest that the extant secondary literature had glossed over or explained away interracial participation in Voodoo. This raised questions about what other complexities were being excluded from these accounts and what the fluidity of this supposedly African American cultural production could tell us about African American and, perhaps more broadly, American culture.

Voodoo has long been viewed as an African American phenomenon largely because of racialized perceptions of cultures that treat them as if they were insular or distinct. In this case, the history of racial discrimination against African Americans and the pejorative view of all things African that accompanied the depressed social standing of Black people in the United States has directly affected the perception of Voodoo in New Orleans. The point here is not to dispute the African cultural impact on Voodoo or the existence of African antecedents in the rituals of practitioners of Voodoo in New Orleans. Indeed, Voodoo may very well demonstrate ties between cultures created in Louisiana, Africa, Haiti, and a great many other sites throughout the Americas. However, most salient in the practice of Voodoo in New Orleans is the unique impact of the immediate cultural context in New Orleans, the American South, and the United States. The view of Voodoo as an African American or largely African phenomenon requires an understanding of culture as stagnant, whole, and complete. Rather than being a monolithic and unchanging set of traditions handed down from African ancestors, however, the practice of Voodoo in the Crescent City represents a dynamic subculture practiced by a racially diverse group of professional and lay practitioners that was constantly growing to incorporate social and economic influences from the wider American culture as it was expressed in early twentieth-century New Orleans.

The specific focus of this book is a group of practitioners who, thanks to the efforts of the Works Progress Administration's Louisiana Writers' Project, the

Columbia-trained anthropologist and famed African American novelist Zora Neale Hurston, and the amateur ethnographer Harry Middleton Hyatt, immediately preceding and during the Great Depression were able to add their voices to the historical record and perhaps for the first time leave written accounts of the practice of Voodoo in New Orleans from a practitioner's perspective. The experiences, structure, and ritual formula described by these practitioners demonstrated a preoccupation with power relations, both social and economic, in the lives of professional practitioners, or "workers," as they often called themselves, and their clients. Most notably, the racial strife of Jim Crow segregation, the material deprivation of the Great Depression, and the accompanying domestic power struggle between the sexes all left indelible marks on the practice of Voodoo in New Orleans. In particular I focus on the deployment of explicitly and implicitly stated notions of race, economics, and gender that litter the accounts of Voodoo practitioners in early twentieth-century New Orleans. Centered on these, the most salient influences on Voodoo practitioners in New Orleans, this project seeks to portray Voodoo as these practitioners themselves did in the late 1920s and 1930s.

In essence, what I argue here is that Voodoo in twentieth-century New Orleans is proof positive that as citizens of a diverse society we share responsibility for the creation of culture, whether that culture is viewed favorably or pejoratively. The creation of culture in a multicultural nation is most frequently the product of the interactions between racial and ethnic groups. Communities create their identities with reference to other communities. Sometimes they view outside communities as "others" and shape their identities so as to mark themselves as distinctly different from those "others." Those kind of identity politics are at the heart of the classification of Voodoo in New Orleans as a mostly, or largely, or centrally African or African American phenomenon. Frequently, though, relationships with other racial groups are characterized by much more complicated positions taken by members of a community. Even in the face of views that mark some members of American society as normative and others as liminal and undesirable, members of all these communities may incorporate practices and belief structures across the boundaries of race, class, and gender in their creation of culture, thus, in the case of Voodoo in early twentieth-century New Orleans, opening the door for members of both the normative and liminal communities to participate together to create a single culture. This can be said of American culture in general. I argue here that it was *the search for power* that led practitioners, male and female, Black and white, rich and poor, to seek out Voodoo. Workers exploited these perceived dichotomies, incorporating the social and economic advantages of whiteness and wealth by association with affluent and interracial clientele. Racialized perceptions of power and spirituality led an interracial population of practitioners to a set of spiritual practices demonized by popular association with Africa and with Blackness. Thus it was the quest for power—social, economic, and personal—that made Voodoo in New Orleans a dynamic religious subculture, constantly changing to meet the needs of a community as diverse as the city itself.

This book is divided into two parts. The two chapters that make up part I describe the unique people and phenomena that defined and distinguished New Orleans Voodoo at the beginning of the twentieth century. Chapter 1 seeks to establish the lasting cultural impact of Voodoo on the city of New Orleans. Because of her influence on the culture of Voodoo in New Orleans as described by practitioners in the early twentieth century, the chapter takes as a starting point the mythology surrounding Marie Laveau, the Crescent City's most famous Voodoo queen, and illustrates the importance of this nineteenth-century figure as the mythohistorical progenitor of the style of Voodoo practiced in twentieth-century New Orleans. Tied into this mythology are the complex notions of racial and gender identity and the practice of Voodoo as entrepreneurship, which helped to define not only the practice of Voodoo but the broader culture of New Orleans in the early decades of the twentieth century. Chapter 2 describes the early work of the Spiritual Church's Mother Leafy Anderson, who brought her own brand of Christian religious worship to New Orleans circa 1920. I illuminate the connections between Anderson's organization and the preexisting culture of Voodoo to demonstrate the influence of these practices, what I term here the *Laveau legacy*, on the wider spiritual culture of New Orleans. Anderson would spend much of her career in New Orleans dealing with the cultural impact of this legacy in everything from the association of Black spirituality with criminality and racial or cultural backwardness to the incorporation of Voodoo-style rituals into the churches of her and her followers.

In referring to the distinctive culture being created and re-created in New Orleans at this period, I most frequently employ the term *Voodoo* as opposed to terms like *hoodoo* or *conjure*, which are frequently used to refer to African American magical-religious traditions throughout the United States, or *Vodou*, a reference to the indigenous religious traditions of Haiti. While the move in much of the previous scholarship on African diasporic religion away from the use of the term *Voodoo* may represent a laudable attempt by researchers and authors to lend authenticity to the religious traditions they write about and move us away from the racism that has negatively colored the cultural traditions of people of African descent, my hope is that the use of *Voodoo* here will move us to embrace the dynamism and diverse influences that led to the creation of New Orleans Voodoo. Not all of these influences and changes were positive. They include the racialization and commodification that proceeded hand in hand with the popularization of this spelling of *Voodoo*. However, practitioners frequently employed the term and used it interchangeably with terms like *hoodoo*, and I employ it here in an attempt to foreground the perspective of the practitioners who shaped the work described here on Voodoo and power.

Part II deals with the ritual practices of workers in the early twentieth century and the inclusion of contemporary cultural biases in those practices. In chapter 3, I examine the impact of the segregation and racial discrimination of early twentieth-century New Orleans on the practice of Voodoo. I look at the impact of the racial politics of American folklore studies, the imposition of segregation in Louisiana, and New Orleans's unique history of American versus Creole identity politics to assert that race was important to Voodoo largely because it was important in the United States generally, and the American South and New Orleans specifically. I contend that the incorporation of Jim Crow–era notions of race into Voodoo is evidence of the dynamism of Voodoo as a subculture and its ability to adapt to the racial climate of post–*Plessy v. Ferguson* New Orleans. Further, I argue that Voodoo should be understood as a product of both its chronological and its geographic milieu, particularly with respect to how practitioners understood race. I conclude that the notions of race that justified Jim Crow also contributed to the understanding of Voodoo as an aspect of African American folk culture. This devaluation through racialization, a characteristic phenomenon of African diaspora religions that has persisted into the late twentieth and early twenty-first centuries in the United States, becomes evident when we compare the United States with nations where identification of religious practices with African culture actually served to legitimate rather than demonize or criminalize them.[3] In Brazil, for example, the association with Africa served to make Candomblé, an Afro-Brazilian religion with strong parallels to Voodoo, more legitimate in the eyes of the law. The seeming marginalization and racialization of Voodoo point to the role of the local social climate, in this case racial norms, in constricting the religious culture of New Orleans workers.

In chapter 4, I look at gender and sexuality in the practice of workers in New Orleans. I posit that the adoption and re-creation of certain Catholic saints, especially Saint Rita, by practitioners of Voodoo in this period is further evidence of the dynamism of Voodoo as practiced in New Orleans. I seek to demonstrate how workers read current gender norms into their rites and formula and navigated perceptions of gender to sell solutions to gender-specific problems, especially domestic conflicts between men and women in which financial control, sexuality of a domestic partner, and spousal abuse were all at issue. The gendered rites and accounts of workers present fresh insight into the great domestic conflicts under way in the homes of Voodoo practitioners and perhaps many others in early twentieth-century New Orleans.

Chapter 5 supports the position that Voodoo was dynamically changing in keeping with the culture of New Orleans and of the United States by looking at the inculcation of wider economic values by practitioners of Voodoo in the early twentieth century. Focusing on rites employed in the late 1920s and throughout the 1930s, I track the importance of money, employment, and currency to the work of Voodoo practitioners. I suggest that the extreme importance of jobs among the concerns of professional Voodoo practitioners and their clients is a reflection of the nation's high unemployment rates during the Great Depression and that the growing importance of a cash economy was directly related to the use of currency in the rites of Voodoo practitioners in the period.

In chapter 6, I further examine the growing importance of economics to Voodoo by looking at the apparent shifts in practice in the early twentieth century. I focus on the legal troubles of workers in the first decades of the twentieth century and examine the ability of Voodoo practitioners and Spiritual Church leaders to alter their relationship to legal authorities using economic resources and the structure and infrastructure of "church." I posit that the accumulation of wealth and property was directly related to the changing status of Voodoo in the eyes of the law. This new status allowed Spiritual Churches to operate free of the kind of legal persecution that had plagued workers in the decades before 1920. The most important example of this new status was that a number of Spiritual Churches were declared tax exempt, an explicit acknowledgment that these organizations, long associated with the practice of Voodoo, were legitimate religions in the eyes of the state of Louisiana. This acknowledgment suggests larger questions about the extent to which the racial identity of a religious community and its economic resources affect its legal legitimacy and the extent to which freedom of religious practice in the United States is affected by these same factors.

My conclusion is that examination of Voodoo as practiced in early twentieth-century New Orleans suggests the folly of using racial classifications to distinguish between cultural forms. Instead we must focus on the material realities and historical contexts in order to understand culture in general and religion, here Voodoo, more specifically. Undue focus on African origins rather than common history and material circumstances among people of African descent has hindered the discourse on the traditions commonly called Afro-Atlantic or African diasporic religions, of which Voodoo as practiced in New Orleans may be the United States' most well known representative. Discussions of Voodoo in New Orleans that focus on African origins or take them as a starting point seemed to be inextricably bound to attempts, both past and present, to draw deceptively hard lines between people of African descent, their cultures, and the heterogeneous societies in which they live. In an urban metropolis like New Orleans, the ideas and practices of one group, if they were ever confined to one racial group, moved fluidly across the boundaries of race, even where those boundaries were codified by the laws of Jim Crow. Driven by the culture of privation that characterized the Great Depression and the consumerism that overtook the United States as a whole from the late nineteenth to the early twentieth century, Voodoo belied the power of segregation and racism to legislate and dictate boundaries between the supposedly distinct cultures of African Americans and whites in New Orleans. In so doing it demonstrated its connection to the material and social circumstances characteristic of its historical contexts. By promising power, both social and economic, to the powerless, workers' attention to their and their clients' material reality and the social contexts they inhabited attracted practitioners across racial, class, and gender lines.

The ritual technology of Voodoo essentially played off social technologies of difference that marked race and gender as unchangeable categories. By marketing their services to those who believed that their race and gender, accidents of birth, were inescapable social and economic disadvantages, workers used the social cleavages perpetuated by racism and sexism. Though fate had seemingly doomed their clients to the perpetual disadvantages associated with racial and gender identities, workers' power could overcome these disadvantages and grant opportunities for employment, revenge, love, and domestic stability, among other things. Further, even those on the dominant end of these social spectra made use of Voodoo when they felt constricted by their racial, gender, or economic circumstances. This made the populations Voodoo might appeal to seemingly boundless.

Perhaps most impressively, members of the Spiritual Church movement demonstrated the ability to overcome the racialization and criminalization of Voodoo by creating churches that the state would acknowledge as legitimate religious organizations despite the long history of legal persecution of practitioners associated with Voodoo. Both workers and Spiritual Church leaders incorporated cultural norms from the surrounding nation and city to create and re-create their rituals, businesses, and organizations. In turn they exerted a lasting influence on the culture of New Orleans. Thus the broad twentieth-century cultural trends of consumerism, racism, and sexism in the United States fed this subculture, which in turn helped to characterize the culture of one of America's most distinct metropolises.

Therefore, in answer to my initial question, What is African American culture?, I have found that, as the term *African American* suggests, Black culture is American culture. To the extent that all Americans share a material and social world, they share a culture. Voodoo in the early twentieth century was a product of the unique cultural milieu of New Orleans, including widespread national trends toward gender bias and consumerism. The realities of ostensibly distinct racial and class groups also informed that culture. Thus the dynamic between Black and white New Orleanians and the dynamic between New Orleans and the rest of the nation all informed Voodoo. The malleability of Voodoo allowed it to meet distinct, often divergent needs while still referencing held national realities demonstrating the fluidity and interdependence of culture in America and the broad appeal of Voodoo's promise of power.

I

LAVEAU AND ANDERSON

1

THE LEGACY AND CULTURE OF VOODOO IN NEW ORLEANS

n September 1947 the *New Orleans Item* published an intriguing story about a housewife on Carrolton Avenue who had become alarmed one morning when, while sweeping her front steps, she discovered three slices of cake "unobtrusively tucked under her doorstep."[1] Frightened for her life, the woman immediately called the police. According to the *Item*, the woman had nearly fainted, and the police, rather than dismissing the woman as a crank caller, had "listened with concern." The author of the article turned to local culture to explain the woman's alarm and the authorities' accompanying concern, suggesting that as residents of New Orleans, both the woman and the police had recognized the seemingly innocuous cake as a threat "all at once": to them, it was obvious that the cake was a gris-gris, the material manifestation of a Voodoo ritual. The police learned in the course of their investigation that the woman was a landlady who had filed eviction notices for some of her tenants, and they now believed that those tenants were retaliating via Voodoo. The *Item* claimed that "analysis" had suggested that the cake contained nail parings, pulverized rent receipts, a tomcat's antenna whiskers, "remains of a rooster's virility," and the grease from a candle burned to Saint John the Baptist, all of which positively identified the cake to the locals as a gris-gris and the work of Voodoo.

It is difficult to imagine what analysis or source could have yielded such detailed results to this journalist, but his report does point to his knowledge of the material culture and rituals associated with Voodoo. In the article, the author traces the origins of Voodoo from Africa to tropical islands off its coast, finally to New Orleans's own Congo Square, Bayou St. John, and the Crescent City's "greatest practitioner of all," its most famous nineteenth-century Voodoo queen, Marie Laveau. While he claims that Voodoo had diminished in both influence and importance in New Orleans by the mid-twentieth century, he also maintains that it pervaded the entirety of the city and that its practitioners were both Black and white. The author indicates that the central rhetoric and ideology of Voodoo revolved around the concept of power. He compares communism, the most feared political ideology in the United States in the mid-twentieth century, to Voodoo, the most menacing cultural practice in New Orleans. He claims that just as the rhetoric of "party-liners" was littered with persistent use of the term *unity*, the rhetoric of Voodoo practitioners similarly revolved around the concept of "power," even in matters of love, employers, and life and death.[2]

While apparently favoring sensationalism and folklore over research that would include the perspective of actual practitioners, the author of the aforementioned article does hit on some points that are important for understanding how and why workers and their clients engaged in the religious and magical rites known as hoodoo or Voodoo. By the mid-twentieth century, Voodoo as a collection of religious and magical practices was familiar to many in and around the city of New Orleans. A group of saints, most of whom are recognizable from Roman Catholic and Christian lore, were employed by practitioners along with a group of magical formulas and mystical texts to secure social and economic benefits in the material world.

The author of the article in the *New Orleans Item* suggests, as have many of his contemporaries and scholars since, that Voodoo as practiced in New Orleans originated in Africa or Haiti. Unfortunately, the legal proscriptions against slaves' meeting together or with freed people in antebellum Louisiana and regulations against fortune-telling, practicing medicine without a license, and obtaining money "under false pretenses" after emancipation made practitioners of Voodoo subject to legal prosecution and thus loath to practice in the open. The clandestine nature of these rituals made it unlikely that any outsider would obtain firsthand knowledge of the rituals or belief structure of Voodoo practitioners. It was similarly unlikely that any practitioner would record his own or his coreligionists' activities, for fear of legal reprisals. The questionable legal status of these practices also made their institutionalization difficult, complicating the establishment of uniform standards of practice or inclusion for a canon or community of Voodoo practitioners in New Orleans. Thus, the set of practices employed by practitioners, the belief structures that informed them, and the origin and lineage of those practices went almost completely undocumented by any inside, reliable source for nearly the entire nineteenth century. It is therefore difficult to establish when and where Voodoo as practiced in New Orleans originated.

Further, the rituals and beliefs reported by practitioners in the early twentieth century were extraordinarily malleable. Evidence suggests that rituals varied from one practitioner to the next, probably owing to the absence of an institutionalized structure or authority. So in addition to the lack of evidence regarding the origins of Voodoo in New Orleans in the nineteenth century, what evidence we have about practices in the succeeding period suggests that those practices may have been dynamically shifting to meet the needs of practitioners. This in turn implies that what workers, clients, and outsiders classified as Voodoo by the turn of the twentieth century may have differed drastically not only from any predecessors in Haiti or antecedents in Africa but also from similar practices in nineteenth-century New Orleans. Therefore, this study approaches Voodoo as both geographically and temporally specific to New Orleans from the end of the nineteenth to the middle of the twentieth century. Rather than being essentially African as scholars to date have claimed, New Orleans Voodoo as practiced in this period was a dynamic set of historically contingent spiritual and religious practices whose practitioners drew overwhelmingly on the immediate social and economic contexts of the early twentieth-century United States and of New Orleans specifically for the purpose, direction, and shape of their rituals and ideology.

In effect, then, while presumptive on the question of origins, the aforementioned *New Orleans Item* article may have hit the proverbial nail on the head in asserting the cultural pervasiveness of Voodoo in New Orleans and the centrality of power to the rituals. Many Western religions have attempted to separate spiritual concerns from the material world. By contrast, practitioners of Voodoo in early twentieth-century New Orleans employed these rituals with the understanding that they would yield tangible benefits in their lives. Those rituals were, generally speaking, attempts to counter what practitioners viewed as disadvantages in power. The power clients and workers sought to obtain was most often social or economic. They frequently attempted to employ Voodoo to take fuller control of the individuals with whom they interacted and the material circumstances under which they interacted with them. Workers necessarily provided services for a fee, and their clients expected an immediate result in exchange for that fee. In turn, workers offered money, candles, and other ritual "sacrifices" or payment to the saints and spirits employed, expecting observable returns in exchange. Voodoo is therefore a business, perhaps in a more obvious way than some other American religions. Despite its potential to alter uneven power relations, the racial stigma attached to Voodoo in the Jim Crow U.S. South made it unappealing to those with access to more traditional avenues of social and economic influence. This racialization was buttressed by a focus on Voodoo's purported origins in dark corners of Haiti and Africa. Thus, Voodoo was most frequently employed by those who believed themselves to be at a social and economic disadvantage or felt constrained by social norms of class, racial, and gender classification. It might be most accurate to say that Voodoo as practiced in New Orleans generally revolved around the promise of power for those who lacked power in relation to whatever adversary they challenged via ritual and magic.

Long regarded as the most powerful Voodoo practitioner in New Orleans, Marie Laveau became *the* symbol of Voodoo's influence in the city. Since her death in 1881, Marie Laveau has become a cultural icon in New Orleans. Her celebrity, while widespread across racial, cultural, and geographic lines, was not unambiguous. She was well known enough that after her death numerous local newspapers published accounts of her life, some national periodicals mentioned her in connection with stories about Voodoo, and she was also mentioned in a number of academic studies. However, not everyone in New Orleans welcomed the association of the city and its population with the cultural legacy of Voodoo. Negative perceptions in periodicals and local-color stories of the religious practices of Marie Laveau seemed to be a part of a stigma, due again to the racist equating of savagery with Blackness, and Blackness with Voodoo. Thus, the infamous queen and Voodoo were associated with immorality, backwardness, and superstition. In spite of these stigmas, however, Marie Laveau's legend became part of the complex cultural landscape of New Orleans, and thus her legacy carried, along with the negative perspectives on Voodoo, associations with everything that made New Orleans unique and intriguing.

The Laveau Legacy

It was increasingly common by the twentieth century for those who identified themselves as professional practitioners of Voodoo, or workers, to claim descent from the famous Voodoo queen to mark her as the source of their own spiritual power and lend authenticity to their rites. While Voodoo was associated with cultural backwardness and immorality, Laveau was a powerful figure in New Orleans folklore. Thus, on occasion even those attempting to eschew the barbarism and immorality attributed to Voodoo practitioners proudly claimed connections to Laveau.

Unpacking this ambiguity is key to understanding how Voodoo overcame the stigma of racialization and cultural marginalization to become a highly recognizable, even highlighted component of New Orleans's exotic culture. By the early twentieth century, Voodoo had become woven into the cultural tapestry of the Crescent City. Despite attempts to racialize and thereby demonize the practices of workers and their clients by claiming that they were employed only by gullible Blacks and the most lowly whites, citizens and outsiders of both races and genders began to identify Voodoo as a component of the rich and unusual cultural landscape that characterized New Orleans. The mythology surrounding Marie Laveau as a figure, the seemingly infinite permutations of her biography, and the debates among those who remembered her or stories about her reveal attempts to lay claim to Marie Laveau by any number of groups and individuals in the city, not just the African American population. African Americans, Afro-Creoles, white New Orleanians, workers, Catholics, and Spiritualists all put their own spin on the Laveau legacy in attempts to somehow claim association with one of the most famous figures in the city's history. By the twentieth century her supposed tomb had become a tourist attraction, with sightseers crossing her crypt with red brick as part of faux Voodoo rituals and leaving offerings as part of quotidian cemetery tours. Whether or not claims made on the Laveau legacy were accurate, the association with power, economic savvy, and local culture evoked by her name help to explain why even locals who eschewed association with Voodoo attempted to lay claim to Laveau.

In turn, the mythology that arose around the figure of Laveau included accounts of her practicing almost every ritual, economic, and social tradition associated with early twentieth-century Voodoo. In recounting Laveau's rituals as identical to their own, workers active decades after Laveau's death depicted themselves as having staunchly held to trends and rituals she created or popularized. It is likely that they frequently read their present practices into the mythology in order to legitimize their work in the eyes of clients and colleagues. Their practice of these rituals established Marie Laveau as a cultural icon central to their brand of Voodoo. Following Laveau's death, many believers traveled to her gravesite to ask for favors and thereby claim some of her power as their own. While many other saints and spirits populated the metaphysical landscape of Voodoo in New Orleans, Marie Laveau was the central personality and source of power for many of the workers in the early twentieth century. Workers were ideologically linked to Laveau, who was culturally anchored to New Orleans. Therefore, for workers as well as the clients who sought them out and the outsiders who remembered Laveau as one of the city's most important cultural icons, Voodoo was indelibly etched on the culture of New Orleans.

The goal here is to unpack the meaning of the widely varied, frequently contradictory accounts of the life, power, and spiritual work of Marie Laveau. Other scholars have done careful research to distinguish between the historical Marie Laveau and the legends that arose after her death.[3] Rather than retreading that scholarship, I will demonstrate how the Laveau mythology functioned for the workers for whom she was such an important figure and how debates about that mythology by New Orleanians seemingly uninvolved in Voodoo mark Laveau as a figure, and Voodoo as a cultural artifact, in the collective consciousness of the city. As important as the ostensibly Catholic saints that populated the pantheon of Voodoo practitioners, by the early twentieth century the recently deceased Voodoo queen was viewed by practitioners and outsiders as the originator, innovator, and archetype of Voodoo as practiced in New Orleans. Her mythohistorical biography as told and retold by New Orleanians marked her and her work as unquestionably linked to the social and economic politics of race and entrepreneurship in early twentieth-century New Orleans. Therefore, by examining the specific stories told about Laveau, we can begin to understand how the unique cultural milieu of New Orleans shaped and characterized the practice of Voodoo. In short, the Laveau mythology, the precedents it set, and the way in which Voodoo practitioners both reacted to and shaped it to fit their circumstances constitute what is distinctive about the practice of Voodoo in New Orleans. In turn, the existence and the collective image of Voodoo is one of the most unique aspects of the culture of the Crescent City.

From Whence Voodoo Came

With the evidence available to date, there can be very little certainty about when and how Voodoo originated in New Orleans. Scholars have traced the name *Voodoo* in its many variations to both Africa and Europe. This apparent contradiction results in large part from the fact that any attempt to etymologize the term involves comparisons with similar terms in whatever culture the researching scholar views to be the root culture of Voodoo. Without any account by practitioners of when and how they began to use the term, its origin is as uncertain as the phenomenon it describes. The first French settlements in the colony of Louisiana were established in 1699. Scholars who privilege a discussion of African origins in attempting to understand Voodoo in New Orleans look to the earliest importations of slaves to the French colony, which began in earnest after 1716 in the face of labor shortages that were problematic for the economic development of southern Louisiana.[4] This approach is predicated on the supposition that spiritual practices retained from Africa are the root of Voodoo as practiced in New Orleans. The clearest support for this position comes from comparisons between traditions observed in Louisiana and those common in regions of Africa from which enslaved people in the colony hailed. This approach is problematic in that we have little or no evidence of what slave religion was like in French colonial Louisiana. The earliest accounts of slave religion come from vague eighteenth-century travel accounts and histories of French Louisiana. It is likely that non-Christian religious practices among slaves would have been clandestine. As early as 1724, colonial authorities began implementing the Code Noir in Louisiana to govern the behavior of enslaved Africans. That code required, among other provisions, that slaves be baptized Roman Catholics and that they be married within the Catholic Church.[5] This would have effectively made practice of any African religion illegal and punishable by colonial authorities. That being said, some of the earliest descriptions of the spiritual practices of slaves, by colonial authorities in Louisiana or practitioners themselves, appear in reports relating to the trials of slaves prosecuted for some form of spiritual practice.

Outside of this kind of primary-source data, the earliest histories of Voodoo date to the 1790s for Haiti and the 1880s for New Orleans. Unfortunately, there has been a great deal of doubt regarding the credibility of these histories. In his essay "Conventionalization, Distortion and Plagiarism in the Historiography of Afro-Caribbean Religion in New Orleans," the anthropologist Stephan Palmié examines the literature produced on New Orleans Voodoo in both English and French and argues convincingly that there has been rampant plagiarism by authors on the subject, who substitute descriptions of Vodun ceremonies in Haiti and especially the *chanson africaine* recorded in the Caribbean accounts of Moreau de St.-Méry at the end of the eighteenth century, for firsthand accounts of practices in New Orleans.[6] Acceptance of the salacious, racialized image of New Orleans Voodoo propagated by authors in the nineteenth and twentieth centuries based on these questionable accounts has brought into question the value of accounts produced well into the last decade of the twentieth century. Further, the questionable authenticity of earlier reports on Voodoo in New Orleans and the lack of more credible scholarship specifically establishing African origins of known rituals or practitioners in the city suggest that trying to understand Voodoo as the product of African cultural retentions may be less helpful than a focus on periods for which we can speak to the work of specific practitioners and rites.

The more meticulous scholarship produced since the dawn of the millennium, largely concerned with the mid- to late nineteenth-century Voodoo queen Marie Laveau, has not taken up the project of reexamining the question of origins in this early literature. While the most current scholarship explicitly rejects the racism and sensationalism of these earlier projects, the works of authors like Ina Fandrich, Martha Ward, and Carolyn Morrow Long cannot quite serve as correctives on New Orleans Voodoo's origins, as their central topics are at a great chronological distance from an origin story for Voodoo in the Crescent City.[7] It is important to note here that while I accept Palmié's conclusions about the questionable "facticity" of much of the scholarship on Voodoo, as with him it is not to deny African origins for Voodoo. I posit instead, first, that much more research must be done before we can convincingly establish an origin on the continent for Voodoo in New Orleans, and second, that there has indeed been a "conventialization" of highly questionable data on the earliest practice of Voodoo in New Orleans.[8] Thus I argue, not that Voodoo *cannot* be traced to Africa but rather that it *has not* been, at least not convincingly. Finally, because of the difficulty of establishing any origin for practices in the city, if one wants to understand what Voodoo in New Orleans was like for those who practiced it, it is best to privilege the sources from which we may "hear" the voices of practitioners.

One of the earliest such accounts, of a trial involving the spiritual practices of slaves in New Orleans, has been termed by one scholar the "Gri-Gri Case," in which several slaves were tried in connection with the use of a "charm" supposedly intended to kill a plantation overseer and the slaves' legal owner.[9] The mere existence of this case points to three interesting facts: First, it confirms the enforcement of the criminalization of slave religion in colonial Louisiana, especially in this case, where it is connected to an attempted insurrection. Second, the case does not even appear in the historical record until a decade after the ceding of the colony of Louisiana to the Spanish by the French in 1763, suggesting that we may need to treat prior reports of Voodoo in New Orleans with some skepticism. Third, the association of slave religion with insurrection and crime would seem to support the necessity of maintaining secrecy and detract from the reliability of these early colonial era accounts of Voodoo in and around New Orleans.

Ostensibly the most reliable early accounts of Voodoo in New Orleans appear in newspaper reports of trials in which people of African descent, both enslaved and free, were prosecuted for spiritual gatherings. These accounts began to surface in the nineteenth century, during the American period, after the colony of Louisiana had been transferred from Spanish control back to the French and finally to the United States after the Louisiana Purchase of 1803. During the American period, when practitioners of Voodoo were prosecuted their descriptions of their spiritual practices might actually serve as a defense rather than the self-incrimination they might have constituted under French or Spanish colonial authorities, who forbade non-Catholic religious observances by the enslaved. Most of these arrests were for illegal assemblies of slaves, especially in conjunction with free people of color and/ or whites. While reports of these arrests date perhaps from the 1820s, one of the most instructive appeared in the 1850s.[10]

A series of court cases in the summer of 1850 resulting from the arrest of apparent practitioners of Voodoo may represent the earliest firsthand descriptions of these gatherings from an insider's perspective in New Orleans. On June 27, 1850, a group of women, free women of color and slaves, were arrested for assembling illegally. Reports were that though more than a hundred people may have been present when the police raid began, only eighteen were arrested, all of them women. Of these, two were white women, fifteen were free women of color, and one was an enslaved woman. In a similar raid on July 2 a free woman of color was arrested with three of her slaves. From these raids a series of court cases arose in which women involved in these illicit meetings had an opportunity to add their voices to the historical record. The apparent public interest in these cases, suggested by the reports of significant crowds at the hearings, may have contributed to the women's willingness to speak on the record. Most important among the complainants was Betsy Toledano, a free woman of color arrested in the June 27 raid. In a complaint filed after the raid, Toledano charged in a civil case that her arrest while performing religious ceremonies had been illegal, and that the arresting officers of the municipality had wrongly imprisoned, fined, and assaulted her and her companions. Toledano's suit failed on the basis that the meeting had been broken up due to the illegal gathering of slaves with free people of color and whites, not because it was a religious service. When Toledano was arrested again at her home in what is now the French Quarter on similar charges, she again added her voice to the historical record, defending her right to practice the religion of "the mother-land," presumably Africa.[11]

These reports tell us, perhaps for the first time, several things about the practice of Voodoo in New Orleans. First, they tell us that the practitioners considered what they were doing to be a religion. A number of gatherings of slaves and free people of color in New Orleans dating from the colonial period are often mentioned in conjunction with Voodoo, most notably weekly dances held at the famed Congo Square, just outside the boundaries of the colonial city. Later practitioners questioned whether any religious or spiritual services took place at these gatherings.[12] Indeed, it would have been imprudent for slaves or free people of color to practice any religion other than Catholicism in the view of authorities given the colonial prohibitions against doing so. Second, they tell us that Voodoo attracted mainly African Americans, inasmuch as most of the practitioners arrested at these gatherings were of African descent. Toledano's claim to practice the religion of the "mother-land" is one of the earliest claims by an admitted practitioner to an African origin for the practice of New Orleans Voodoo. However, it is crucial to note the presence of white practitioners in even the earliest reports of these religious practices. Thus, rather than being an exclusively African or African American religion, Voodoo in New Orleans seems to have had an interracial component from its earliest verifiable existence. Third, we find some of the first reports of ritual implements in cases in which, unlike in the aforementioned "Gri-Gri Case," those implements were not incriminating evidence. Newspapers reported the presence of an altar, color prints of the saints, banners, bowls containing various stones, and a number of goblets and vases.[13] While Toledano and others did not testify to the meaning of these artifacts, it is likely, given the religious nature of those services, that they had some spiritual significance. In addition, the police raids of 1850 may have resulted in one of the first recorded appearances of Marie Laveau in connection with the practice of Voodoo.

On July 2, 1850, Marie Laveau appeared in the papers in connection with a judicial complaint she filed against the municipality for confiscating a wooden statue at the June 27 raid of Toledano's gathering. Her claim to one of the implements confiscated in the raid of this religious ceremony is one of the first confirmed connections of Marie Laveau to the practice of New Orleans Voodoo. The newspapers suggested that Laveau was in fact the leader of the group, and eventually the statue she claimed was released to a woman described as a quadroon, that is, a person who is one-quarter African American, in exchange for the payment of related court costs. In the summer of 1859 Laveau again appeared in the papers, in connection with a case brought against her by a neighbor for disturbing the peace in connection with "fighting and obscenity and infernal singing and yelling" at a building she owned.[14] It is reasonable to assume that this second case was also religiously connected given the account nine years earlier. Ironically, then, these raids intended to stop the practice of Voodoo may provide us with the first verifiable accounts of the religion as practiced in New Orleans in which practitioners' "voices" are present.

Brown or Yellow, Black or Creole, Mulatto, Quadroon, or Octoroon

Witnesses who claimed to have known Laveau during her lifetime offered a number of distinct, often contradictory descriptions of her physical appearance. When Marie Laveau died in 1881, the arguments about every aspect of her life, including whether she had ever even practiced Voodoo, had only begun. Some of the most salient debates about Laveau among New Orleanians in the early twentieth century concerned her racial identity. According to legend, Marie Laveau was born a free woman of color in antebellum New Orleans. This identity in and of itself, because of the complex history of racial interaction in Louisiana, is weighted by notions of power, education, and privilege. The combination of identities that converge on Laveau as a Creole free woman of color in nineteenth-century Louisiana, while tethering the Laveau mythology firmly to the cultural history of Louisiana, also elicited images of cultural divisions in the city of New Orleans. These cleavages were linguistic, interracial, and intraracial. Individuals interviewed about Laveau attested to distinct, often contradictory memories of her aesthetic, centering on her language, skin color, and dress, that were clear indicators of cultural orientation meant to situate her firmly on either side of the cultural and racial divide between African American and Afro-Creole. Considered together, these memories and accounts suggest that citizens of New Orleans across racial, cultural, and geographic lines attempted to claim this important mythohistorical figure as a member of their communities. Laveau and her story of power had firmly entrenched her in New Orleans culture, and neither her purported racial identity nor her status as queen of Voodoo was enough to tie Laveau to the culture of any one community.

For much of its history, Louisiana was a French colonial possession. Thus, even after the territory that encompassed New Orleans was ceded first to the Spanish in the 1760s and then to the Americans in 1802, many citizens maintained their French cultural orientation. This resulted in noted conflicts between the French-speaking Creoles and the incoming English-speaking American population. *Creole* was used by both the French and the Spanish to denote citizens of their colonial possessions who were born in the New World. For some time into the American period, many French-speaking Creoles attempted to carve out a distinct space for themselves in New Orleans. The local government actually went so far as to divide the city into three distinct municipalities during the antebellum period in response to Creole citizens' efforts to maintain political autonomy and distinct educational institutions. Complicating matters were disparate racial views held by the distinct cultural communities. In French colonial possessions a three-tiered racial order that allowed for distinct legal and social status for free people of color, those of African descent who, through a gift of their owners, through their own industry, or as a result of being born to free parents, were themselves free from slavery and bondage. This created a middling class of Blacks in French colonial possessions, often well educated and propertied, in contrast to African-descended people in the United States, and frequently connected to the white French population through blood ties.

The American understanding of racial identity granted no unique status to these individuals or their descendants and thus viewed race as a zero-sum proposition. Anyone of African descent was considered Black or Negro socially and legally. The frequent intimate interracial relationships, ostensibly more frequent than in Anglo-American territories, often resulting in biracial children, created a distinct group in New Orleans of African Americans who were mulatto, or biracial, as well as quadroons and octoroons. Individuals in the latter two groups were often phenotypically indistinguishable from whites but had one grandparent or great-grandparent of African descent. The latter two racial categories were frequently associated with the city and the supposedly characteristic phenomenon of race mixing. This led to a blurring of racial lines with which Americans emigrating into New Orleans during the nineteenth century, who viewed people of African descent as inferior and looked with disdain on both intimate relationships with them and the children born of such liaisons, were uncomfortable. Because of the comparative frequency with which race mixing produced people of lighter skin complexions in New Orleans prior to the Louisiana Purchase, this race mixing became associated in the American collective imagination with the French-speaking Creole culture of the people who were native to Louisiana. Incoming Americans, who quickly assumed political and social control of the city, then began to associate Creole identity with miscegenation and thus with many of the stigmas accorded to African parentage. To avoid this, many white Creoles abandoned French language and cultural norms in order to be included as full members of the white race according to the American standard. In contrast, viewing Creole identity as a mark of sophistication, education, and unique history and culture, Afro-Creoles often clung to their Creole identity, some hoping that it accorded them a status above African Americans, who were portrayed by whites as the antithesis of all these things.[15]

Thus, debates about Marie Laveau's physical appearance often suggest attempts to position her on either side of the cultural divide between Creole and American. Claims that she had a lighter skin color than most African Americans and curly hair and wore exotic, brightly colored clothing reflected attempts to invoke perceptions of Creole identity that conflated French language, miscegenation, and Voodoo. Descriptions that strongly refuted remembering Laveau as fair skinned reflect attempts to claim her power, influence, and status as a cultural icon in New Orleans by African Americans excluded by the Afro-Creole community, who were often viewed as elitist and exclusionary by their English-speaking counterparts. There is some evidence to suggest that outside of New Orleans's African-descended population of either cultural orientation, whites in the city had begun to claim Laveau as a part of their cultural history as well. Laveau's racial status as Black, in the sense that she was of African descent, is rarely if ever challenged, but descriptions of her ranged from tall, thin, and nearly white to short, fat, and decidedly brown. While in individual cases it is not always clear exactly what witnesses were trying to argue by stating that Laveau was more or less Black, the vehemence with which they entered either side of this debate made it clear that this aspect of the Laveau mythology clearly held meaning for them. Further, considered together, attempts to claim Laveau reveal her significance to multiple cultural and racial communities in New Orleans.

Many witnesses exhibited a surprising willingness, even a need, to claim some relationship with Marie Laveau, often accompanied by a seemingly contradictory eschewing of Voodoo. Gloria Jones was a resident of New Orleans's Seventh Ward, long viewed as an enclave heavily populated by the Afro-Creole population. Louisiana Writers' Project (LWP) interviewers met with Jones about the wishing spot, a debated location rumored to be either on Lake Pontchartrain or Bayou St. John and associated with Laveau, where Voodoo practitioners went to pray or ask the spirits and saints for favors. Interviewers described Miss Jones as "very light-complexioned" and said that she professed to be dignified and accordingly disliked talking about Marie Laveau. However, Jones did tell interviewers that participants in Voodoo rituals dressed in colorful clothing and sang in Creole. She maintained that her grandmother had known Laveau but said that her family had not entertained her talk of the Voodoo queen. Even though Jones's address and the description of her as fair skinned suggest that she might have identified as Creole, she did not question the importance of Creole culture for Voodoo practitioners at this point, acknowledging the music explicitly and the dress implicitly as Creole. In contrast, however, she did attempt to distance herself from any association with Voodoo by professing to be "dignified" and eschewing any talk of Voodoo, even if it meant shutting out her grandmother. Much as the stigma of race mixing challenged white Creoles' status as fully white and thus civilized, associations made between Creole identity and Voodoo served a similar purpose for the Afro-Creole community. Jones sought to distance herself from her grandmother culturally by rejecting any stories about Marie Laveau or Voodoo. Simultaneously she clung to her association with Laveau by claiming not only that she knew who Laveau was but also that she had a personal connection to her, albeit a secondary one.[16]

Despite Laveau's association with the Creole community and that community's association with race mixing, some individuals disputed references to Laveau that seemed to mark her as somehow less Black than members of the non-Creole, African American community. In 1940, LWP workers interviewed Joseph Morris, who, remembering Laveau from his youth, described her as tall, portly, and brown skinned. He asserted in no uncertain terms that Laveau was not racially mixed or "a very light woman" and said that a picture in which she appeared to be had simply faded.[17] He also claimed that when he had seen Laveau and others dance in Congo Square, they wore "usual ordinary clothes," perhaps contradicting accounts of Laveau and her followers wearing exotic colorful Creole costumes.[18] He said specifically that Marie Laveau was "not a mulatress" and distinguished himself from Voodoo practitioners, whom he described as believers not in Voodoo but "in Marie Laveau," speaking to Laveau's centrality to the culture of Voodoo. He also distinguished himself from this group by saying that he was not "familiar with her practices," but he said that he remembered Laveau's house and that he had called her "grandma" in his youth. Mr. Morris seemed eager to identify Laveau with the Black community and to claim some personal relationship with her. But like Gloria Jones, he denied an association with Voodoo, which might create a cognitive liaison between Blackness and cultural backwardness.[19]

Not all African Americans refused to claim Laveau's practices as part of their cultural heritage, however. In contrast to Morris, Oscar Felix, an older gentleman who claimed to have participated as a singer in Laveau's ceremonies when he was a boy, described Laveau as a "good-looking brown-skinned woman, tall and like a queen. . . . Oh, yes, I am positive she was brown skinned."[20] Like the noted late nineteenth-century Afro-Creole activist and author Rodolphe Desdunes,[21] Felix did not seem to have a problem reconciling brown skin and Creole cultural markers, also maintaining that Laveau wore a "handkerchief around her head with two twists in the front," probably a reference to a tignon, a headdress worn by Creole women. In addition, unlike many of the witnesses who viewed participation in Voodoo rites as shameful, Felix openly admitted his participation, which he continued long after Laveau's death, and maintained that it was positive for his race that researchers were recording information on Laveau and Voodoo.[22]

The donning of the tignon held particular meaning for many of those interviewed about their memories of Marie Laveau.[23] Researchers spoke with an older woman who, having lived around the corner from Laveau, claimed that she had heard, though not witnessed, the Laveau rites, which she dismissed as "nonsense." This woman described the Voodoo queen as tall, "thin," and "very pretty." She said that Laveau "wore her hair dressed with curls falling on her shoulder" but "never wore a headdress or tignon."[24] The reference to shoulder-length curls may be a suggestion that Laveau was of mixed race, but the assertion that the tignon was absent implies that it had become a fixture in the Laveau mythology the informant contested.

According to one tradition, the tignon was a simple, colored madras handkerchief worn by Creole women. In the 1780s, during the short period of Spanish rule in Louisiana, Governor Don Estevan Miro ordered that women of African descent not "wear feathers, nor curls in their hair, combing same flat or covering it with a tignon," which was said to be a headwrap worn by slaves.[25] The tignon served not only to cover the hair, one of the most conspicuous physical characteristics that would mark this population as unique, but also as a reminder of servile status. The implication was that their hair was part of an aesthetic that made Creole girls of mixed race attractive to white men, a proposition that obviously disturbed the governor, among others. By the twentieth

Black Woman in Tignon, by Ellsworth Woodward, ca. 1910.
Courtesy of the Collections of the Louisiana State Museum.

century many believed that rather than enforcing modesty, the brightly colored coverings attracted attention to these women and became a distinct marker of Afro-Creole femininity and beauty.[26] In memories of Laveau, the tignon carried associations with race mixing, an interracial standard of beauty, and Creole identity for many of the witnesses who claimed to have known, seen, or heard stories about the Voodoo queen. Some ascribed this identity to Laveau, remembering her in the tignon, and others objected to it by contesting this part of her purported aesthetic.

Some of those who linked Laveau with the Creole community sought to identify her linguistically as Creole. Mary Washington claimed that Laveau spoke broken English but fluent French, that Laveau's mother was from Saint Domingue (modern Haiti), and that she wore a "madrasse," another name for the tignon. While the historical record may not bear out the immigrant status of Laveau's mother, the Creole population of New Orleans did in fact swell with the migration of thousands of émigrés after the Haitian Revolution, and reference to language may have been one of the most definitive ways to identify Laveau as Creole.

The connection between Marie Laveau and Creole culture was often made geographically as well as by aesthetic descriptions. An inordinate number of informants recalled her living on St. Ann Street between Burgundy and Rampart Streets. This location is now on the edge of the French Quarter, which encompassed the entire city of New Orleans during the colonial era. The suburbs, or faubourgs, as they were called locally, surrounding the city were built during succeeding generations to accommodate the expanding population. Therefore, this downtown area, north of Canal Street, which traditionally marked the border between the older Creole city and settlements of the incoming American population, was frequently identified with Creole culture. An article published in the *New Orleans Item-Tribune* in 1928 even identified the section of the city where Laveau lived as the "quadroon quarter" of New Orleans.[27]

In a 1922 *Times-Picayune* article, William Nott reported that a contemporary of Laveau's recalled that residents "below Canal Street," white and Black, had feared her power.[28] The author of a *Daily Picayune* article published just after Laveau's death in April of 1881 remembered her as a living receptacle of the city's history, having met every important person who spent time in New Orleans.[29] Laveau was thus a cultural landmark of sorts. Not only her appearance but her address was tied to unique historical and cultural markers in the city.

The majority of descriptions of Laveau identify her as Creole, fair skinned, and often wearing the tignon. This does not necessarily mean that this was the most accurate description of Laveau, but rather that it most closely fit her image as passed down in New Orleans's popular culture. A remembrance of Laveau as a quadroon or octoroon of beauty and stature resonated with the popular image of the city's racially exotic population in a way that a remembrance of her as brown and portly might not have. Laveau's aesthetic was as much a part of her legend as was her career as Voodoo queen. She was not just a practitioner of magic but identifiably the product of the unique cultural and

Marie Laveau, by Frank Schneider after George Catlin, ca. 1921–1923.
Courtesy of the Collections of the Louisiana State Museum.

racial history of New Orleans. It may be impossible to discover what Laveau really looked like, but a remembrance of her as racially mixed is an implicit identification with the city and with the Creole culture, so frequently equated with exotic, biracial individuals. Similarly, those who remembered Laveau as brown skinned appeared to be struggling to hold a place for darker African Americans in the cultural legacy of New Orleans. Acknowledging Laveau as an important part of that legacy, they remembered her not as representative of a population viewed as beautiful because of their aesthetic distance from the majority of the Black population but as decidedly Black and therefore somehow inclusive of a larger portion of the city's African American community.

Marie Laveau's identity as Creole was also characteristic of connections drawn between Voodoo and Creole culture. New Orleans popular culture conceived of Voodoo as the combination of African traditions and "the fetish worship of our Creole negroes" that were the "habits and customs of old Louisiana."[30] Isolated accounts of Laveau suggest that she may have played on the association between Creole identity and Voodoo. Raymond Rivaros, a former sexton of St. Louis Cemetery No. 2, told the LWP that at dances on Lake Pontchartrain songs were performed in French and Laveau wore a tignon, whereas he had never seen her wear the headdress anywhere else.[31] He also believed that none of Laveau's associates ever saw her do her "real work," which was conducted in secret. This implies that the ceremonies Laveau held in public were self-consciously performative of a Creole identity. Another witness who recalled the dances at Lake Pontchartrain and Congo Square reported that Laveau appeared mulatto and normally wore a handkerchief-like headdress and a plain blue dress but wore "fancy things for dances."[32] On Sundays at Congo Square, slaves were allowed to attend drumming and dancing ceremonies, which have long been considered a social safety valve by scholars.[33] The participation of slaves at this circumscribed time and place supposedly provided an opportunity for meetings between slaves and freed people, which were otherwise banned because of their association with insurrections. Many witnesses remembered that Laveau danced at these ceremonies, though the most convincing asserted that no Voodoo occurred there. If Laveau self-consciously sang in Creole or French and donned the tignon in the most public of the ceremonies she supposedly performed, at Lake Pontchartrain and observed by journalists, this suggests a deliberate deployment of the purported connection between Voodoo and the exotic Creole identity to add to the proceedings.

Early twentieth-century accounts about Laveau and her racial identity also reflect cultural concerns about the contemporary period. Informants who told stories about Laveau's predecessors and her progeny sometimes went beyond vague descriptions of her appearance and claimed to have actual knowledge of both her parentage and her offspring. One informant maintained that Marie was a quadroon whose father was white and whose mother was a "mulatress." This witness also asserted that Laveau had a daughter named Malvina who was darker than her mother and did not practice Voodoo, as it was on the decline in the period after Laveau's death.[34] The implication here may be, as asserted by authors like Martha Ward, that the story of darkening children and forgotten Voodoo culture may reflect the waning influence of Creole culture in New Orleans.[35] A Black woman interviewed when she was over eighty asserted that Laveau had raised a daughter who married "a pure white man."[36] Emile Labat, a Black undertaker who believed that his father had buried Laveau, mused aloud to researchers that much of the confusion about where Laveau was buried, a hotly contested issue at the time and since, might have been caused by family members who wanted to pass for white destroying the records that identified her tomb.[37] While this may be an unlikely scenario, it points to a concern by both the elderly woman and Labat that the city's Creole population might be declining, but here through intermarriage with whites rather than with African Americans as implied in the story about Malvina. It is often difficult to determine from the available interviews whether this change was viewed positively or negatively. It does suggest, however, that there was a discernable change in the New Orleans population by the beginning of the twentieth century that was being read into the Laveau mythology.

Even though Laveau's Afro-Creole identity was rarely, if ever, in dispute among informants who claimed to remember her, what that identity said about her relationship to the rest of the African American community was a slightly more contested issue. John Paul Smith, a seventy-two-year-old white man from Spanish Fort, on the edge of the city near Lake Pontchartrain, claimed that he remembered Laveau from frequent visits she made to a cabin in the area when he was a boy: "She never allowed any niggers in at those dances. She just catered to the white sports."[38] Taken by itself this comment is not terribly surprising; there were frequent mentions of business Laveau conducted mostly for white patrons. Smith added that at those dances she only worked with attractive octoroon girls and that "she never fooled with the niggers around here.

The only one she went with was Indian Jim." "Indian Jim" is a common moni-ker for Dr. Jim Alexander, a supposed Voodoo doctor and a contemporary of Laveau's. Some suggested that he was called Indian Jim because he appeared to be of mixed descent. Smith, however, stated unequivocally that Indian Jim was the product of a Black mother and an Indian father. In all, Smith seems to have been implying that Marie Laveau was too good, or too powerful, to consort with Blacks who were not of mixed heritage. It is also probably significant that during his interview he never explicitly identified Laveau as Black or Creole; rather, he described her as a "good looking woman" with black hair "sort of combed with curls." While very few, if any, informants denied that Laveau was a member of the Creole community, Smith may be the only identified witness who applied to Laveau a common twentieth-century stereotype that presumed that Creoles and people of mixed decent thought of themselves as superior to African Americans.[39] And while he did not identify her as white, he certainly seemed to distance her from the Black community in New Orleans.

It is also possible that Smith was attempting to claim the history and cul-ture embodied by the Laveau legend for members of the Spanish Fort com-munity who were neither Black nor Creole. It was not only African Americans in New Orleans who wanted to identify with Laveau In 1941, LWP researchers interviewed Leo Bronson, the operator of Pelletier's Antique Shop, on Royal Street in the French Quarter, not far from Laveau's residence in downtown New Orleans. Bronson claimed that his mother-in-law had bought Laveau's home after her death and found a dried, petrified snake in the house (a large snake sometimes called "Grand Zombi" that was, according to the Laveau my-thology, frequently used by Laveau both at Congo Square and Lake Pontchar-train) a claim that researchers doubted after checking the records and finding that no one with his mother-in-law's name had owned the Laveau property. If he fabricated this story, Bronson was no doubt aware that association with a mythohistorical figure like Laveau could enhance his business as a peddler of material culture. This suggests that whites, even those with no connection to Voodoo, often recognized the romance in having known Marie Laveau. It is doubtful that Smith and Bronson were the only white men to make such claims, and their readiness to associate themselves, even secondarily, with a controversial figure like Laveau in the midst of Jim Crow and segregation in the late 1930s and early 1940s demonstrates the universality of her association with the Crescent City.

Altars in the Front, Altars in the Back:
Politics of Ritual Practice in the Laveau Mythology

Stories about the rituals Laveau performed suggest that the Laveau mythology was infused with not only the history of the nineteenth century but also the politics of ritual practice in the twentieth century. The mythology surrounding Marie Laveau could be incredibly detailed, not only delving into her personal history and genealogy but including accounts of her own rituals and performance of Voodoo. Workers seldom noted differences between their own techniques and those of Laveau. Instead they emphasized the similarity between the rituals, suggesting that they had preserved the rites and ritual practice of the powerful Voodoo queen. Establishing similarities between their modern rites and Laveau's allowed twentieth-century practitioners to lay claim to the Laveau model of practicing Voodoo. They established Laveau as an independent practitioner working largely out of her home, performing clandestine rituals employing saints, altars, candles, and other paraphernalia. In turn, by estab-

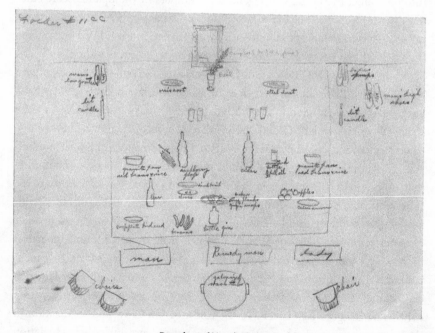

Drawing of Voodoo altar.
Northwestern State University of Louisiana, Watson Memorial Library, Cammie G. Henry
Research Center (Louisiana Writers' Project, folder 44 [part 1 of 2]).

lishing how Laveau practiced, they could claim to have followed, learned from, and duplicated much of this model, thereby legitimizing their own practices.

None of the informants described ritual manuals left by Laveau about how to practice.[40] In fact, reports suggested that the Laveau ceremonies were largely clandestine in nature. Those who claimed firsthand knowledge of Laveau's practice, remembering those practices fifty or more years later, most frequently stated that they had participated in the Laveau ceremonies as children. Invariably, though, those who claimed to have participated in this intimate fashion in their youth also practiced Voodoo professionally and frequently altered and adapted practices to meet their current needs. It is possible that their current practices or those learned since their childhood may have influenced their recollections of the Laveau rituals. It was also important that their memories of their earlier practices be aligned with their contemporary work. What I am suggesting here is not that this material be put aside as inaccurate; rather, it may tell us what early twentieth-century workers had invested in Laveau as a mythohistorical figure. Workers constructed the mythology to portray Laveau as a leader and founder to be emulated, both in her command of the ritual practices and in her quest for power.

Some workers interviewed in the 1930s recalled very specific ritual details about Laveau's practices. Raphael, a seventy-two-year-old African American male who claimed to have worked for Marie Laveau as a teenager, singing at her weekly ceremonies, recounted his experiences to LWP researchers. He said that Laveau kept an altar in the front room of her house for good work, "good luck charms, money-making charms, husband-holding charms, etc." A number of saints decorated this altar, according to Raphael, most notably Saint Peter. In the back room of her house she kept an altar for bad work, or "charms to kill, to drive away, to break up love affairs, and to spread confusion." On this altar were statues of a bear, a lion, a tiger, and a wolf. Raphael said that she would also work in the house of other Voodoo practitioners. On Mondays, for example, she performed what he called *parterres*, which LWP workers translated from French or Creole as "on the ground," though a more accurate translation might be "by the ground/earth/land." At these rites a feast was prepared for the spirits on a white tablecloth laid on the floor. The foods varied, but among them would be congri, or boiled rice and cowpeas, and various fruits. Colored candles were placed in the four corners of the room, the colors dictated by the purpose of the ritual. Women danced, accordion music was played, and songs were sung. Raphael claimed that periodically twelve well-to-do white women would "engage Marie" to participate in a *parterre,* at which they paid the dancers ten dollars each, and they danced barefoot and "almost nude" at a place on Bayou St. John.[41] In a separate statement Raphael claimed that Marie Laveau worked without an altar when she did "bad work," perhaps referring to the *parterres.*[42]

Raphael's accounts of the Laveau ceremonies were entangled with descriptions of his own power and practice. He said that both he and his brother were involved in the work.[43] So in recounting the Laveau mythology for researchers he incidentally or intentionally promoted his own power. Mostly because of the dates he gave for his work with Laveau, researchers discounted the possibility that Raphael had actually studied his craft under Marie Laveau, as he claimed. Raphael's story contains many of the formulaic descriptions of the Laveau model for practicing Voodoo observed by workers in the beginning of the twentieth century. He also took the opportunity to impugn his competition. He made a brief mention of Nome Felix, alternatively known as Oscar Felix, a worker who also claimed to have participated in the Laveau ceremonies in his youth and continued as a worker into the twentieth century. Raphael claimed that Felix was a "fake," misrepresenting himself as having known Laveau. He also claimed that Felix had learned his work from Raphael and his brother Paul. In attacking Felix's connection to Laveau, Raphael may have been seeking to strengthen his own claim of connection to the Voodoo queen. In claiming that Felix had been his student and not Laveau's, he may also have been claiming responsibility for whatever power and reputation Felix had been able to attain as a worker.

Oscar Felix participated in an "Opening," or initiation, performed for LWP researchers who were posing as aspiring workers in order to observe these rituals that was nearly identical to rites he attributed to Marie Laveau. Researchers recounted that the Opening took place in an unfurnished room of a house in secret. He insisted that the altar for the ceremony must be on the floor. It started with a white cotton cloth, reportedly the size of a tablecloth, adorned with a picture of Saint Peter leaned against the wall. Felix added white and green candles lit, one on either side of the altar, and a quart bottle of cider and another of raspberry pop, in front of which were placed other colored candles. The altar was also adorned with a plate of steel dust to the right of the picture, a plate of orrisroot to the left, and a plate of dried basil in front of it. Researchers also noted the plate of cake they called "stage planks,"[44] a box of gingersnaps, mixed birdseed, bananas, powdered cloves, cinnamon, apples, two pans of congri (composed of red beans and rice), olive oil, and a bag of sugar. A camphor branch was leaned against the picture of Saint Peter, according to the researcher because there was no palm branch, and there was a glass containing gin, sugar, and water with "a spray of large basil" in front of it, along with a bottle of local beer and a court notice. Researchers claimed that Felix began the rite by knocking on the floor three times, having them do the same, and praying in French. Again this is very similar to the setup for a rite described by Felix that he claimed was performed by Laveau and her followers on St. John's Eve. The question remains, to what extent is Felix's description of the Laveau ceremonies reflective of his own rites, and to what extent did maintaining the traditions of Marie Laveau and having practiced with her during her lifetime validate the practices of modern workers?

Undoubtedly, the similarity of his own rite to the one attributed to Laveau lent credibility to his own practice. This, combined with his age and the great chronological distance from the time he would have been able to observe the Laveau rites and the time in which he was reproducing them for LWP researchers, suggests that perhaps his current practice influenced his memory of the Laveau ceremonies. Often, contemporary elements, many of them seeming to characterize practices used by workers in the 1920s and 1930s, were included in the mythology surrounding the work of Marie Laveau. Substitutions such as Felix's of the camphor branch for a palm branch, based on the availability of ritual objects, were common in Voodoo in the twentieth century. This kind of constant innovation would have yielded significant changes in ritual practice, thereby creating some distance between how Voodoo was practiced in the late nineteenth century and how it was practiced in the early twentieth century. Clearly, whether or not the descriptions given for the Laveau rituals are accurate for the nineteenth century, they outline a methodology for practicing Voodoo that is reflective of rites in the early twentieth century. In addition, by the twentieth century many workers and residents of the city regarded Laveau as a kind of founding figure in the establishment of Voodoo as it was practiced in New Orleans. Most did not imply that she created Voodoo or that she was the first to practice it in the city. Rather, she is usually represented as an innovator who added certain forms to the practice of Voodoo or broadened its appeal, suggesting that even in shaping the image of Laveau innovation and creation were important, and that workers' tendency toward innovation was embraced in their collective memory of the history of their practices, which centered on Laveau.[45]

Workers' claims to have known Laveau linked their own power to hers. Raphael's and Felix's claims centered on their having participated in the Laveau ceremonies in their youth. Other workers claimed to have learned their technique directly from Laveau. Mary Washington remembered that she had rescued Laveau from drowning on the banks of Lake Pontchartrain and that Laveau herself had mentored her in the work. Speaking about Spiritual Churches, Washington said, "They run their business like Marie Laveau did," suggesting a connection between rites resembling spiritual possession in both traditions and a resonance with the spiritual work of Laveau even outside the community of self-identified Voodoo practitioners in New Orleans. Marie Dede based her connection to Laveau on close familial ties to the Voodoo queen, asserting that Laveau had spent a great deal of time at her home and that her father, who knew Laveau well, had told her that "Marie Laveau was the cause of them other folks starting that hoodoo business in the treme [i.e., Treme, one of the oldest faubourgs in New Orleans, just west of the French Quarter]."[46] By making this claim, Washington not only rooted her own power in the Laveau mythology but also suggested that other spiritual practitioners in New Orleans were part of a wider community that had Laveau to thank for establishing or popularizing their current practices. Similarly, one informant posited that the tradition of sweeping red brick dust on front steps in New Orleans had originated with Laveau.[47] Many locals in the early twentieth century believed this ritual warded off evil or gris-gris, which might be left on their front steps.

Often the Laveau mythology merged figures from the past and present. In one case, interview material gathered in 1940 stated that Laveau worked with two other practitioners, called Grandjean and Titi Albert. Grandjean was the name of a Spiritualist famous in New Orleans for conducting séances during the Civil War era. Conversely, the 'Tit Albert is a mystical text frequently mentioned by practitioners in the twentieth century.[48] Thus the Laveau mythology was not only about the time it purported to describe but integrated these other figures, practices, and adjacent periods.

Another interesting aspect of the accounts about Laveau's ritual performances was the suggestion that she only performed certain rites on certain days or nights. Some said that Laveau's designated meeting night was Friday night, while others said that they only knew her to perform at certain places on Mondays or Wednesdays.[49] This presents an interesting parallel to Spiritual Churches in the early twentieth century, which held services dedicated to certain saints, spirits, or rites on similar weekly schedules. The idea that Laveau had regular services on particular nights may tell us more about the functioning of the community in the period in which these stories were being told than in the period they claimed to describe.

Despite the number of accounts of how Laveau practiced Voodoo, a large part of the mythology insists that Laveau practiced her rituals in secret. Anita Fonvergne claimed that as a child she had seen Laveau in the graveyard and that persistent rumors that she was buried in the St. Louis Cemetery on Claiborne Street, on the outskirts of Treme, could be attributed to the fact that Laveau would do her "bad work" there in private after leaving more public ceremonies at Congo Square.[50] Raymond Rivaros, a former sexton at St. Louis Cemetery who claimed to have gone to Marie Laveau's house when she was practicing told researchers that he thought that none of Laveau's workers knew how she worked because in public she simply stated the price for the work but never allowed anyone to see how it was done.[51] Similarly, Oscar Felix told researchers that while Laveau did participate in dances at Congo Square, "these weren't the regular ceremonies because those were never held in public."[52] All these people thought of the Laveau model of practicing Voodoo as secret. The access to this information about purportedly clandestine ritual fifty years after Laveau's passing may indicate that twentieth-century workers were assuming a congruity between their practices and those of the Laveau era rather than recalling decades-old, intricate ritual details from their childhoods.

As intrinsic as secrecy and Voodoo were to stories about Laveau's life and practice, some suggested that the Voodoo queen's political acumen explained her success in operating her business without being prosecuted for practicing Voodoo. Many believed that she was able to influence the outcomes of court cases because she knew and did favors for important judges and police officers. These stories suggested that Laveau had managed to curry favor with important people, thereby avoiding problems and increasing her power, not only in reach but in kind, from the spiritual to the sociopolitical. Such professional multitasking would be ardently replicated by workers and Spiritual Church heads who employed lawyers to mitigate some of their troubles in the twentieth century and told stories of their associations with Louisiana politicians.

Even after her death, the mythology surrounding Laveau is said to have had an effect on practice, with sites tied to her death also becoming associated with her power. The debated site of her tomb in the St. Louis Cemetery was often visited by individuals who crossed the grave with red brick in order to solicit her power or favor.[53] One informant who claimed to have visited Laveau's grave said that it was particularly crowded on certain days and that she had seen people place money, along with offerings of wine, preserves, pralines, and candles, in the vault where they believed she was buried.[54] In addition, stories about Laveau drowning in Bayou St. John or Lake Pontchartrain appear in more than one interview from the early twentieth century, and at least one informant told researchers that Laveau's followers believed that if they submerged at the spot where she supposedly died in Bayou St. John, any spell cast on them would be washed away.[55] This sanctification of supposed sites of Laveau's death again demonstrates the investment later practitioners had in the Laveau mythology.

Economics

A great deal of the power assigned to Marie Laveau in the mythology surrounding her life and practice was not only supernatural but economic. By the beginning of the twentieth century, and undoubtedly long before, New Orleanians, like most Americans, understood the extraordinary influence that accompanied wealth. In the mythology surrounding Laveau in the early twentieth century, she was not remembered as using Voodoo to surpass or compete with the economically powerful; rather, she was remembered as using supernatural means to accumulate economic power of her own. Laveau's practice of Voodoo supposedly allowed her to amass a great deal of wealth, mostly in return for magical and spiritual services rendered to wealthy white clients. Despite New Orleans's history of African-descended property owners and business people, there was no question who controlled the majority of the city's economic resources. In the public imagination wealth was generally considered one of the privileges of whiteness. In that vein, the Laveau mythology attempted to explain her apparently contradictory status as both Black and wealthy by attributing her wealth to access to the white community. Some of the stories even asserted that she had acquired her home from a white benefactor to whom she had provided Voodoo-related services.[56]

This relationship to white wealth often complicated perceptions of Laveau's connections to the African American population in New Orleans. Some stories assert that in addition to making money by performing Voodoo rituals for white women, who supposedly lined the street outside her home with extravagant carriages, Laveau worked as a sexual procuress, obtaining quadroon or octoroon girls to serve as concubines to white men for a fee.[57] These accounts are undoubtedly tied to the city's history of *plaçage*, formalized relationships in which white men maintained a quadroon or octoroon mistress in a certain degree of material comfort without ever marrying her and sometimes while married to a white woman. Interestingly, some of the mythology surrounding Laveau's access to white wealth entailed a negative or at least questionable relationship to African American women. Similarly, many of the individuals interviewed about Laveau who spoke to the high cost of her services also posited that this price did not apply to African Americans and that Laveau did not work for Blacks who could not afford her price.

As with much of the Laveau mythology, however, there are contradictory stories. Some suggest that Laveau had a special relationship to the poor, Blacks, and others in need. Some, while not contradicting the perception that Laveau became wealthy working for whites, contended that she helped the poor free of charge while gouging her wealthy clients. One of the accounts repeated by more than one witness claimed that Laveau and her followers often deposited food, money, and other offerings for the poor in the hollow bark of a tree at Congo Square.[58] She was also remembered as sheltering both African slaves and Native Americans at her home. Some of these, especially the Native Americans, are remembered as traders with whom Laveau had some kind of business relationship, adding the role of entrepreneur to her other accomplishments.[59]

While there were stories about every other aspect of Laveau's life, those interviewed about her knew surprisingly little about the existence of a husband or mate. Some had some vague notion that there was a man in her life, but many did not know whether she was married or what man, if any, she was in a relationship with.[60] The obscurity of Laveau's marital relationship and her image as an economically powerful woman are not unrelated phenomena in the Laveau mythology. I would suggest that much of this is due to her image as a powerful and independent woman who established her economic influence through her own business in Voodoo. Stories about a husband, especially one gainfully employed, who in the nineteenth century would have been expected to financially support Laveau, might have complicated the mythology's portrayal of her power.

43

Laveau as an economically empowered woman was an imposing figure on the cultural landscape of New Orleans and the community of Voodoo practitioners. Her story drew together notions of spiritual and economic power that were crucial to understanding the practice of Voodoo in the early twentieth century. Unlike religions that eschewed an association between spiritual power and material wealth, the Laveau mythology painted a vibrant picture of one form of power helping to generate and sustain the other. This connection was crucial to the perceptions of workers in the twentieth century. The necessity of mingling the roles of spiritual leader and entrepreneur, as well as the perception that the ability to garner significant wealth was integral to the Laveau model, was established in the numerous accounts of her life and work as a Voodoo queen. This model of spiritual practice left an impression on the religious culture that had to be engaged by spiritual leaders operating in New Orleans in the early twentieth century. Among the most prominent of these may have been Mother Leafy Anderson, the purported founder of the Spiritual Church movement in New Orleans.

Anderson, frequently accused of practicing Voodoo at her own church, was forced to deal with the cultural legacy left by Laveau in fighting the stigma of Voodoo. Laveau's importance in the city as demonstrated by the racial tug-of-war that saw diverse communities attempt to claim Marie as their own was something that Anderson would have to contend with forty years after the Voodoo queen's death in order to establish herself as a spiritual practitioner in New Orleans. Problems with the law and a demand among spiritual practitioners in the city that the Spiritual Church mother be able to meet needs that workers in the city had been meeting since Laveau undoubtedly impacted her work. Her adaptation to the Laveau model demonstrates the importance of that model to the city's spiritual culture. Similarly, her ready adaptation to those circumstances demonstrates her connection to the spirit of innovation that drove the continuation of Voodoo in New Orleans.

2

"MESSIN' AROUND IN THE WORK"

The Leafy Anderson Model and New Orleans Voodoo

I n the 1930s, researchers from the Louisiana Writers' Project interviewed Mary Johnson, a long-time worker and apparent proponent of the Laveau model of Voodoo practice, at her home uptown, just south of Canal Street. She told researchers that before Leafy Anderson, the supposed founder of the Spiritual Church movement in New Orleans, started her church in New Orleans, she sought Johnson out for advice, probably on the basis of her reputation in the city as a successful Voodoo practitioner. Despite vociferous contentions by some that Leafy Anderson practiced Voodoo and by others that the Spiritual Church she founded in New Orleans was free of these practices, Mary Johnson was certain that Anderson practiced Voodoo, stating unequivocally that "Leafy was messin' around in the work." According to Johnson, Anderson was concerned about how her operation would fare with legal authorities and whether she could turn a profit. Anderson apparently told Johnson that she believed New Orleans would be a profitable city to do business in but that she was concerned about law enforcement given the decades or even centuries of suppression of Voodoo. Anderson would have to adjust to the legacy of the Laveau model in terms of both law enforcement and ritual practice in order to successfully run her Spiritual Church in New Orleans. Her solution was to create a "legitimate church," perhaps suggesting a more institutionalized structure for her spiritual practices than that of Laveau's followers. She also believed that she needed some "contact and protection" to deal with law enforcement. Though she eschewed the practice of Voodoo in her organization, many in the city doubted the veracity of claims made to this effect, and some Spiritual Church leaders openly practiced rituals that resembled those mentioned in the stories about Laveau and common among workers in twentieth-century New Orleans.

Information about Leafy Anderson prior to her arrival in New Orleans is fragmentary and largely dependent on accounts by her followers in New Orleans. Between 1913 and 1920 Anderson supposedly established a network of missions and churches beginning in Chicago, purportedly her city of origin, and moving through Arkansas, Tennessee, Florida, Mississippi, and finally Louisiana. Once she reached New Orleans in 1920, however, Anderson was able to establish churches and a system of training other ministers, or "mothers" and "fathers," as they were called, which led to the proliferation of Spiritual Churches according to the model that would become so significant in New Orleans. Beginning uptown, this movement spread, with Spiritual Churches being established across the city and surviving Mother Anderson's death in 1927.[1]

The Anderson model centered on spiritual work within the context of a church. With a charter and the financial means to include the accoutrements of Christian religion, Mother Anderson, while not completely immune from legal persecution, created a space for her organization, which frequently fared better vis-à-vis legal authorities than some of her predecessors in the city who functioned under the Laveau model as independent, home-based workers. Using profits from the church, she was also able to acquire property and infrastructure that lent legitimacy to her claim that hers was a bona fide religion. These funds also gave her the means to bribe local law enforcement, for whom the appearance of religious legitimacy might not have been a deterrent from persecuting her and her followers. The stability of the church and the money earned also provided the means to hire a lawyer to defend her interests and those of her congregation. Financial resources added to religious legitimacy, which added to the stability of the Spiritual Churches as institutions, which in turn improved their ability to generate income. This was a cycle that characterized one of the central contributions of the Spiritual Church, and what I have labeled in this chapter the *Anderson model* of spiritual practice, to the community of Voodoo practitioners in New Orleans.

This business model allowed Anderson to give birth to the Spiritual Church movement in New Orleans. But that movement could not have survived without taking into account the local context and spiritual market. For some Spiritual Church heads, the spiritual marketplace they entered often encouraged them to incorporate the practices of local Voodoo practitioners into their structure to better serve a community already acquainted with Voodoo. In addition, the Anderson model created a structure adopted by some local workers.

Within that structure, professional practitioners of Voodoo continued their own rituals and practices, but often with fewer conflicts with legal authorities and more profits. Thus, the citywide culture of Voodoo that I call the Laveau model greatly influenced the practices of the Spiritual Church movement, and the Anderson model simultaneously changed the way Voodoo functioned in New Orleans. After Anderson established her church and the organization that would give birth to more than a dozen like it, Voodoo practitioners in New Orleans had a framework for practice that generally worked within the bounds of the law. Further, rather than simply dismissing or rejecting workers, as many of their Christian counterparts did, some noteworthy members of the Spiritual Churches used their Christian-based religious organization's malleable structure to incorporate aspects of Voodoo on their own terms. Mary Johnson believed that the Anderson model of business and institution building was successful. She told researchers that she thought Anderson had done "some good" in New Orleans.[2]

Voodoo in the Church

Criminalization of Voodoo was part and parcel of the culture in New Orleans, and Mother Anderson would have to contend with that culture when she began to operate her church in the city. The earliest verifiable reports of Voodoo practitioners in New Orleans were related to their prosecution by legal authorities in the city during the antebellum period. That trend did not cease after the Civil War, and Voodoo practitioners' relationship with the law would have implications for Leafy Anderson's Spiritual Churches well into the twentieth century. Local authorities' hostility to the practice of Voodoo was part of the culture and would have direct consequences for Mother Anderson and the Spiritual Churches.

As early as the mid-nineteenth century, local officials enacted laws aimed at, or seemingly with, Voodoo practitioners in mind. In 1858 a city ordinance forbade African Americans from gathering for worship services without the supervision of a white congregation. It was under this prohibition, aimed at preventing revolt, and similar laws prohibiting free people of color from meeting with slaves that Voodoo practitioners were prosecuted during the Laveau era. With emancipation, this law would no longer suffice to prosecute Voodoo practitioners, and in 1879 city ordinance 5046 prohibited "disorderly conduct,

. . . exposing the body, loitering in public places and made it necessary to support dependents in a legitimate manner and provided for punishment not only of offenders but of police who failed in their duty to enforce the ordinance."[3] The restrictions contained in this ordinance not only identify it as an assault on the practice of Voodoo, as practitioners at raided services were often said to be found nude or nearly so, but also indicate that the law viewed Voodoo practitioners as disorderly, licentious, and incapable of supporting themselves without resorting to artifice.

The 1879 ordinance was followed two years later by another prohibiting assembly in squares, parks, and other places without proper authorizations and repeating the prohibition against exposing parts of the body.[4] The preoccupation not only with gathering for religious purposes but with public spaces reflects an insistence by the law on not only stopping the practice of Voodoo but hiding it from the sight of the public. In 1894 the Louisiana Medical Practice Act required graduation from an accredited medical school and a license from the state board of medical examiners in order to offer therapeutic treatment of any kind.[5] This is particularly important given that many twentieth-century practitioners were investigated by the state board and associated law enforcement for practicing medicine without a license while providing treatment for injured or ill clients. Later ordinances, such as those passed in 1897, "prohibiting trance artists, voodoos and similar tricksters," as well as outlawing "all phases of fortune-telling, pretended power to effect marriages, and inducing clients through publicity making fabulous statements," even more directly targeted Voodoo practitioners and related professionals as a group. After a lull around the turn of the century, new ordinances were passed in 1916, 1922, and 1924 to replace, reiterate, or update nineteenth-century counterparts. Thus, two decades into the twentieth century, when Mother Anderson arrived in New Orleans, there were local precedents for prosecuting spiritual practices associated with spiritual healing and supernatural control of romantic or professional relationships going back at least sixty years. In addition to dealing with the legal perception of Voodoo, Anderson would also have to deal with her congregation's expectations regarding these kinds of practices, both positive and negative.

Anderson's Spiritual Church organization had a complex relationship with the workers who practiced Voodoo in New Orleans, often expressed as animosity by Spiritual Church members toward the practice of Voodoo. When Zora

Hurston began her ethnographic research of Voodoo in New Orleans in the late 1920s, shortly after Anderson's death, she reported that while the first Spiritual Church Anderson founded, the Eternal Life Christian Spiritual Church, was free of hoodoo, the other eleven congregations affiliated with Anderson and her "co-workers," as they were known in the Spiritual Church, had been "stolen by hoodoo worshipers."[6] The implication was that Anderson was not aware of or complicit in the connection of her Spiritual Church to the community of Voodoo practitioners in New Orleans. By contrast, Mary Johnson's contention that Anderson sought her advice before establishing her organization in the city, along with other evidence provided by subjects interviewed by the Louisiana Writers' Project in the 1930s, brings the oppositional dichotomy between Anderson's practices and hoodoo or Voodoo in New Orleans into question. The contention here is not that Anderson simply used the Spiritual Church label to cover the practice of Voodoo, as many of her contemporary critics asserted. Rather, I am positing that the lines between the Spiritual Churches and the community of Voodoo practitioners were not as firm as either this perspective or Spiritual Church members' frequently stated contention that they did not practice Voodoo implied. In contrast to Spiritual Church members who defended Anderson's memory after her death from the stigma of practicing Voodoo by asserting that she never participated in such practices, many Spiritual Church members embraced the practices of workers. If Mary Johnson's recounting of her meeting with Anderson is accurate, that trend extended back to the founding of the Spiritual Church movement in New Orleans. It also suggests that from the beginning Anderson was interested in incorporating techniques, whether spiritual or operational, from the Laveau model of spiritual practice as described by Mary Johnson, based on her purported thirty-seven years of experience as a worker.[7]

The closeness of the relationship between Anderson's Spiritual Churches and the practices of workers can also be inferred from the beliefs expressed and activities engaged in by her co-workers. Alberta Price, one of Anderson's closest associates, had apparently been with her since she relocated to New Orleans from Chicago. After Anderson's death, perhaps in an attempt to claim Anderson's estate, estimated to be worth $8,860.92 in 1928, Price claimed to have been Anderson's niece, an assertion that was undoubtedly plausible owing to both the inordinate amount of time they apparently spent together and to the fact that she had represented herself as such in the past. An agent for the

Italian Homestead, through which Anderson acquired the building on Amelia Street for the Eternal Life Christian Spiritual Church, remembered Price conducting much of Anderson's business for her when she was ill.

A number of witnesses suggested that Price, who was "second to Mother Anderson" in her organization,[8] may have been involved in practicing Voodoo. Most convincingly, a maid at Charity Hospital told LWP researchers that she had known a woman who, when the doctors at the hospital apparently could not cure her health problems, sought out "a hoodoo woman named Price" who lived on North Derbigny Street between Conti and Bienville. The Homestead agent who noted Price's importance to Anderson's organization also noted that Price had moved to the neighborhood of Bienville and Broad Streets, less than a mile from the location given by the Charity Hospital maid, after the church organization lost its title to Anderson's property for failing to make payments after her death in 1927.[9] The maid's statement suggests that Price, Anderson's closest co-worker, had apparently become known as a "hoodoo woman" by the late 1930s. The maid said that Price had diagnosed the woman's neck problems as being the result of a friend's having stolen her menstruation cloth and buried it in the graveyard because she coveted her husband. These kinds of rituals, specifically those aimed at joining or separating couples, will be discussed in chapter 5. For now it is sufficient to note that this was a formula commonly used by workers in the city. Both the diagnoses and the cure suggest at least a belief by the witness that Price, one of the founding members of Anderson's Spiritual Church, was employing a ritual formula common among workers.

Other associates of Anderson's, while not openly practicing Voodoo, did express ambiguity about the relationship between Voodoo and some of the Spiritual Churches' practices. Father Thomas, the founder of St. Paul Spiritual Church No. 1, who had been trained and financially backed by Anderson, said that he had disagreed with Anderson on a number of issues, one being the role of Black Hawk in the Spiritual Church. Black Hawk was a Native American spirit popularized by Leafy Anderson in New Orleans. Father Thomas told researchers, "Dere may be a little hoodoo in dat Black Hawk business. . . . Nobody knows but Leafy Anderson."[10] Thomas expressed uncertainty about Black Hawk, saying that some Spiritual Church members' reports about him and the results of soliciting his aid had been positive, while other members' reports about their experiences with Black Hawk had been frighteningly negative. His own discomfort came from the fact that Black Hawk was not mentioned in the Bible, and he believed Mother Anderson may have confused Black Hawk with another saint. He also believed that some members had left his church because he "didn't know what to give people when dey wanted to do harm"[11] and had sought out Spiritual Church leaders known to be associated with Voodoo. According to Father Thomas, these individuals eventually returned to him reporting negative or malicious experiences with Black Hawk and requested his aid in countering the pernicious effects of their experiences. While he was apparently unable to ascertain the precise relationship between them, Father Thomas appeared to have some ambiguous feelings about Black Hawk and Voodoo and chose to avoid work with Black Hawk in favor of more traditional figures, like Saint Paul, maintaining a close association between his church and a more traditional form of Christianity.

Thus even for Spiritual Church leaders who had been associated with Anderson's organization, the line between her work as a Spiritual Church mother and Voodoo was blurred. This is not to draw a one-to-one correlation between invoking Black Hawk and the use of Voodoo by Spiritual Church members. Rather, Father Thomas's account suggests that so much of Anderson's work was conducted in secret that even those who worked with her were not sure where her Spiritual Church practices ended and Voodoo began. This suggests a fluid relationship between Anderson's practices and the rites employed by workers in the city. There was no hard and fast line between these practices even among those closest to Anderson.

The fear of saying anything negative about Anderson or her co-workers, specifically implicating them in the practice of Voodoo even after death, may also indicate that the public believed her to be practicing Voodoo, specifically Voodoo that could be used to attack them if they disparaged members of her community. Zora Hurston claimed that similar to the way Laveau's power was invoked by Voodoo practitioners in the city after her death, some of Anderson's followers believed her to be present at some of their meetings after her death.[12] The researcher Robert McKinney noted that in the 1930s, years after Anderson's death, Pauline Smith, a member of Anderson's church, said fearfully that she would not speak about Anderson or Alberta Price. Another witness who had attended Anderson's church a number of times said that while she had not been privy to the details of Anderson's work, she did know that Anderson called individuals who were afflicted with "something real bad" to her home to be serviced in private. The interviewer noted that this witness too became unwilling to give information, saying that she did not "want to be mixed up in no hoodoo or spiritualist bisness." Her fear was that she would "be er round hyar wid something ailin me an Ah won't know what de cause of it." The fear of reprisals via Voodoo was common among individuals interviewed about both workers and Spiritual Church leaders. Some researchers who interviewed individuals to get information about Marie Laveau long after her death noted a similar sentiment among some of them, and this anxiety seemed to follow Anderson and her co-workers as well. Pauline Smith's fearfulness suggests that even members of the Spiritual Church congregations believed that Anderson was connected to Voodoo.[13]

Failing to meet the local demand for Voodoo rites could have hurt Anderson's ability to maintain and expand her organization in New Orleans. One of her followers who attempted to found his own church after her death had to abandon the endeavor for financial reasons. He too implied some discomfort with the relationship between the Spiritual Churches and Voodoo. Eli, or Elias, Williams had worked with Anderson and according to some had been groomed to succeed her after her death. Because of conflicts with Alberta Price, he branched off after Anderson's death and founded his own church.[14] He told researchers that he believed that "the people" wanted "hoodoo practices" and that there was money to be made from performing them. He clearly indicated that he had had no interest in providing these services, and while he did not draw a correlation between his intransigence and the economic problems that forced him to close his doors and take up work as a servant or butler, it may not be a stretch for us to draw this correlation or to assume that Anderson had drawn it.[15]

The blurring of the line between Anderson's practices and those of workers in the city may have resulted in part from a demand for these rites and practices created by their ubiquity before she started her organization. As Anderson's visit to Mary Johnson implies, when she moved to New Orleans she was entering a spiritual market previously dominated by workers. Even if Anderson had intended to create something completely new in New Orleans or to copy her model from Chicago, *sans Voodoo,* she would have had to contend with clients that were familiar with the operations of workers and thus wanted those kinds of spiritual services provided. Like Father Thomas after her, she may have found that failing to provide these services resulted in a loss of membership and income, and while Thomas's account implies that he stuck to his guns, allowing those who wanted Voodoo-style rituals in order to harm others to leave his congregation, Anderson may have decided to be more accommodating. Whatever the case, it seems relatively certain that the practice of Voodoo in New Orleans had an impact on the Anderson model, and vice versa.

Building a Church: The Anderson Model of Institutionalization

Institutionalization is at the heart of the Anderson model. The workers who operated in New Orleans prior to the Spiritual Church movement were generally content to run their businesses from their homes, sometimes with charters from one school or another giving them the right to practice. However, Anderson's Spiritual Churches presented a new and malleable format for indigenous spiritual and religious practices. As previously stated, some of these rites common among workers in New Orleans may have been added to the practices of Spiritual Church heads who legitimately viewed themselves as carrying on a distinct body of practices but incorporated these or similar rites in order to meet an existing demand. A number of Spiritual Church heads obtained charters to found Spiritual Churches after operating as workers with no such institutional forms surrounding their practices. The organization built by Anderson, which allowed co-workers to establish churches independently, altering practice as they saw fit, under the legal protection of a charter that sanctioned their work as part of a legitimate religious institution, appears to have been an innovation at the time.

In October 1920 Leafy Anderson legally incorporated her church by obtaining a charter from the Office of the Recorder of Mortgages for the Parish of Orleans that recognized the Eternal Life Christian Spiritual Church as "a body politic in law." Article 2 of the charter defined the church as "strictly religious," and claimed that the object of the church was to demonstrate the "true doctrine of Christian Spiritualism," but the charter established the right of the church to "buy, own, or sell property."[16] While a more detailed statement of the church's doctrine would undoubtedly have been reserved for a mission statement of some kind, the close proximity in the charter of the statements of the religious and financial missions suggests the intimate connection between them for Anderson's organization. The purpose of the charter and the structure it established for the church was to give the institution a form viewed as legitimate in the eyes of the law. Apparently central to doing so for Anderson was the right of the organization to own, buy, and sell property. In the view of the public, the difference between a legitimate religious organization and a group viewed as a sect or cult often has less to do with the doctrine of any specific faith and more to do with the adoption of the appearance of organized religion. In the United States, organized religious communities have church buildings. The ability to acquire such infrastructure almost immediately changes the status of a religious community. Infrastructure and resources often lend legitimacy to a community of religious practitioners. Churches are thought to contain certain material objects, mostly those common in the churches of the Christian majority, such as altars, pews, and so on. Again, these things would be just as important to Anderson as a legal charter in establishing her model of religious organization as legitimate in the public imagination. Of course, a charter was less visible. Further, as the example of workers arrested in the early twentieth century despite possessing certificates granting them the right to practice one or another magical art suggests, the official recognition implied by possession of a charter added little legitimacy to workers' practices. Anderson seems to have brought the understanding to the community of workers in New Orleans that to be a church or religion was to act like a church or religious organization. In the United States, churches owned property both "real and personal."[17]

Anderson also established the method of acquiring the funds to buy and sell property for the church that was legitimate in the eyes of the law. The charter explicitly stated that the laws of the church would not "act in conflict with the laws of the United States or of this state, to receive donations and bequests of all kinds." By establishing Eternal Life as an organization that took donations with the ability "to donate help, giving and helping the needy and deserving," Anderson marked the monetary exchanges of her organization. These exchanges, of the kind traditionally associated with Christian religious organizations, were in keeping with common notions that such organizations were maintained through the charity and generosity of their congregations rather than by the profit motive. There is of course a contradiction in the notion that the products of economic success, namely, the infrastructure that would make a religious community readily identifiable as a legitimate church, are divorced from, or at least partially removed from, the engines of commerce that generate the funds necessary to purchase them. This contradiction is integral to the way legitimate religious organizations are imagined in the United States. However, the recognition and inculcation of this contradiction in the charter for her church also characterized the Anderson model, which would become so intertwined with the community of workers and Voodoo practitioners in New Orleans.

Anderson's importance as an institution builder was acknowledged by her death notice on December 13, 1927, in the *Times-Picayune*, which identified her as the "President and Founder of the Eternal Life Christian Spiritualist Church."[18] Though Anderson's charter established the original location of her church as 2059 Jackson Avenue, the Longshoremen's Hall, where she initially held meetings, she eventually purchased property on Amelia Street through the Italian Homestead, a member of the Federal Home Loan Bank system.[19] Mother Dora Tyson, one of Anderson's first graduates and among her closest associates, stated explicitly that Anderson's organization and instruction offered her students "ways to earn money" and attracted some seventy-five persons to learn this model from her in her first year of instruction. Mother Dora also maintained that Anderson had established churches in Indiana, New Jersey, and a number of other states.[20] Mary Johnson confirmed as much when she said that Anderson had told her that she also had a church in Chicago and was seeking Johnson's advice, especially in reference to dealing with the law, because being arrested in New Orleans might hurt her reputation and organization back in Chicago and "kill" her "in nine states."[21] This suggests that Anderson's model may have been constructed after many dealings with legal authorities in various states. These prior incidents, along with her ability to cater to the needs and spiritual demands of the local culture, may account for some of her success in the city. The *Times-Picayune* account, as well as the recollections of Tyson and Johnson, tell us that Anderson, like Laveau, was viewed by both the public and her followers as a professional and economically savvy figure as well as a religious leader. This was a component of the Laveau mythology as well, but exemplified by Anderson and the Spiritual Church heads who succeeded her.

After Anderson died, her organization fell on hard times, losing her apparently substantial holdings. A succession of Anderson's estate filed after her death suggests that her assets may have amounted to more than $8,800, and this figure may not have included the building that was officially owned by the Eternal Life Christian Spiritual Church, a corporation that lost the property to the Italian Homestead, which foreclosed a year after Anderson's death because of the congregation's inability to pay the rent.[22] Anderson's church on Amelia Street was valued at $5,110.92.[23] The property may have been lost in part because of a lawsuit filed against Anderson for some $6,700 by a contractor who claimed that Anderson had not paid him for work valued at that amount. There are some indications that there was a lien on Anderson's property when she died.[24] The *Louisiana Weekly* reported on April 19, 1930, that members of the church on Amelia Street believed that it had been sold by the preacher, Reverend Alberta Price Bennett, without their knowledge. The congregation was evicted by the Italian Homestead after being four months behind in its rent.[25] The fate of Anderson's own church after her death suggests that while the model of institution building established by the Spiritual Church movement contributed to the religious market in New Orleans, there was still room for improvement.

Despite Anderson's precautions and apparent savvy in dealing with law enforcement, her own problems with the police also suggest that there was still room for improvement in the Anderson model and that innovations made in response to the specific circumstances she encountered in New Orleans may have been crucial to creating her organization. Anderson was arrested twice during the 1920s, first in June 1921 at her Amelia Street church for fortune-telling and again in April 1925 for holding a "Voodoo Meeting" on a fish-fry permit.[26] One of the officers that arrested Anderson in 1921 said that the police had received a tip that Anderson was "operating a confidence game in the back of her church." He claimed that when he approached Anderson for her services and then identified himself as a police officer, Anderson tried to bribe him with a roll of bills.[27] This echoes Mary Johnson's report that Anderson said she had paid off a police captain in order to operate in the city without fear of legal reprisals. How the officers knew enough about her operation to suspect her is uncertain, but Anderson may have realized at this point that her formula for practice at her church required some adjustment. This realization may also be connected to Anderson's supposed insistence on secrecy in providing certain services to church members.

Even Anderson may have been slow to realize that it was the physical infrastructure as well as the legal that protected her from law enforcement. In 1925 she was arrested at the home of a Spanish fisherman named Vegas at 1237 Desire Street, in the Lower Ninth Ward, at the opposite end of the city from her church on Amelia Street. While this suggests the spread of Anderson's influence across town, perhaps speaking to the success of her organization, it also seems to indicate that Anderson may not have understood that it was not only her charter and position as a leader in her church that protected her from legal persecution, but the building itself and the implications of practicing within a space outsiders regarded as sacrosanct.

In addition to building a church and providing certain services in relative secrecy, Anderson employed a lawyer to handle her affairs. One of the officers who arrested Anderson in 1921 identified her lawyer as a state senator named Stafford, who had defended Anderson and got her out on bond after she was arrested. Another officer, who remembered monitoring and attending Anderson's meetings at Longshoremen's Hall, confirmed that her lawyer was named Stafford. An associate of Stafford's, Daniel Wendling, said that he had defended Anderson in a disturbing-the-peace case for Mr. Stafford, and she was released.[28] While Laveau was presumed to be connected to powerful figures, there are no stories in the mythology surrounding her life about her retaining a lawyer to fight legal battles for her. Laveau was instead remembered as using Voodoo to manipulate judges and police. Problems with the law for spiritual and religious practitioners in New Orleans had been constant since the nineteenth century, but it appears that it was Anderson who first made a legal-defense team a part of the collective consciousness of the community of workers in New Orleans, as well as of her own community of Spiritual Church co-workers.[29]

Ritual and Practice

Both public and private healings were integral to Anderson's model of religious practice at Eternal Life Christian Spiritual Church. Mother Dora Tyson recalled that at her Church on Jackson Avenue Mother Anderson cured the sick. Father Thomas said that Anderson healed with holy water and her bare hands, sprinkling the water on the sick and stroking the ailing area, saying, "Lawd free dis puson from dat evil dats troubling him." She also healed some ailments in a private room. Father Thomas said that Anderson treated individuals who approached her at the pulpit and appeared to have some money, charging them a fee for the healing. The processes conducted there were known only to those healed, but Father Thomas maintained that these people went into the room sick and came out well.[30] A woman who attended services at the Amelia Street church believed that private treatment was given to persons not because of their apparent wealth but because of the severity of their afflictions, but she confirmed that they were charged a fee.[31]

Anderson provided a number of other services for her followers. Dora said that prominent white lawyers, judges, doctors, and other professionals consulted Anderson about their future, for which she charged a substantial fee. She recalled that the Longshoremen's Hall services attracted more than five hundred persons three times a week, on Sundays, Mondays, and Thursdays at 8:00 p.m. Anderson apparently held training classes for her co-workers on Tuesday. In addition to learning to provide healing services, her students learned to "prophesy," probably a reference to the kind of services Anderson provided to these affluent individuals. She also taught her followers to read the Bible and "see spirits." Dora recalled that on Friday nights Anderson also held meetings at Cooperative Hall, downtown, marking her influence as citywide, apparently stretching from uptown to downtown and all the way out to the Lower Ninth Ward. [32]

Many of Anderson's services would have been familiar to Christians, that familiarity drawing them into a space where she could also offer services less familiar in Christian churches. Dora said that at her public services Mother Anderson wore a yellow and gold garment she referred to as a Father Jones dressing robe and a "Black Hawk mantle." She was also known to wear a solid white robe and sometimes a full dress suit for an occasion called Father Jones Night, dedicated to a "great guiding spirit" who controlled the other spirits and instructed Mother Anderson on how to "master all evil." [33] A visitor to the church recalled the white robe worn by Mother Anderson during services but remembered it being adorned with "a string of crosses" around Anderson's neck and waist. She remembered Mother Anderson fainting regularly while preaching and having to be attended by her co-workers. She also remembered Anderson's co-workers, in white dresses with purple waist pieces marked with crosses, falling to their knees during Anderson's sermons, as well as a great deal of call and response between Anderson and the congregation. She would call "sinners" up to the pulpit and bless them when they asked to be saved, exhorting them to change their lives and attend her church regularly. [34]

Mother Dora remembered that Mother Anderson opened her services with hymns, reading of the scripture, prayer, and reading (perhaps fortune-telling). The services at Eternal Life were accompanied by "a red hot six piece swing band," made up of known jazz musicians, "that played the hymns in jazz time and style." This addition was obviously influenced by the popularity of jazz and New Orleans's long association with it. At the end of services, Anderson took up a collection and told selected individuals about their future.[35] Father Thomas said that Anderson began services with a greeting, sang, and then blessed the congregation. She then "read the past, present and future of those who wanted to know what the spirits could tell Anderson about them. At the end of service she cured the sick with the help of her co-workers."[36] With the exception of the worldly music, communicating with spirits, and prognostication, many of the rituals resembled those that could be found in the churches of any number of Christian denominations. Holding to an overall Christian structure allowed Anderson to attract the majority of New Orleanians who considered themselves Christian to her churches. The spiritual innovations allowed her church to offer something more than Christian churches did, including new ways to deal with the exigencies of daily life.

The additions to Anderson's services that might have seemed foreign to Christians were hardly random. Mother Dora Tyson indicated that Anderson understood the importance of adapting practice to the local context. Among other things that Dora picked up from Mother Anderson while training under her was the use of Black Hawk, a Native American saint used to aid both "good and evil people." Interestingly, Mother Dora reported that though Mother Anderson used a similar saint called White Hawk, the latter's power was limited to Chicago. Similarly, Anderson "found" Black Hawk, who served Louisiana exclusively.[37] While one Spiritual Church leader noted that descriptions of Black Hawk varied, Corinne Williams, a member of Mother Dora's church, confirmed that Black Hawk was a saint and reported that she herself had seen him and that he had gotten her a job after she was out of work for six months. Williams described Black Hawk as an Indian chief dressed in a white robe with long feathers in his hair and carrying a candle in his hand. She claimed that when he visited her, he flew down from "out of the ceiling." She said that when he entered she felt cold and that when he left she felt warmth. She described him as flying with ease, like an angel.[38]

Mother Dora confirmed that these temperature changes accompanied Black Hawk's presence and more specifically described his physical appearance. She said that Black Hawk was about six feet tall, with high cheek bones and wavy black hair. The three feathers in his hair were red, yellow, and white. She described him as walking on air and said that he was always accompanied by a silent black dog when he visited her church.[39] Mother Dora said that she met with Black Hawk regularly to discuss her "affairs" and that Spiritual Churches honored him and paid their respects to him on Wednesday nights. Though she followed the example set by Anderson here, Mother Dora explained that even in a single generation change and innovation had set in, as her church honored Black Hawk on Tuesdays, though she acknowledged Wednesday as the "proper night." At the Black Hawk services, Dora put two candles near his picture, prayed to him, and played music that she said he and other spirits found pleasing. Mother Dora believed that Anderson had made Black Hawk a saint, exclusive to spiritualism, when he visited her and revealed himself as having founded spiritualism in America prior to America's discovery by "de white man." Mother Dora said explicitly that Anderson had the power to make saints, as she had done with Black Hawk.[40] When asked why Black Hawk was exclusive to the South, Mother Dora replied that Mother Anderson had granted him that position because he was a southern Indian.[41]

In Mother Dora's estimation, Anderson had as much power over Black Hawk as he did over anyone in her congregation. It was she who granted him his position in her church and she who decided his jurisdiction, for lack of a better word. Unlike many Christian denominations' view of saints as the agents in relationships they formed with largely passive earthly devotees, Mother Anderson seemed to be the creative and dominant partner in her relationship to Saint Black Hawk. In fact, Dora recalled seeing Mother Anderson call on Black Hawk in front of witnesses simply as a demonstration of her own power. Again, Mother Anderson was the source of power here, rather than being beholden to the saint for his. Following suit, Mother Dora described herself as calling on Black Hawk with similar authority and even described him as good for making wishes, which she got him to grant for her congregation. The understanding that Anderson and her followers exerted this kind of influence over these saints also allowed them to dictate how the saints functioned. In Black Hawk's case, by making him local to Louisiana, Anderson again demonstrated her understanding that she had to shape her practices to the local contexts. In so doing, she not only responded to the preexisting culture, which characterized the Laveau model of practicing Voodoo but added something distinct to that culture.

The Anderson model of institution building provided not only for the creation and expansion of her church but for the proliferation of churches created by students she trained. The training classes allowed her to add to the income she could accumulate by charging her students tuition. The classes also created a structure for training new Spiritual Church mothers and fathers that had the potential to be extraordinarily inclusive. Unlike the one-on-one apprenticeship structure described by workers, Anderson's model, which was undoubtedly more expansive, could educate more individuals not only in the ritual techniques of the Spiritual Church but also in the organizational structure for creating such an institution. As stated above, Anderson held the training classes each Tuesday night, collecting one dollar per student for each lesson. In addition to teaching students to read or prophesy, heal, pray, and see spirits, she taught them to get jobs for people, indicating the importance of economic concerns for both the co-workers and their congregations. One of her students remembered that she issued her first certificates of completion, at the cost of fifteen dollars per certificate, in 1923 to seventy-five to eighty graduates after fifty-two weeks of classes. After presenting the certificates of completion, Anderson was known to financially back churches founded by some of her students.

Her model of teaching students to prepare them to found their own independent churches not only allowed them freedom to choose rituals to practice but apparently provided them a great deal of institutional freedom as well. While many of Anderson's former students were complimentary toward their former teacher, some had complicated relationships with Mother Anderson. Some viewed themselves as following in Anderson's footsteps and spoke about their close personal connection to her. Others thought of Anderson as their competition for parishioners and influence. Still others took a more complicated view, seeing themselves both as Anderson's followers and as her competition.[42]

What these varied perspectives point to is the independence possible in Anderson's model of institutionalization. While many of the students she trained felt indebted to Anderson for helping them begin their own organizations, they also felt free to establish their own practices and institutions, sometimes contrary to the wishes of their teacher. While this formula led to strife between her and a number of the co-workers who trained under her, it also created opportunities for diversity and expansion of the kinds of practices included within the framework established by the Spiritual Churches. This is evidenced by the existence of a generation of Spiritual Church heads operating in New Orleans by the late 1930s who had not trained under Anderson at all. Some of them established churches independently, imitating Anderson's model. Others trained with some of Anderson's co-workers. If those closest to Anderson, trained by her and loyal to her memory, felt free to alter rituals, then it would be difficult to consider ritual innovations as invalid in these other churches, especially by the time the church reached this second generation of Spiritual mothers and fathers. For some Spiritual Church heads this freedom presented the opportunity to incorporate practices similar or identical to those employed by workers in New Orleans. As Anderson's protégé Eli Williams stated, many of the churches were simply catering to the demands of their congregations. It also allowed workers who wanted to avoid trouble with the law or to practice in what was perhaps a more obviously Christian framework to adopt the Spiritual Church as a model for how to institutionalize their own spiritual practices, which previously would have been characterized as Voodoo.[43]

Evidence suggests that many of Anderson's students were attracted to her organization not only because of the spiritual opportunities but also because of her business acumen and the economic opportunities operating a successful Spiritual Church presented. When speaking about Mother Anderson, many of her former students, Spiritual Church heads, and even workers in the city expressed admiration for her economic success. Further, many of those who went on to found Spiritual Churches of their own reported working in relatively menial and low-paying occupations before becoming associated with Anderson's organization.[44] This could be particularly problematic for African Americans, who because of segregation and workforce discrimination had fewer job prospects than did their white counterparts. Frequently, low-paying jobs in service industries or as domestics for white families represented the only employment opportunities available to many African Americans, especially in less industrialized cities. Spiritual Church heads' stories about being called into the churches often involved being rescued from these menial jobs or working at these jobs when they saw a spirit, Christian or Spiritual, that drew them to the work. Like many spiritual practitioners in New Orleans in this period, Anderson's followers suggested that they often understood her power in economic terms, her economic success being an indicator of her spiritual power. Equating spiritual and economic power will be discussed in reference to the wider community of Voodoo practitioners in the city in more detail in chapter 4. Here it suffices to say that at least one of Anderson's students spoke of her indicating that the spirits had to be paid and that she worked with expensive spirits rather than ones that did not require pay, judging even spirits in economic terms. It is probably important to note as a caveat that Anderson's model of doing business did have an air of charity in that more than one witness claimed that while she insisted on being paid, it was the wealthy who paid for services, while the poor often were not charged for help.[45]

It is also noteworthy that while Anderson seemingly discriminated on the basis of class in determining whom she charged for services, she apparently did not discriminate on the basis of race. Numerous reports of Anderson's followers mention whites as well as Blacks. The students she trained also included whites, who Mother Dora said paid the same fees for instruction as did the Black students. Even on the occasion in 1925 when Anderson and twenty members of her group were arrested for illegally holding a meeting, a quarter of the participants arrested were white. Likewise, attendants at Anderson's funeral noted the presence of many whites, many of whom they described as affluent, openly grieving.[46] Thus the Anderson model seems to have extended her influence not only across the city but across the color line.

Anderson's model of religious practice brought the appearance and legitimacy of "church" to many spiritual practices in New Orleans previously regarded only as "voodoo." Her system of training students and subsequently aiding them in founding churches that were not institutionally or ritually bound to her own allowed co-workers whom she trained to incorporate the rituals of workers. This allowed them to cater to individuals who previously might have sought out workers for assistance or to combat individuals they believed were trying to harm them with the help of a worker. Further, the context of a Christian church provided an air of legitimacy that went along with sharing the general religious character of the majority of the city's residents. That advantage was not lost on workers who had a history of negative experiences with law enforcement and a stigma associated with practicing Voodoo. Some of these individuals copied Anderson's model in order to legitimize and/or Christianize their own practices. Anderson's model also allowed her and her successors to accumulate financial resources, which in turn helped them to acquire the infrastructure and accoutrements to make them indistinguishable from their Christian counterparts, allowing them to act the part of "church." The interaction between Anderson's Spiritual Church model and the preexisting community of workers represented by the Laveau model, steeped in New Orleans's history and lore of Voodoo, created a unique community of spiritual and religious practitioners in the city. Some members of this community considered themselves workers and readily identified with Marie Laveau and the culture she represented. Others considered themselves members of the Spiritual Churches and eschewed any association with Voodoo, while simultaneously incorporating rituals identifiable with that tradition. Still others called themselves workers or co-worker but incorporated the practices of both, demonstrating the fluidity between these groups and their dovetailing in early twentieth-century New Orleans.

The early twentieth century saw the participation of myriad religious practitioners who, like Leafy Anderson, had to accommodate, refute, or include the legacy of Voodoo in New Orleans. The workers, co-workers, queens, doctors, and Spiritual Church mothers and fathers all belonged to a community anchored to New Orleans by historical figures like Marie Laveau and the Laveau and Anderson models. These models were informed by the racial and social politics that permeated New Orleans, as well as by a history of practice that determined the boundaries of practice based on decades of navigating the traditions of Voodoo practitioners and legal prohibitions against the practice of Voodoo, which also were tied to the racial and economic politics of the Crescent City.

II

THE WORK

3

DAME ZOMBI MEETS JIM CROW

Race and Voodoo in New Orleans

Due undoubtedly to the persistent stories of workers' use of grave dirt and the spirits of the dead in their rites, a researcher from the Louisiana Writers' Project sought out Louie Haley, the sexton of St. Roch Cemetery, for an interview about his experiences with Voodoo practitioners who frequented the graveyard. Haley assured the interviewer that "ennytime ya see a nigger wench and a white woman come into th' cemetery together, ya kin expect some monkey-shines."[1] For Haley, the crossing of the racial boundary in the graveyard was a very specific signal that Voodoo was afoot. Despite explicitly stating that it was the interracial character of the company of women that tipped him off, the sexton seemed sure that it was the African Americans in these groups who were somehow responsible.

Like many of his contemporaries, the sexton seemed to think of Voodoo as a kind of racial knowledge, endemic to the African American community. During the aforementioned interview, seemingly in support of this perception, Haley described a gris-gris he had stumbled upon at St. Roch's that involved a live chicken tied up just out of reach of a supply of food and water. Haley told his interviewer that to get information about what he had found, he simply asked "some nigga wench" who came into the cemetery. That is, rather than seeking out a professional practitioner, he thought it adequate to find anyone Black, who he presumed would understand why the chicken had been left in the cemetery. Haley told the interviewer that the Black woman he questioned explained to him that the rite was designed to punish someone who had committed a crime for which someone else had been jailed, undoubtedly buttressing his racialized perception of this kind of rite. In further support of his perception of the direct correlation between Blackness and Voodoo, he recounted a request made of him for grease from the bell of the church the cemetery served by a worker who was Black. He added that most of the Voodoo paraphernalia he found in the graveyard was "in th' back, in the nigga section," employing the apparently segregated space in the cemetery to support his perception of a segregated cultural landscape that cordoned off Voodoo behind a black border that belied the cooperation he observed between Black and white practitioners.[2]

Haley's contempt for the Black workers he observed seemed tied, at least in part, to his perception that Blacks were responsible for the involvement of whites, especially white women, in these uncivilized enterprises. In the handful of stories he recounted during his interview, he mentioned the involvement of whites but reserved his judgment for the African Americans. Near the conclusion of the interview he lamented that on a handful of occasions he had seen three attractive blondes come into the cemetery with "a ole nigga wench" and dig around at the back of the cemetery. Haley did little to hide his disappointment at the spoiling of these perfectly good white women by this apparently aged Black worker, openly whining: "Dammit, I coulda gone in for them dames myself."[3]

Louie Haley was not alone in his presumption that the responsibility for Voodoo, even among whites, should be laid on African Americans and that white practitioners were somehow ruined or beneath some standard of whiteness. The certainty that Voodoo in New Orleans was an intrinsically Black phenomenon, despite persistent reports of white participation, has continued from the first reports of these practices in Louisiana to the publication of the most recent scholarship on the subject. This contradiction has obscured the fact that the story of Voodoo in New Orleans is largely one of interracial participation and a shared culture by the city's residents that flouted the color line imposed by Jim Crow. More than one account suggests that interracial partnerships between workers were not uncommon and that in such partnerships the dominance of the African Americans involved was by no means certain. Evidence suggests that even if we do not refute the supposition that the origins of Voodoo were African, Caribbean, or African American, in early twentieth-century New Orleans this spiritual subculture included participants who were both Black and white. Voodoo became part of the exotic cultural landscape that characterized New Orleans as a whole, just one of many cultural traditions for which race proved an inadequate boundary.

The goal of this chapter is to establish two points. First, in order to best understand Voodoo as it was practiced in twentieth-century New Orleans, we must focus less on its purported African origin and more on the deep impact of the racial politics of the U.S. South and their effect on the practices of workers in the city. While the African origin and the centrality of African traditions are maintained both by contemporaries and by more current scholarship, they are nearly impossible to prove, as there is little or no documentary evidence left by practitioners of Voodoo in early twentieth-century New Orleans establishing which of their practices had been learned on the African continent and which were created and established locally. The reproduction of racial ideologies necessary to justify the segregation of the races in Jim Crow Louisiana was definitive in labeling Voodoo as an African or African American phenomenon despite the gap in empirical evidence for that label. The need to reify a firm line between Black and white in New Orleans necessitated this classification, despite the participation of whites throughout the city, so that Voodoo could be cited as evidence of the backwardness of African American culture, the need to separate the races, and the danger for the white community in not doing so. This racialization of Voodoo in New Orleans, as well as the certainty of the distinct differences between Blacks and whites, is most salient in the rites of workers, which imply not only physical but metaphysical differences between the races, requiring a racial distinction between Blacks and whites even in the performance of magical rituals.

Second, this chapter seeks to establish the truly interracial character of the community of practitioners in New Orleans and the wide appeal of Voodoo for residents throughout the city regardless of race, religion, or geographic location. The data collected by ethnographers on Voodoo in New Orleans in the early twentieth century make clear that despite their acceptance of the premise that Voodoo in New Orleans was an intrinsically African phenomenon, the reports from practitioners themselves established not only the participation of whites but also the local influences on many of the rites and practices common by the 1930s. Whites were able to establish businesses as workers and were accepted by both Black customers and fellow professional practitioners. This was possible because attempts to define Voodoo as an African American phenomenon were belied by the reality of Voodoo's reach beyond the color line, exemplified by the participation by both Blacks and whites as both professional practitioners and clients.

Despite efforts by journalists, scholars, and novelists to label Voodoo as Black and by Black Protestants from uptown New Orleans to label Voodoo as the work of Afro-Creoles from downtown, the practice of Voodoo was widespread across racial and geographic lines in the city. Voodoo as practiced in New Orleans is a unique cultural phenomenon, characterized by influences in the city as diverse as Creole cultural identity, Protestant and Catholic Christianity, racial segregation, and consumer capitalism. The practice of Voodoo was widespread in the city despite distinctions of color in an era in which every aspect of life was subject to Jim Crow segregation. Ritual practice in early twentieth-century New Orleans was greatly influenced by the historical context and by the social and economic challenges common to many New Orleanians. These influences widened the appeal of Voodoo, allowing it to touch the lives of many who faced those challenges and eventually establish itself as a salient marker of New Orleans's rich and layered cultural heritage. In the end, the common association between Voodoo and the city of New Orleans may demonstrate the impossibility of cultural containment along racial lines. Study of Voodoo in this period suggests that in a multicultural society, even when history and circumstance conspire to create new cultural formulations that are rooted in the distinct experiences of one particular community, as interactions between that community and outsiders expose new observers to these formulations, outsiders invariably become participants and the nature of these formulations are altered. It would seem that U.S. culture marked Voodoo's development and practices. Like many American cultural traditions, Voodoo in New Orleans was clearly influenced by its multicultural context. If indeed Voodoo began as an African or African American religion, by the twentieth century African religion had become New Orleans religion and, more broadly, American religion.

African Culture in New Orleans

The view of Voodoo as practiced in New Orleans as predominantly or centrally African is part of a larger cultural project in the twentieth-century United States to establish the distinct nature of African American folklore and mark it as somehow separate from mainstream U.S. culture. Early twentieth-century segregationists contributed to this project, seeking to draw firm social and cultural lines between whites and African Americans. Academics and ethnographers, perhaps unknowingly, have abetted this process by studying Voodoo and other aspects of African American culture in a vacuum, as if they did not influence, and were themselves not influenced by, surrounding cultural norms.

Lastly, the state, in the form of the Works Progress Administration–sponsored Federal Writers' Project, also participated in a demarcation of African American culture that is central to the understanding of Voodoo in New Orleans as an essentially African cultural phenomenon. This position, supported by the earliest research on Voodoo in New Orleans, has in turn been reified even in the most recent scholarship.

Much of the work on Voodoo in New Orleans conducted in the 1920s and the 1930s racialized these practices based on research models that presumed the "Blackness" of these rituals and reinforced that perception by studying them among African Americans in isolation. Two scholars, Zora Hurston and Newbell Niles Puckett, both proceeded from the racialized presumptions not only of African origins for Voodoo in Louisiana but also of the ubiquity of Voodoo cognates in African American communities throughout the United States. Puckett, a sociologist and folklorist at Western Reserve University, undoubtedly using secondhand reports of snake worship in New Orleans among Voodoo practitioners in the nineteenth century as a point of departure, assumed that these practices had been "carried to Hayti by slaves from Ardra and Whydah." He believed that because of war between France and Spain, these rites had been carried in 1809 by Haitian planters, with their slaves, from Cuba (where they sought refuge from the Haitian Revolution) to New Orleans. These migrations, he maintained, were the "principal sources of the voodoo religion in the United States."[4] Rather than establishing these connections with ethnographic research among his informants in the city though, Puckett used established migration patterns as grounds to assume the connection between Voodoo in New Orleans and similar practices in Haiti and West Africa.

French culture was important to Puckett's theory of Haitian origins for New Orleans Voodoo. He accepted that Haitian émigrés had sought refuge in Louisiana because of the common language and culture. Inexplicably, however, Puckett minimized the importance of New Orleans's unique historical context in favor of racializing Voodoo. While Puckett conducted significant portions of his research in and around New Orleans, his project was concerned with African American folklore throughout the U.S. South. He maintained that throughout the South, because slave owners provided "proper medical attention" and protection for bondmen because their productivity as planters was dependent on the physical health of slaves, magic and conjure persisted among slaves, who were looking for methods to exact "indirect revenge or revenge by witchcraft" against other slaves. He explains that "lacking overt and natural means of obtaining justice, the slave turned to his conjure-bag and after the Civil War, when the master had given again to the Negroes, their desire to avoid expensive medical attention focused their attention again on the all-powerful 'root-doctor' or 'hoodoo-man,' as the healer of diseases."[5] In Puckett's formulation, slaves, who used Voodoo to attack one another because their captors prevented them from harming one another, and freedmen, who could assault one another at will in the absence of the care of white masters, continued its use for medical care. Thus, Puckett regarded Voodoo as an African American phenomenon predicated on slaves' need to attack one another and on the poverty of post–Civil War Black populations. In addition, by lumping New Orleans practitioners in with Black conjurers throughout the South, Puckett effectively obscured the importance of New Orleans's unique culture, which connected it to Haiti and for him explained the origins of Voodoo.

Puckett's presumption of the benevolence of the American slave owner is interesting. Also intriguing is what his assumption that other slaves were the primary targets of conjure doctors says about the bias of a white researcher, originally from Mississippi, and his acceptance of the racist presumptions about the violent and dangerous nature of people of African descent commonly held in this period. If the lack of "overt and natural means of obtaining justice" was the motivation for preserving magical practices, as Puckett suggested, why would a slave use Voodoo to attack another slave, with whom he was equal in social standing, rather than the slave owner, in comparison with whom he had no power?[6] Puckett, in a blanket statement asserting the universality of conjure practices among African Americans, wrote that "one might safely say that any inexplicable or unexpected calamity, both in Africa and in many parts of Negro America, is often blamed on witchcraft."[7] He also maintained that similar practices were common in the "Negro quarter" in New York, Atlanta, Philadelphia, and Pittsburgh, all cities with sophisticated, cosmopolitan African American populations.[8] This claim may be more about casting a shadow on Black culture as a whole than it is about any objective observation of folklore traditions. It also ignores the possibility of geographically and culturally specific influences on conjure in distinct geographic locals in the South, generalizing about conjure and portraying it as a racial knowledge common wherever there were African Americans. It does not consider the influence of developments specific to New Orleans or any of the other aforementioned cities.

In addition, Puckett introduced a seeming contradiction to this racialized formulation by maintaining the European origin of many of the practices characterized as Voodoo in the early twentieth century. Puckett maintained that the use of salt in reference to luck, the belief in reptiles living in the body of a person being relieved of a curse, the use of a black cat bone and love powders, and even the practice of sticking pins into a three-dimensional image of a victim—the iconic Voodoo doll—were all of European origin.[9] Whether Puckett was any more correct in rooting these practices in Europe than he was in rooting others in Africa is irrelevant. What is at issue here is the logical contradiction of pointing to non-African origins of all these practices while maintaining that in the practice of Voodoo "the African influence greatly predominates over the European."[10]

Also interesting is the contradiction Puckett's own research methodology presents for the perception of Voodoo as an African American, rather than a more generally American, cultural phenomenon. Puckett admitted that both Blacks and whites "still believe in the power of the 'voodoo-doctor'" and that whites, specifically white women, also employed themselves as workers.[11] Further, in order to gain a more complete insight from informants without paying the exorbitant fees they might ask for information, Puckett began practicing as a Voodoo doctor in New Orleans. After making himself into a professional Voodoo practitioner, Puckett noted that a kind of camaraderie among workers led to an exchange of trade secrets and materials in which he actively participated, allowing him to gather data for his project.[12] He noted that while he had never been initiated and therefore lacked the connections that this could bring him, his accumulated knowledge and Voodoo-related paraphernalia were enough to make him credible to fellow workers and clients. The implication here is that both purveyors and purchasers of magical services in New Orleans were less interested in a worker's racial identity, as Puckett was a white professor, then they were in his expertise in Voodoo.

Similarly, Robert Tallant, a Louisiana Writers' Project editor and author of *Voodoo in New Orleans,* a book he produced in the 1940s from fictionalized and conglomerated accounts of interviews conducted by the Works Progress Administration, found himself the subject of numerous inquiries regarding the practice of Voodoo once his book was published.[13] An Alabama man wrote to Tallant's publisher asking for the address of a drugstore on Rampart Street that dealt in Voodoo materials and inquired about a book on mixing roots. The publisher replied to the inquiry, maintaining that this was not information to which the publisher was privy, and wrote to Tallant joking, "I honestly think you should go into the Voodoo drug business!" For the writer of the letter, however, Tallant's statuses as an author, a white man, and in all likelihood a nonbeliever were irrelevant; he was a potential source of information and therefore power.

Racialized perceptions of Voodoo were not limited to white researchers. Similar to Puckett, the famed African American novelist and Columbia University–affiliated ethnographer Zora Hurston asserted that "shreds of hoodoo beliefs and practices are found wherever any number of Negroes are found in America."[14] Hurston posited that hoodoo beliefs were strongest along the Gulf coast, especially in New Orleans, because these portions of the former French territory of Louisiana had been settled during the Haitian Revolution by Haitian émigrés, who had fled there from Saint Domingue because it was the nearest French province. She maintained that while Haitian "hoodoo rituals" were "modified of course by contact with white civilization and the Catholic Church," they were "predominantly African."[15] Hurston held to this premise despite the tremendous influence of local custom and belief peculiar to Louisiana, which she herself noted. The perception of Voodoo as a kind of racial knowledge intrinsic to all communities of African descent and the insistence on the centrality of African traditions in Voodoo despite the wide variety of New Orleans influences on these practices speak to perceptions of the great social and cultural distance between Black and white.[16] Early twentieth-century racial essentialism is as much to blame for perpetuating these views as any objective observation of Voodoo practitioners.

Between her own ethnographic studies of folklore and African American religious practices and her connection to state-sponsored Works Progress Administration projects that included studies of Black culture as something distinctive, Hurston's work on hoodoo seems situated at a nexus of projects in the early twentieth century that began to acknowledge the cultural contributions of African Americans in the United States but stopped short of recognizing that the traditions that formed within Black communities altered the cultural landscape of the country as a whole, helping to create and re-create it. Hurston and the WPA instead studied African American culture as something distinct, perhaps inadvertently feeding the notion that it was also somehow incompatible with the culture of white Americans.

The *Journal of American Folklore,* in which Hurston published her findings on New Orleans Voodoo, is itself an artifact of the development of folklore studies and the inclusion of African Americans in that field. That inclusion demonstrates the understanding of African American culture as separate from the wider American culture. In a departure from European folklore studies, understood as the study of peasant populations of the European continent, American scholars included outsiders in folklore studies. Influenced largely by the presence of American Indians and other non-European people "classified as savages or primitives," the American Folklore Society, founded at the end of the nineteenth century, marked folklore as a discipline worthy of study and these non-European people as worthy of inclusion in studies by folklorists, ethnologists, and anthropologists. There was debate among scholars of American folklore about whether the studies should focus on "folk" that were part of local marginal societies, dependent on larger societies, or on "folk" from foreign, non-Western, small-scale societies. But in both cases the subjects of folklore studies were outsiders to the larger, Western, in this case American, society in which they lived. Almost from its inception, the *Journal of American Folklore,* the literary arm of the American Folklore Society, included not only Native American and "Old English" folklore but also the "Lore of Negroes in the Southern States of the Union."[17] We will table for the moment the notion that the geographic divide between North and South implies that something about southern culture made it the bailiwick of folklore studies and by consequence primitive. Much like the Native Americans, African Americans were included because of a presumption that as they were granted "opportunities for civilization," their culture as it had been would fade out of existence. For this reason, folklore in the understanding of American scholars "could not be associated with a living system of belief *precisely* because folklore was viewed as dead or dying in this cultural evolutionary scheme."[18] This meant that by including African American culture in the study of folklore in America, scholars were implicitly marking that culture as primitive and backward.

Zora Hurston, a student of Franz Boas, a Columbia University anthropologist and founding member of both the American Folklore Society and the *Journal of American Folklore,* studied folklore in the South, including Voodoo in New Orleans, and in 1931 published much of her data in an article entitled "Hoodoo in America" in the journal. Anthropologically trained folklorists like Hurston looked at African American folklore as a combination of European and African elements but focused on the African.[19] While men like Boas understood the folklore of their subjects as mirroring their lives and revealing their larger culture, they were searching not for connections to the present culture in which these stories were recounted but for remnants of a "traditional culture" that was dying or passing into obscurity. The problem, as one folklorist of the period noted, was that even though the argument for African retentions was rooted in attempts to combat racist notions that there was no culture in Africa to be retained, it was in itself as racist as arguments for "white origins" in assuming that "an original American Negro tradition can only emanate from black-skinned Africans."[20] I would add that this also suggests that "black-skinned" Americans cannot create the culture of white Americans, or specifically in the case of Voodoo, white New Orleanians.

In the 1930s, many interviews with Voodoo practitioners in New Orleans were conducted by members of the Louisiana Writers' Project, the local incarnation of the Federal Writers' Project. One of the best-known endeavors of the Federal Writers' Project was the Slave Narrative Collection, researched in seventeen states from 1936 to 1938. This project suggests that federal authorities, like the scholars of the American Folklore Society, implicitly acknowledged that African American cultural memories were worthy of study. Initial plans for the Federal Writers' Project did not provide for collecting slave autobiographies, but after sporadic interviews with former slaves, often by individual Black employees in southern states, the Washington office began a coordinated regional project to continue these efforts. This larger project was sparked in large part by narratives submitted to the Federal Writers' Project by the Florida Writers' Project, with which Hurston was employed for a time.[21]

The ethnographers and researchers in this period who concluded that African American folklore was unique and worthy of study, undoubtedly due to racialized notions of culture and perceptions that Blacks and whites did and should occupy distinct geographic, social, and cultural spaces, established that African Americans had a unique folklore and history that they communicated in their communities. The view that much of this folklore was passed down relatively unaltered from time immemorial fails to acknowledge the creativity in the communities that molded these traditions to fit contemporary circumstances. It also is party to the suggestion that this dynamic culture was somehow limited to the African American community, especially in the case of Voodoo, and had little or no impact on the surrounding cultural sphere inhabited by non-Black New Orleanians.

Despite the observations of some of the earliest ethnographic studies of Voodoo practitioners in New Orleans, the presumption about the racial nature of these practices and the research methodology that resulted from that presumption often buttressed the notions of Voodoo as the near-exclusive purview of the city's African American community. Harry Middleton Hyatt conducted interviews with conjure practitioners throughout the U.S. South. While he had previously done folklore studies among both races in Adams County, Illinois, he believed an interracial study to be "unwise and impossible in the South." He asserted that logistic concerns like the gasoline rationing resulting from the beginning of the Second World War limited his ability to conduct separate studies among whites and African Americans in the cities in which he worked and that, conversely, the concentration of African Americans "in or near cities, or in country districts" made it more feasible to restrict his studies to this community.[22] This decision was again a logistic one and not a theoretical one. In fact, Hyatt maintained that "white people also believe what you will read in Hoodoo."[23] However, the focus exclusively on African Americans undoubtedly had an effect on the data he collected and gave the appearance that these practices were more prevalent or centered in Black communities. In keeping with southern standards for racial segregation, Hyatt also maintained that all his interviews had been conducted in the homes or hotels of Black people. He made certain to note that he had never interviewed a Black person in a white person's home.[24] Thus it was the social norms predicated on racism and segregation that created Hyatt's one-sided ethnography of conjure practices in the South. It might have been difficult for later scholars who encountered Hyatt's work to maintain the centrality of the African nature of Voodoo in light of the dynamic changes occurring within in the practice if he had studied these practices among individuals with no racial connection to Africa.

Unfortunately, the focus on the cultural connection of Voodoo to the African American community and its essentially African nature is not limited to the research of scholars working during the Jim Crow era. While attempting to validate the practice of conjure in African American communities as religion, rather than simply consigning it to the perceivably less prestigious category of magic, Yvonne Chireau viewed what she referred to as "the aggressive spiritual practices . . . initially employed as sources of resistance by Black people" as "African-based beliefs in spiritual power."[25] She seems to have been comparatively uninterested in examining the social ramifications of connections between the European-derived beliefs about magic retained by Anglo Americans, including the use by conjurers of what she described as Euro-American magic manuals like *Albertus Magnus* and the *Sixth and Seventh Books of Moses,* and those of conjurers.[26] Chireau insightfully noted that conjure as practiced by African Americans was not confined by the color line and had a noted effect on whites. That being said, her project focused on the influence of African-derived spiritual beliefs on African American traditions of magic. She also noted adaptations of older beliefs and practices to their new American cultural context and framework but deliberately centered on the retention of ancient African "spiritual moorings while in America."[27] The certainty that the key to understanding these practices lay in their African past rather than in their American present is probably not unrelated to the notions of earlier scholars who were certain that these practices were ubiquitous among communities that shared an African lineage.

Even scholars who have had the insight to look to the present context to understand Voodoo and similar practices in the United States have adhered to largely racialized perceptions of these practices. In *Conjure in African American Society* Jeffrey Anderson directed the discussion more toward the significance of the U.S. context in the growth and development of similar magic practices that he termed conjure. He maintained that nineteenth-century Blacks built conjure upon an African foundation, but he insisted that the "European and American Indian elements were as important in the practice of conjure as those originating in Africa." Anderson posited that conjure exhibited "immigrant African origins coupled with an essentially American experience of assimilation." What resulted, in his formulation, was "a practice as American as anything brought from Europe."[28] This perceptive insight aside, Anderson writes almost exclusively about these developments as they pertain to the African American community.[29] Focused on the nineteenth century, he maintained that the source of conjurers' power was the "African American" belief in the potency of hoodoo, and he wrote specifically about the continuity of that community's belief in conjure. He even went as far as to express some incredulity at the participation of whites when he described Hyatt's assertion that whites' belief in hoodoo was surprising.[30] Thus, noting the importance of the American context and the cultural exchanges in that environment has not eliminated the notions of Voodoo or the wider traditions included under the designation "conjure" as racial phenomena.

In the case of Voodoo in New Orleans, examination of firsthand accounts suggests the developing importance of Voodoo for the city's cultural identity as a whole. This broader cultural significance is facilitated by the crossing of racial boundaries by practitioners and integral interracial participation in what became a complex flow of cultural influences, including the consumerism Anderson notes and the Catholicism alluded to by both Hurston and Puckett, all of which imprinted themselves on the practices of workers. Thus, Anderson hit the mark in asserting the truly American character of these kinds of practices, but viewing conjure practices in an exclusively African American cultural context minimizes the appeal for all Americans in need of the saints' assistance. Voodoo became part of the cultural identity of the Crescent City. Practitioners of both races influenced these practices and therefore this characterization. Images of the iconic Voodoo queens and doctors ceased to be limited, if they ever were, to African American folklore, and Voodoo, rather than being just a "black thing," became a "New Orleans thing."

I am not contending that the migrations of African slaves from Haiti to Louisiana at the dawn of the nineteenth century and the passing of certain traditions were not integral to the establishment of Voodoo in New Orleans. Indeed, a number of African American practitioners as late as the twentieth century claimed that they had learned their trade from parents and grandparents who in turn traced their knowledge to Haiti or Africa.[31] These claims may in fact reflect one of the earliest assertions of pride in an African cultural heritage, predating the twentieth-century movements of Marcus Garvey and Elijah Muhammad. Rather than aiming to refute these claims, I assert that because the reports of Voodoo as practiced in New Orleans in the nineteenth century are secondhand at best, mostly recorded by whites with a distaste for these rituals and a bias against what they regarded as African cultural retentions among a backward, savage, and hostile population, it is difficult to accept these accounts as accurate and reflective of the spiritual beliefs of practitioners.[32] Because of obstacles such as illiteracy and persecution of non-Catholic religion up to the nineteenth century, the population of slaves who supposedly practiced these rituals left no accounts of their own. Practitioners faced similar challenges throughout the nineteenth century. Therefore, until the twentieth century there were no known records left by practitioners themselves to confirm or refute an African origin for the majority or most central of their practices. In addition, the insistence on the African and African American character of Voodoo in New Orleans, despite myriad American cultural influences, has de-

tracted from an examination of these influences, which are both chronologi-
cally and geographically closer to the firsthand twentieth-century accounts of
workers' practices. Focus on these documented descriptions of Voodoo rituals
and beliefs by practitioners points to the influence of the culture in and around
New Orleans more than it harkens back to a distant African past.

It is also important to examine the racial politics of early twentieth-century
contemporaries who insist on the Haitian or African origins of Voodoo. Cir-
cumstantial evidence that places large numbers of Haitian émigrés in New
Orleans at the dawn of the nineteenth century is compelling, if not completely
convincing. There are also the comparisons of local practices and those common in regions of Africa that supplied slaves to both Haiti and Louisiana,
which are interesting but by no means conclusive. By uncritically accepting
these accounts, which equate the presence of African-descended populations
with practice of Voodoo, we run the risk of reproducing the racial ideologies
of separateness and racial distinctiveness used to buttress Jim Crow legislation
and segregationist ideologies.

In order to demonstrate the comparative barbarity of African American culture, twentieth-century journalists described supposed atrocities committed
by practitioners of Voodoo in the Caribbean or the backwardness of Haitian or
African civilization in general. A 1908 story in the *New Orleans Item* described
the sacrificing of white and Black babies to boa constrictors in the Caribbean
islands. The article claimed that the children were subsequently roasted and
eaten by practitioners and then attributed the source of all these dangerous
practices, even those in Cuba, to "the Black Republic," or Haiti, which the
author described as a nation "absolutely dominated by Negroes and inhabited
almost solely by blacks, who live in a state of primitive savagery and ignorance
such as exists hardly anywhere else except in the African jungles."[33] These statements would not only relay to white readers the intrinsic threat represented
by all "negroes" both in Haiti and the United States but also, by consequence,
justify racial boundaries erected by Jim Crow legislation locally.

Conversely, a 1929 interview in the *Sunday Item-Tribune* with a Sergeant
C. W. Stuart, of the U.S. Marine Corps, who had been stationed in Haiti during
what would become a two-decade-long American occupation of the republic,
used reports of the persistence of Voodoo worship, despite supposed U.S. efforts to stamp out the practices, as proof of the backwardness of the population,
thereby justifying the American military presence there. Speaking of Voodoo

in New Orleans as a thing of the past, as well as the rapid strides in education and sanitation made in Haiti under the auspices of the United States, and juxtaposing those to the pervasiveness of Voodoo even among the highest government officials in Haiti, the author manipulated tropes about civilization of the African in the United States under the paternalistic care of whites to justify the continued occupation of an intransigently backward population in Haiti. Both scholars and journalists in this period viewed what they believed was the decline of Voodoo in African American communities as the result of increasing education (i.e., civilization) in Black communities.[34] Several aged informants interviewed by the Louisiana Writers' Project in the 1930s who had practiced Voodoo in their youth said that they no longer did so, at least in part because of the shame associated with such practices by the younger generations of their families.[35]

Similarly, in order to put a "Black face" on the practice of Voodoo in New Orleans, newspaper reports, especially those on Voodoo-related arrests, made certain to accentuate the racial identity of African American defendants and to suggest the pervasiveness of Voodoo in the Black community. Conversely, in a number of accounts of such arrests the names and descriptions suggest that those arrested in connection with Voodoo were white, but the race of the defendants is not explicitly stated.[36] In these kinds of reports, whites always seem to have gotten information about the gris-gris they encountered from Black neighbors. Even though there are numerous reports confirming the participation of whites in Voodoo, their participation is always attributed to connections with Blacks, crossing of racial lines, or their own ignorance. The contradictions abound as these whites seem to gain knowledge of such things, even though many accounts claim not only that Voodoo was confined to the Black community but also that practitioners were disinclined to speak to outsiders about their practices.[37] This contradiction is resolved in the minds of segregation's proponents, in whose view the majority of Blacks, whether or not they practice Voodoo, have some experience with it, and therefore these are things "any negro would know."[38]

This conception of an African American community that was somehow culturally distinct from the surrounding city, with practices to which all African Americans were privy, which were simultaneously known to white residents of New Orleans and completely secret, is a fabrication of the collective imagination of journalists and authors. However, that perception of racial difference was widespread in the early twentieth century. Despite the opposition to Jim Crow legislation that began in New Orleans and ended in the famed *Plessy v. Ferguson* decision, codifying the separate-but-equal doctrine in American jurisprudence, or the constant intimate crossings of the racial divide evidenced by the conspicuous population of quadroons, octoroons, and mulattoes in the city, many whites and Blacks accepted that there were intrinsic differences between the races.

Today we conceive of racial identities largely as social constructions heavily influenced by contemporary politics, but in the early twentieth century most Americans accepted the immutable physiological distinctiveness of the races. The extent to which this perception was held by workers in the city is evidenced by the use of race as a key component in the rituals of a significant number of workers. Further, workers crossed racial boundaries to sell their services and held to the claim that their power crossed racial boundaries as well. At the same time, they not only accepted the physical immutability of race as a category but also perpetuated the notion that race had a metaphysical reality that should be taken into account in Voodoo rites. A number of informants who recounted specific formulas for researchers in the early twentieth century altered their prescriptions to fit the racial identity of their intended targets or clientele.

Race as a Metaphysical Category

Often race was used in the magical formulas of Voodoo practitioners as a means of identification. The most common method of identifying the target of an intended rite was to write their name down multiple times on a piece of paper that was subsequently included with other ingredients. A number of workers believed that the race of the person being acted upon dictated the color of the ink or the paper used. For instance, a worker might write a subject's name in black ink if the target was African American and in red if the target was white. The name might be written on white paper for a Caucasian target and brown paper for an African American. Often the color of candles burned during a rite corresponded to the race of the person being affected. Since black and white candles held a significance that pertained to the purpose of the rite rather than the race of the victim, often pink, red, or some other color would be burned when whites were targeted, and blue or brown when the targets were African American. The colors of candles used and their corresponding purposes varied widely, however. Sweeteners used in rites often varied according to the race of the target as well. Rites that specified the use of syrup might specify lighter-colored syrup, or "karo syrup," for example, for a white victim and brown syrup for an African Americans. Likewise, rites that called for the use of sugar often required white granulated sugar for Caucasians and brown sugar for African Americans.

Just how important designating race was to affecting a potential subject is not certain. Zora Hurston claimed that one of her mentors, whom she identi-fied as Father Simms, could "read" anyone if given his or her height and color. In this case, since race is one of the only attributes given to identify the individ-ual, one would assume that the race of the subject was of great importance.[39] Conversely, most of the informants questioned by Harry Middleton Hyatt made no specific mention of altering rites according to the race of the client or their intended subject. The significant number of informants who did make such distinctions were quite clear, however. In describing a candle rite one infor-mant stated:

Informant: White can'les [candles] is for white people. They burn that [candle standing] in a white rum and white loaf sugar.

Hyatt: You mean a white person does this?

Informant: No, no. That white can'le is for a white person like if you got chure landlord worrying you a whole lot, choo understand.[40]

Similarly, clients who might be self-employed often sought out workers to act on their own customers or competition, some of these enterprises being more legitimate than others. For example, rites to aid sex workers were also fre-quently mentioned: "Well, dey got some women that hustles, they got candles they burn an' dey got de white candles—dey is fo' white men. De red candle is fo' a dark man. . . . An' dey got a black candle, dey burns dat tuh keep de enemy mens away—dat's like a man whut would come aroun' an' ain't got much money tuh spend. . . . But chew burn de black candle tuh keep de policeman away."[41]

A second informant describing a similar rite added, "Well, wit all dose mens comin'—white mane an' othah wealthy men with money—dese mens goin' come, but de policeman nevah come to her do' [door]." These examples exhibit not only racial delineation of the subjects, but a loaded perception of the relationship between whiteness and social and economic power. This relationship is a presumption made repeatedly by workers about landlords, employers, judges, prosecutors, and any potential subject of a rite who had money and/or power.[42] Clearly, workers recognized the disparity between the races in regard to power and understood that many of their African American clientele were requesting rites to touch individuals whose race, in addition to their position, often left subordinates few means of redressing grievances.

The complexity of the racial hierarchy in New Orleans is also evident in the racial distinctions drawn by workers. One informant who spoke to Hyatt specified not only distinct colors for "burning a candle on" one's boss depending on whether he was white or Black but also an additional colored candle if he was "brown" or an African American with a lighter skin complexion:

Informant: If he's a white man, you gon' a burn a green can'le and his name wrote backwards on that can'le. . . . And you go to the bossman. . . .

Hyatt: What if the boss is a colored man?

Informant: You do the same thing, but choo burn diff'ran can'le. If he's a black man, you burn a red can'le; if he's a brown-skin man, you burn a blue. If he's a dark man, you sue [use] a red can'le on him.[43]

The notion here seems to be that rather than being skin deep, a person's color, even within a single racial group, in part determined who that person was metaphysically. Did workers assume that whites, Blacks, and mulattoes had different souls?

Nahnee, an informant who identified herself as the "Boss of Algiers," the suburb of New Orleans immediately west of the Mississippi River, made a distinction according to the race of the subject in nearly every rite she described to Hyatt. In only one of these was race the lone identifying characteristic of the subject requested. Most rites took into account other factors as well: "If it's a white person, yo' draw de form of a person—if dey tall, or low, or short, or whether dey stout, yo' draw dere form—or if dey wear glasses, yo' put de glasses on it—if it's a white person, it's in red ink yo' draw it an' if it's a colored [person], yo' use black ink. Yo' draw dere form an' yo' write dere name sixteen times."[44]

In one rite she even prescribed the use of a doll, which had to match the race of the subject. Nahnee's consistently taking note of the race of the subject in every rite and making adjustments for it would seem to suggest the extreme importance of race to some workers as not only a physical and social category but a spiritual and metaphysical one as well.

White Face of Divinity

Perhaps the most poignant example of the pervasiveness of racial ideology in the formulations of Voodoo practitioners in New Orleans is the racialization of spirits popular among workers. One of the most interesting spirits was called "Unkus" (Uncle). One informant explained that "we call him Unkus because we call Christ, Our Father," the implication being that Unkus had biblical or Christian origins. The informant noted that Unkus was eight inches high and added: "He's the spirit of the atmosphere. And he got a nose just like a white man. And he's not a negro at all, got a big nose, and he just stand there with a clock in his belly."[45] Among practitioners, racial identity was so intrinsic to defining individuals that they even assigned a racial character to spirits or, perhaps more importantly in this case, denied that they were Negroes. The apparent social impotence of African Americans in the face of Jim Crow legislation and widespread racism apparently made it unthinkable that any spirit with power could be Black.

The same worker described a spirit called Gray Eagle, whom he called upon for help with court cases. Even though he asserted that Gray Eagle was a spirit who "never has lived in the flesh," he assigned him a racial identity:

He's a white man—but he's just like he got on dress coat—but when he broaden's his wings, you kin see he's an eagle. He's not got an eagle face, he's got a man' features—pretty, fine man, and all look like silber, all up in here. But you never see him with black clothes on—you see with all light clothes—and he got nice—he combs his hair like a woman—beautiful appearances . . . but he speaks flat—most like a Jamaica person.[46]

Saint Expedite, a saint not included in the legion of canonized Catholic saints and the apparent creation of folk Catholicism picked up by workers in New Orleans, was described by one informant as Italian. What is most significant here is that none of the racialized spirits apparently unique to the canon of Voodoo workers and Spiritual Churches were African or African American. If segregation resulted in Blacks feeling powerless vis-à-vis whites, it is interesting that workers would not call on African or African American spirits to combat many of the social and economic disparities intrinsic to Jim Crow. African spirits would certainly be a natural ally for workers if we accept the presumption of African origins for Voodoo.

Another interesting case of racial categorization was related by Bishop Jeff Horn, founder of the Jeff Horn Spiritual Catholic Church. He told Louisiana Writers' Project interviewers that he had left Opelousas, Louisiana, for New Orleans when he had visions of God with both Black and white angels. In Christian theology, angels are considered spiritual entities. That not only were they depicted as winged human beings in his visions, a common occurrence, but that Horn highlighted the racial identity of the angels speaks volumes about the importance of racial identity and spiritual power to alternative religious practitioners throughout the city during this period. It also suggests the importance of the local context in understanding spiritual concepts. In the southern United States, where racial identity defined and characterized human beings, it became necessary even for spiritual, nonhuman entities to have such an identity in the understanding of some Voodoo practitioners and Spiritual Church heads. Horn recalled: "There is black angels too, and they flys lak the white ones, all together too. Oh yeah: That's one time all of the colors git together. The Japs, English, Germans, Africans and all of them. All of them angels fly together."[47]

The nature of the relationship between the races seemed important to a great many of the workers interviewed in the 1930s, but not all workers agreed on what the nature of that relationship was or should be. Horn seemed to present an idealized picture of race relations in which the heavens exhibited a model of interracial cooperation. It is interesting to note that at eighty-four years old Horn would have been able to recall a time in the state's history when race relations may have been even worse than under Jim Crow legislation, presumably under slavery.

Race Relations among Voodoo Practitioners

The racial dynamic between white and Black practitioners within the context of New Orleans's alternative religious community seemed to play out in an infinite number of permutations, some of them contradictory. What was consistent, however, was that race had to be navigated by workers. Despite the perception of Voodoo as an African American phenomenon, nearly every informant questioned about the participation of whites knew of white workers, clients, and suppliers active in this alternative religious community. The clandestine nature of many of the businesses and organizations involved in this community of workers and Spiritual Churches was most likely a result of the legal prohibitions against many of the practices associated with Voodoo. Therefore, because many of the individuals involved provided and solicited services in secret, it is impossible to know how many people were involved, much less the percentages of Blacks and whites.

What was most common both among informants and contemporary journalists was the use of generalizations in their responses to questions about the racial demographics of Voodoo practitioners. More than one source supposed, admittedly with no supporting numerical data, that a third of the city's community of Voodoo practitioners and Spiritual Church members was white.[48] When asked about the participation of whites, many informants reported that while most believers and workers were Black, a significant number of whites were involved. On occasion informants spoke about meetings or businesses that actually served more whites than Blacks. Some informants named white workers whom they knew. A couple of Hyatt's informants specified that they knew of a white worker called Madam Helen, though it was unclear whether they were describing the same woman.[49] Journalists who reported on Voodoo ceremonies, whether open gatherings witnessed by the public or clandestine ceremonies broken up by police, almost invariably noted the presence of whites, though in the more public venues they might be spectators rather than active participants, perhaps speaking to the racial stigma attached to practicing Voodoo. It is interesting, however, that the disparities in social and economic power perpetuated by segregation may have given whites a disproportionate influence on Voodoo.

Anyone who delved into the Voodoo or Spiritual Church communities in the early twentieth century could not have missed the presence of one rather conspicuous group of whites: drugstore owners and pharmacists. Many pharmacists and suppliers of paraphernalia to informants interviewed in the early twentieth century were white and had at the very least continuing business relationships with their clientele, which included both workers and workers' clients. There has been a perception promulgated by researchers of an ideo-logical divide between these suppliers and their clientele, with the white busi-ness owners simply supplying goods to the alternative religious community for profit and having no investment, outside of the obvious economic one, in their spiritual practices. This has led to a view of pharmacists as preying on a super-stitious community of believers.[50] They are also viewed as outsiders, connected to but not participating in the subculture from which they profited.

Even Hyatt, who reiterated his certainty that whites had faith in these kinds of practices, expressed some agreement with the perception of the centrality of economic interest among whites in these spiritual practices. A female infor-mant of Hyatt's in Vicksburg, Mississippi, reported receiving a strange bottle in the mail that she believed was a threat or an indication that a woman with whose husband she had become involved was attempting to use Voodoo against her. She told Hyatt that in response she had written to a worker called B. B. McConnick in Algiers, who for a fee mailed her black candles and instructions for dealing with her would-be assailant. Hyatt noted that he believed this was a scheme performed by a correspondent in Vicksburg who passed information to a candle distributor, the aforementioned Doctor McConnick, in New Orleans. He wrote: "McConnick is primarily a distributor of candles—a business man and surely a white man."[51] Hyatt's presumption about the race of the mysterious Doctor McConnick demonstrates his acceptance of the paradigm of the alter-native religious community that presumed that white suppliers were entrepre-neurs and opportunists and Black clientele were gullible victims. This seems particularly obvious when we consider that his informant specified that she did not know whether B. B. McConnick was Black or white. This paradigm is as much a reflection of popular opinions about the credulity of African Americans as it is the result of any research.

It is also worth noting that even acting solely as suppliers, drugstore own-ers would have had the opportunity to participate in an important way in the community of workers. It is logical to assume that in order to maximize prof-its, suppliers of Voodoo paraphernalia would have had to stock the supplies requested by their customers. It is also likely, however, that by selecting one group of spiritual products over another, or keeping some in stock while ne-glecting others, these apparently white drugstore owners could exert a dispro-portionate influence on the material culture of gris-gris and rituals in Voodoo, actively participating in and influencing the culture of Voodoo practitioners.

Race also often affected how authorities dealt with Voodoo practitioners. In 1927 federal investigators connected to the U.S. Post Office questioned merchants on South Rampart Street regarding a white physician in the area who had been caught running a drugstore dealing in Voodoo-related paraphernalia. A U.S. attorney named Edmond S. Talbot called the physician into his office, but the reports never indicated the arrest of the unnamed assailant. According to the papers, the goal of the federal authorities was "to break up what is obviously an imposition and fraud upon ignorant persons."[52] Even though the papers acknowledged that the mail-order business sold merchandise as far away as New Jersey and Texas, they also reported that the inspectors investigating the case claimed the perpetrator's business was "entirely confined to negroes whose superstitious natures have enabled him to found a drug store dealing in such articles as 'goofer dust,' 'eagle eyes' and other charms for good and evil."[53] It is unlikely that all of this physician's clients, both local and mail-order, were African Americans or that either the journalist reporting the story or the U.S. attorney could be certain that they were. In the case of his mail-order clients, even the accused physician may not have been certain. Further, while newspaper reports of Voodoo-related arrests and investigations involving African Americans identify them by name, this physician, the subject of a number of articles in more than one paper, is never identified by name.

Oddly enough, even when this trope was accepted by the researchers, some of the data they collected seemed to directly contradict it. A pair of LWP researchers, a Black man and a white woman, interviewed J. C. Coleman, a white pharmacist and the proprietor of the Ideal Drugstore on South Rampart Street, an apparently popular thoroughfare for procuring Voodoo-related products. The researchers approached Mr. Coleman under the pretense of being practitioners. Coleman spoke of Professor Hubert, a customer with whom he had formed a partnership. Hubert, a worker, apparently bought all his materials from Coleman, who in turn used his printing press and mimeograph machines to handle Hubert's publicity. Coleman also kept a collection of the workers' cards to provide to prospective clients. He offered to print cards for the LWP researchers and also offered them the free use of office space should they decide to go into the Voodoo business. He also advised them on how to avoid legal problems. This suggests that Coleman at least respected the workers with whom he worked. Coleman's offer of partnership and advice also implies a camaraderie between him and his clientele.[54]

Contemporary norms about race also influenced the way many workers dealt with customers. An African American woman reported that she had been employed by a white woman called Madam Helen, who ran a business as a worker uptown in New Orleans.[55] Despite the apparent interracial nature of Madam Helen's clientele, she apparently did not stray from the norms set down by segregation. Her Black assistant reported: "But if they—if the customers would come, and rang the doorbell, I would answer the doorbell and let'em in. But they'd have their room to sit down in. All I'd do, just go round and ring her bell and have another girl—for a white girl to come and receive'em girls, if it was a lady, if it was a gentleman—whoever would come to see her."[56]

Hyatt's informant specified that her employer saw Blacks and whites on separate days and had a white assistant who tended to white patients and issued the Black woman her pay, while the African American woman was confined to tending to Black patients who remained to receive care. If nothing else, this separation, by not violating the standard of segregation, may have improved Madam Helen's appeal to white clientele. It also suggests the pervasiveness of Jim Crow. The need of a white worker to have a white attendant also suggests that the white clients were significant in number, influence, or both.

Many of the Spiritual Church heads in the city made it a point to accentuate the interracial nature of their churches. A white spiritual mother and head of St. Rita's Church, the Reverend Alice Mancuso, made such a distinction. Mancuso claimed that she did not believe in Voodoo, but she admitted that she had trained a number of workers who practiced hoodoo against her wishes. She herself apparently read cards as well, a common practice among those who identified as fortune-tellers or workers. Mancuso asserted that in her interracial congregation "color don't make no difference; some of my best workers are colored." In the same breath, however, she admitted that because it was considered improper for whites and Blacks to sit together, she seated them separately in her church.[57] Despite working with, preaching to, and training African Americans, she was unwilling to challenge segregation directly in her church. Mother Maude Shannon, a Black spiritual mother and head of the Daniel Helping Hand Spiritual Church, told LWP interviewers that she had recently ordained two white women, whom she identified by name, when they visited her and insisted that when her church made donations of blankets and bread to the poor on a monthly basis, they were given "to any race, creed, or color, just so they are poor people."[58]

Althea Morris, a Black woman who called herself a "median," told researchers that she had been trained by a white reverend, Ermine Cadiz, at Little Theresa Chapel of Mercy.[59] The Reverend Lena Scovotto, of the Sacred Heart Spiritualist Church uptown, said that she had even attempted, albeit unsuccessfully, to create an interracial organization of both Black and white Spiritualist preachers that she would lead.[60] Joseph Lyons, "the Prophet," the African American founder of the Emperor Haile Selassi Nu-Way Ethiopia Mystic Light Baptist and Spiritual and Kingdom Church, specifically stated that his congregation had both Blacks and whites because he was not prejudiced and all people were welcome in his church.[61] The interracial nature of the clientele and association was often a powerful image invoked by the heads of Spiritual Churches. While the belief in the impermeability of the racial divide persisted, the ability to cross that divide spoke to their power and influence. In the case of African American church heads, it was particularly significant that they had overcome the boundaries of segregation, so that they were not prevented from serving as spiritual authorities for whites, even when the law and society held Blacks inferior to whites in nearly every other respect.

Sometimes the ability to cross the racial divide seemed to be a prerequisite for doing business in Voodoo. Robert McKinney, of the LWP, reported that when he sought out a well-known Voodoo queen called Madame Ducoyeille, also known as Robinson, in 1936, he took along another interviewer, Hazel Breaux, because he believed he would get more cooperation if a "white writer or representative of the project" accompanied him.[62] He explained her presence to his informants by claiming that he would need her to handle white contacts, and the explanation was accepted perhaps because Madame Ducoyeille, a Black woman, lived with Mrs. Dereco, a white woman, who had studied under the Voodoo queen. Both the researchers and their informants had formed these interracial partnerships because they believed that they would make it easier to broaden their client base across racial lines.

Some Black workers attempted to turn the racial divide to their advantage. The hermaphroditic worker whom Hyatt identified as "Boy-Girl" prescribed a formula for "hustlin' women" to avoid the law after robbing a customer: the sex worker, presumably an African American, was to throw holy water behind him when he departed. The result would be the john's complete unwillingness to return with the police to recover his property. This rather unique worker said: "Someone throws the water on [you] and let the water touches you. And when you go out, well naturally you say 'Well, I'm white and that's a nigger woman; I won't go back there with the law, because there would be too much publicity and scandal.'"[63]

Workers therefore navigated a complex space in which they had to be keenly aware of the norms of segregation precisely because their clientele was interracial in nature. Workers often stated the efficacy of their magic in terms of the ability to affect anyone, white or Black.[64] For Blacks, who were confined by law and custom to an inferior social sphere, the ability to affect whites spoke to the power of workers to penetrate the racial divide and challenge the power of whites. When interviewed by LWP workers, Joseph Lyons called on a white neighbor, a grocer identified as Mr. Baudin, who attested to the Prophet's power. Baudin said that his confidence in the Prophet stemmed from the worker's having cured him of an unspecified "ear disease." Lyons also claimed an interracial congregation of about fifty people, though he did not specify how many were Black and how many were white.

Mother Rita, formerly Eliza Johnson, changed her name when she took over the church of Mother Catherine, a student of Leafy Anderson's and a famed healer in the city, after Mother Catherine's death in 1930.[65] Both women claimed interracial congregations at the Church of the Innocent Blood, which after Mother Catherine's death became the True Light Church under Mother Rita. One of Mother Catherine's parishioners told interviewers that not only did white people attend Mother Catherine's services but several had studied under her as well, presumably to become spiritual mothers themselves. Another said that while she had heard Mother Catherine remark that "in the next world I'll be high up in things; in things of this world I knows my place," Catherine had fed and housed both Black and white tuberculosis victims in her church, obviously not allowing her perception of her "place" to hinder her work among whites.[66]

Observers found Mother Catherine's ability to cross the racial divide almost as impressive as her famed healing ability. Nearly ten years after Catherine's death, one observer said of her congregation, "Strangely, in a southern city traditionally ingrained with color prejudice and race distinction, Black and white men and women worked together in dignity and mutual respect."[67] Mother Catherine had become a healer when she herself suffered a paralytic stroke after being struck by her husband. She had gone to Brother Isaiah, a white man famed as a prophet who healed the sick and the lame on the levee of the

Mississippi River in 1922, for help. When Isaiah turned Mother Catherine away because she was Black, she began praying on her own for "religion and good health" and was visited by a spirit who called her to "organize religious meetings of sinners."[68]

The sting of racism was apparently not an uncommon reason for the ill to seek out alternative religious practitioners. In 1940, LWP workers visited the shrine of the healer E. A. Zatarain Sr. A client visiting Zatarain for help with heart trouble seemingly related to a stroke told one interviewer that she had stopped her treatments at the hospital not only because they were ineffective but also because she had to endure the racial slurs hurled at her by the hospital physicians. When Mother Rita spoke with interviewers in 1940, she made a point of mentioning that the interracial tradition started by Mother Catherine had continued at True Light. She told them that she was currently working on "a special case of a white family that I've got to pray for."[69] One wonders whether the case was special because the parishioners were white and her work with whites might speak to Mother Rita's influence across the color line or because of some circumstances of the case not mentioned by Mother Rita or the interviewer. In any case, these were all apparently instances of racial perceptions having an effect on the treatment of the sick by workers.

This ability of Voodoo to cross the color line did not always come cheap. Zora Hurston recorded a rite imparted to her several times by her mentors in Louisiana for creating a black cat bone, one of the most infamous articles of Voodoo paraphernalia inside or outside New Orleans. It was similar to a rite described to her by a man she identified as William Jones, an informant from Mobile, Alabama, which came with the addendum that the black cat bone would allow the user to disappear by holding it in his or her mouth and that it would "fix you so the white folks will never deny you—never refuse you anything." Again, the power acquired, that is, to influence whites in the Jim Crow South, in this particular worker's formulation required the potential user to sell his or her soul to the devil.[70] The substantial price may speak to both the power of the color line and the power of the worker.

Hurston, in addition to being initiated several times and researching supernatural formulas and rites, also collected folklore about Voodoo. One story that seemingly functioned as a parable about the power of Voodoo as a tool to exact vengeance against those whose race and social and economic power might put them out of a practitioner's reach detailed the vengeance exacted on an "unreconstructed" Georgia planter who employed an entire Black family as servants on his property. When the planter struck the family's daughter in a dispute and killed her, her father, feared as a practitioner of hoodoo, used his power to exact his revenge. The father claimed the body of his daughter and immediately moved away with his family because "they knew better than to expect any justice."[71] Within two weeks of the Black family's departure the planter's wife went insane, attacked him and only him, and had to be institutionalized. Two years later, after the planter relocated his family from Georgia to North Carolina, his son also attacked him and had to be locked away in an institution for the criminally insane. A year after that, following yet another move, the planter's daughter attempted to kill him. Before each incident the planter saw the figure of a Black man resembling the worker and head of the family whose daughter he had unrepentantly murdered. The result, according to the story, was that in his later years not only did his family never recover their faculties but despite his wealth and power, "he skulked about, fearful of every Negro man he saw."[72] This story speaks not only to the power of Voodoo to overcome the social imbalances intrinsic to racism but also to the importance of the social milieu and of the racial climate as a base metaphor by which practitioners understood Voodoo's power. They conceived the power of Voodoo in the contexts in which it applied to their circumstances, in this case the segregated South, rather than in the context of a distant past.

It is interesting, however, in the story just related, that while the worker was powerful enough to alter the destiny of his white employer, he did not use that power to alter his own position with reference to his employer. In other words, until his daughter was killed, the worker and his entire family were economically dependent on the planter, even though the Black community is said to have "both depended upon him [the worker] and feared him." Therefore, the story seems to speak to the power of Voodoo to exact vengeance without greatly disturbing or disrupting the social order around workers. However, the moral here is obviously that neither the planter's white privilege, his economic power, nor his geographic distance could prevail against the power of hoodoo.[73]

The possible upending of certain tropes about exploitation and Voodoo that may be related to the racial identity of the storyteller is also interesting. While many stories insist on the prevalence of African Americans among the clientele of workers due to the gullibility of the Black population, an article in a 1929 edition of the *Louisiana Weekly*, an African American New Orleans paper, specifically noted that a Voodoo doctor named John Scott, who had been arrested and charged with obtaining money under false pretenses, had "fleeced" a few Negroes but had worked his magic, so to speak, on "a large number of white persons."[74]

While both journalists and researchers have consistently attempted to ascribe alternative religious practices in New Orleans to the city's African American population, there was an explicit concern about the crossing of racial boundaries where Voodoo was concerned. This seems to have been implicitly related to a consistent connection drawn between Voodoo and crime, undoubtedly owing in part to the illicit nature of many alternative religious practices. The prosecution of workers under charges of defrauding the federal mails and obtaining money under false pretenses often criminalized their practices. Many alternative religious practitioners also found their work criminalized under municipal ordinances outlawing fortune-telling. Thus, in a very practical sense, workers were facing similar legal challenges as sex workers, bootleggers, and perpetrators of similar victimless crimes.

Workers also shared with participants in underground economies an explicit challenge to established power structures—legal, social, and economic. Building wealth through extralegal means represents an unwillingness to work within the capitalist model as established by the state. Especially among the poor and disenfranchised, it also represents a resistance to the implicit rules that confine those unable to succeed economically on the terms laid out by the state to a lower social class. Despite whatever difficulties led these individuals to the margins of the city's economy, they were unwilling to accept poverty and instead allegedly violated the law to succeed, or at the very least survive economically.

Already pushed to the margins of society by their economic enterprises, sex workers, bootleggers, gamblers, numbers runners, and so on, also represented a danger to the established racial order. Mainstream businesses had to hold the racial line to maintain an air of respectability, their compliance with segregation statutes, and by consequence their continuity. By contrast, interracial interaction was often common in extralegal businesses. Bootleggers increased their profits by selling to both races, as did sex workers and gambling houses. The novelty of these establishments was often that they offered this opportunity to engage in forbidden social interactions. Similarly, there was no profit for workers in providing their services only to African Americans. Quite the contrary. If they could provide services to a more affluent, that is, white, clientele, they could increase their profit and their prestige. The appearance that they were somehow less susceptible to the color line could increase the perception of their power among potential clients of both races and, as a result, their business. Their ability to strike at white subjects for African American clients and white clients' faith in their abilities were implicit challenges to the presumption of the racial exclusivity of social and economic power. The fear of segregationists would be that if workers could cross the color line with impunity, others might attempt to do so as well.

It is possible that the interactions across racial boundaries facilitated by workers providing spiritual services to all did call into question the sacrosanct nature of the divisions between Black and white. A number of members of the alternative religious community were noted to have engaged in intimate interracial relationships, perhaps the most conspicuous disregarding of the mores of Jim Crow segregation. One of the most infamous Voodoo doctors of the late nineteenth century, Dr. Jim Alexander, or Indian Jim, as he was sometimes called, was said not only to have served both Black and white clients but also to have had a white wife. Residents of the city also remembered a scandalous incident in which several prominent white women were arrested at his home while participating in a presumably Voodoo-related rite.

In 1889 a news story on a police raid of a dance purportedly held by Alexander reported the attendance of a well-known prostitute, as well as nude white women, some of whom were underage, all in the company of Black men.[75] Similarly, an article published in 1885 marking the passing of Jean Montanet, also known as the infamous Dr. John, noted that in addition to having a number of Black wives whom he had purchased prior to emancipation, he also had married a white woman, with whom he had at least one child.[76] The author of the Dr. John account also noted that John's influence extended not only from the Black to the white community but across Canal Street, the traditional boundary between the Creole and American communities in the city, speaking to the broad appeal of the most successful Voodoo practitioners in New Orleans. In fact, a 1906 *Daily News* article claimed that Lafcadio Hearn, the author of the Dr. John account, was known in his private life to associate only with African Americans, not the least of whom was Marie Laveau, his supposed consort.[77] These accounts, especially in the nineteenth century, were always given amidst descriptions of the workers' wealth, power, and influence. The implication was invariably that true power—the magic, cunning, and wealth accumulated by these infamous men—allowed them to cross the color line with impunity. Social and cultural distinctions that bound others were of no concern to those who accumulated power through the employ of Voodoo. By contrast, a racial transgression by a white individual, namely, the author and journalist Lafcadio Hearn, was seen to degrade his person, characterized by a "forbidding, if not actually repulsive" appearance due to being "ill-dressed, unkempt," and "slovenly."[78]

The researchers who interviewed workers in the early twentieth century encountered more than one who was apparently engaged in an interracial relationship. When LWP workers interviewed an African American worker called Madam Maika in New Orleans in 1939, she and her two sons were living with a white man in a small duplex home. While researchers seemed certain of cohabitation between the couple, they were less sure that the man was officially Madam Maika's husband.[79] Similarly, Peter Palao, investigated by the LWP, was alternatively known as Pedro the Statue Maker because he and a business partner apparently supplied many of the statues of saints and other religious paraphernalia that adorned several of New Orleans's Spiritual Churches in this period. LWP workers also interviewed a witness who said that Palao was married to a white woman and passing for white himself, though it is not clear whether his wife was a victim of this deception or party to it. Interestingly, in the report on Palao the researchers cast aspersions on the "whiteness" of Palao's wife, who was reportedly of Italian heritage, questioning whether she, despite her appearance, was also passing.[80]

There was also the issue of the intraracial divide. Sometimes it separated workers, but others were able to penetrate that divide. After taking over Mother Kate Francis's interracial congregation at St. Michael's Temple Number 1, relocated downtown from its original uptown site, Mother Fairwell noted a downturn in attendance among Mother Kate's congregation.[81] She supposed that it might be "because these Creole people down hyar don't understand the work of Mother Francis lak them people way uptown do."[82] When interviewed after her death, a number of Mother Kate's co-workers suggested that there had been some competition between her and the "Creole Negroes in the downtown section of the city whose beliefs rest on the Catholic side." Some of her co-workers said that Mother Kate, presumably to combat the Creole Negroes' influence, wanted to band all her co-workers together in a society "for the

Lawd" and march them on Sunday to Corpus Christi Church, the largest Black Catholic Church in the country at the time.[83]

Among many workers there was a keen awareness of the intraracial cultural divide. Zora Hurston identified the men under whom she studied and by whom she was initiated in New Orleans as Catholic or Protestant, Catholicism being one of the most salient markers of Creole identity.[84] The imposition of Jim Crow accelerated what one historian has called the "submergence of ethnicity—both black and white" in New Orleans, identification as Creole giving way to a simplistic system of biracial classification. Among African Americans, however, this process was a great deal slower and more contested,[85] perhaps largely because of the sheltering of some of the city's Afro-Creole population who were seeking reprieve from the unpleasantness of Jim Crow in the downtown neighborhoods with which they were by this time traditionally associated.[86] In addition to being located downtown, locals of African descent clung to Creole identity through their continued identification with the Catholic Church despite the influx of English-speaking Protestants. This division between Creoles and Americans dated from the demographic shifts that saw large numbers of Americans pouring into formerly French (and Spanish) New Orleans after the Louisiana Purchase in 1803. In the 1850s, at the height of this cultural conflict, local legislators actually divided the city into distinct municipalities almost entirely along the Creole-American cultural divide. While this system did not endure to the end of the nineteenth century, the perception of cultural difference and the exoticism of New Orleans due to these distinct populations persisted.

By the beginning of the twentieth century, Canal Street had long been the traditional divide between old, Creole, Catholic, formerly French-dominated downtown New Orleans and the more recently added, Protestant, American, uptown districts. There was also a frequent association between biracial parentage, lighter skin tones among Blacks, the city's notorious quadroon and octoroon populations, and Creole identity.[87] Further, this Creole population was often connected to the practice of Voodoo. An article published in a local paper in 1881 actually identified Voodoo practitioners as "that curious sect of superstitious darkies that combined the hard traditions of African Legends with the fetish worship of our creole negroes."[88] The article noted that with the death of Marie Laveau the last of that "class whose peculiar idiosyncrasies were derived from the habits and customs of old Louisiana" was also dying out.[89]

These statements represent a simultaneous indictment of and identification with this population being both maligned and claimed as "*our* creole negroes" (emphasis mine).

Another journalist wrote of the songs supposedly sung by the city's earliest Voodoo practitioners: "In the early days of voodooism these songs were tribal in their language. . . . Later the Creole patois crept into the songs—crept into them just as the white blood crept slowly into the veins of the Africans and made mulattoes, quadroons, octoroons of this race."[90] The author brings her cultural line up to the present by asserting that by the early twentieth century the "Creole Patois" had been replaced by English but that all the prayers, snake worship, and bloodletting had remained consistent for two hundred years.[91]

New Orleans journalists continued to suggest that it was the downtown neighborhoods associated with the Creole community that harbored the "superstitions" associated with Voodoo.[92] Further, around the turn of the century many explicitly stated that the waning belief in Voodoo could be attributed to the rising education of the Black community. An article in a paper ironically called the *New Orleans American* maligned this supposed remnant of Creole culture by associating contact with Voodoo with interactions with "the lowest element" of the Black community, asserting that more educated African Americans eschewed any association with workers.[93]

Madam Murray, an informant of Harry Middleton Hyatt's, stressed that though she had been born in New Orleans, she was not Creole. Immediately, though, the cultural association between Creole identity and participation in Voodoo fell flat as Madam Murray displayed extensive knowledge of the work despite not identifying as Creole. She did recognize the association between the two, though she pointed out that she could not decipher the words to a song associated with a particular rite because it was in Creole (a local variant of French).[94] The Spiritualist mother Dora Tyson told the researchers that it was the French people downtown who still used the spirit of Marie Laveau in their work, implying a distinction between the way co-workers uptown and workers downtown operated. Upon examination, the geographic distinction between the uptown and downtown workers and American and Creole identity also does not hold firm, however. Lala Hopkins, a self-proclaimed worker, operated on the downtown side of Canal Street. When speaking to researchers about her mentor, Marie Comtesse, Lala asserted that her teacher had studied under Laveau, undoubtedly the most famous worker in the city, Creole or otherwise.

Lala specified that Comtesse had a dark complexion, spoke "creole and French," and hired Creole dancers for ceremonies. Lala, like Madam Murray, said that she did not have skill in the Creole language and so had to hire Creole girls to sing Creole songs at certain ceremonies. Here Lala used almost every cliché about the association between Creole identity and Voodoo to establish a genealogy of power that went back to the Creole community in the person of Marie Laveau herself. [95] However despite being involved in Voodoo, living downtown, and having a Creole teacher, she had to enlist the help of others to maintain the Creole linguistic component of her rites.

This conflict between Afro-Creoles and African Americans was in no way peculiar to practitioners of Voodoo, but it did add a New Orleans flavor to Voodoo that was not present among conjure practitioners elsewhere in the United States. Workers inculcated this dialectic from the surrounding cultural mélange that was early twentieth-century New Orleans. The idiosyncratic colonial history of Louisiana added Creole cultural identity to the racial politics of Voodoo. The stories about Marie Laveau and the later influence of Leafy Anderson also made this New Orleans religion distinctive. The racial and, more specifically, interracial politics in the city permeated everything from the Laveau mythology to the ritual music of twentieth-century practitioners. All these things informed the practice of Voodoo in the early twentieth-century Crescent City and made it something unique.

By contrast, the racial classification of Voodoo was part of a larger project by the dominant culture throughout the U.S. South and beyond to push New Orleans into the biracial system of classification and segregation that characterized the codification of the Jim Crow system. In addition to the unique ideas about Creole cultural identity, workers shared the pervasive racial ideologies that marked African Americans as an "other" in the early twentieth-century United States. What they seemed less inclined to accept were the racial limits on their own practices, clientele, and personal and economic power that these distinctions were supposed to necessitate. Black workers served an interracial clientele and both trained and were trained by white workers. Whites, like Blacks, practiced Voodoo to augment their own social and economic power. This apparently included not only local practitioners but in Newbell Niles Puckett's case a white academic and researcher recording and analyzing the rituals of the Crescent City's workers. The continuing portrayal of Voodoo in and around the city as an African American phenomenon is a distortion that is the legacy of racism, slavery, and Jim Crow segregation. In order to gain a clearer understanding of these practices and their impact on the culture of New Orleans, we must view them as a New Orleans, rather than simply an African American, tradition, and we must examine the exchanges occurring between this subculture and the wider society in the city and beyond. This kind of examination points to the centrality of the local culture in New Orleans in the making of twentieth century Voodoo.

The point of this chapter is not to argue that the majority of Voodoo practitioners were white or even that they were not Black. Rather, I hope to complicate the perception that Voodoo is a Black cultural production by asserting that it is a New Orleans one. Even though researchers and ethnographers to date have clearly demonstrated or even stated a bias toward collecting data among African Americans when researching Voodoo, largely owing to our acceptance of notions of culture as racially bounded, we still maintain the expectation that their data are an acceptable confirmation of those notions of Voodoo as a racially bounded subculture. Again, it is not my intention to counter the perception that most Voodoo practitioners were African American. While that perception is based on a problematic acceptance of biased research and reporting during a time when such racial differences and boundaries were presumed to be unquestionable, the lack of convincing statistics on the number of non-Black practitioners of Voodoo would make a counterargument equally problematic.

What I am suggesting is that any notion of culture that allows us to look at a population that is constantly exchanging ideas and material resources with other populations and dismiss the impact of that exchange as negligible only hinders our understanding of what that culture is and how it functions. In the case of Voodoo in New Orleans, even though the evidence suggests that at least since the mid-nineteenth century whites have been involved in Voodoo, we dismiss their role as peripheral because it complicates our image of Voodoo as Black culture. The significant, possibly even disproportionate impact of white practitioners in helping to create and re-create what Voodoo is or was has thus been ignored or understated because it does not fit neatly into the racial lines we have drawn around Voodoo. Catering to a white clientele, buying from white supporters, and claiming the prestige of whiteness when whites participated in these rituals suggests that our insistence on viewing New Orleans Voodoo through black lenses may have obscured as much as it has illuminated about the practices and perception of practitioners. For practitioners Black and white, Voodoo was about power, and the need and desire for power stretched across the color line in early twentieth-century New Orleans.

Is the conclusion, then, that as long as the cultural productions of the African American community are birthed and reared in a multicultural New Orleans, it is incorrect to speak of an extant African American culture in the Crescent City? The answer is a definitive no. However, it would be helpful to do away with value-laden qualifiers like *predominantly* or *centrally* when referring to Voodoo as African American. These terms suggest boundaries that lead us to put a wall between the terms *African* and *American*. It starts us down a path that allows or even pushes us to view African American culture as distinct from the larger American culture rather than constantly drawing on and contributing to it. By consequence, culture, like race before it, becomes a conversational and, more importantly, an ideological boundary that reinforces notions that African American people are separate, alien outsiders in America. All Americans imbibe African American culture and often use it to define what it is to be American.[96]

All New Orleanians participated in the creation of Voodoo, from the early French Roman Catholics whose veneration of the saints had such an important impact on practitioners to the white women who validated practitioners by attending their rituals and financed their continuation by paying for ritual performances and the paraphernalia used in the production of gris-gris, the cemetery officials and sextons who cordoned off the Black sections of cemeteries, inadvertently helping to hide them from the prying eyes of the majority of white visitors and making them perfect for the practice of "Black magic," and the white pharmacists who facilitated the perpetuation of Voodoo by acting as suppliers, to say nothing of the white women who operated explicitly as both workers and clients in the community of Voodoo practitioners. These people were not outliers but cocreators of New Orleans Voodoo, and the Black clients and workers, along with their white counterparts, created rituals and practices that spoke to and of all these influences in their quest for power, weaving racial ideologies into their ritual formulas and their motivation for performing them.

4

"YES ISE A WOMEN FIXER"

Gender, Sex, and Power among New Orleans Workers

In the late 1930s a worker from New Orleans identified as the Mind Reader, because of rites she employed using flowers as a tool of divination, described a rite whereby using her finger- and toenails, specifically on a Friday, she could suppress the will of a man. The formula required her to cut and parch the toenails, sprinkling the resulting powder into her shoe. The fingernails, likewise finely parched, would be sprinkled over her subject's food and then ingested. She claimed that the outcome would be a man "under your feets and right in the palm of your hand."[1] In short, after the rite was completed, the subject would comply with any wish of the worker or the client for whom she performed this rite.

Such rites were all too common among workers in and around New Orleans in the early twentieth century. Nahnee, the Boss of Algiers, had a number of these rites. She claimed that one in particular would result in the subject being placed "under" her, where he or she would "jis' dance" while her client made the "music."[2] Madam O. Lindsey, of Algiers, had a number of rites specifically aimed at controlling a man, including one that she claimed would allow her client to "put her foot onto" the target's neck.[3]

The number of workers who provided researchers with ritual formulas pertaining to male-female relationships suggests that they were a major concern for both professional Voodoo practitioners and their clients. Workers performed and described rites that dragged the battle of the sexes from the quotidian domestic sphere into the realm of the metaphysical. While the rites described above might suggest that workers in New Orleans had a bias that skewed toward employing Voodoo as a weapon for augmenting the position of women in the seemingly timeless competition between the sexes, in fact, just as workers in this period reasoned that limiting their customer base racially might do them a disservice, they also played both sides in gendered conflicts. The aforementioned rites are evidence of apparent insecurities in a significant number of relationships between men and women revolving around who controlled the home, insecurities that seem not to have been exclusive to women.

Workers made their power available to both men and women who felt that their gender put them at some disadvantage in reference to the opposite sex. Workers described rites to change power dynamics in the home, curb spousal abuse, prevent or prematurely end pregnancies, and shift control of financial power in a domestic relationship. Workers used their power to help men and women target each other, their power seemingly not mitigated by gender loyalty but by the ebb and flow of commerce and the needs of their customer base. Because of the advantages that accompanied masculinity in this period, Voodoo may have been employed more often by women, but workers did not limit their clientele by gender and instead helped both men and women control members of the opposite sex.

With the help of workers, women could overcome some of the social and economic disadvantages vis-à-vis the men in their lives, and men could regulate female behavior in a way that even the gender-based privileges of patriarchy did not allow. However, just as workers did not claim to alter the reality of racial distinctions, they accepted the distinctions and basic logic of the early twentieth-century gender roles that created these power imbalances. They accepted that men and women were inherently different and occupied disparate roles in society and in the home. At the same time, they created rites that could make men subservient to women, bend the will of women to alter courtship norms, and help each sex overpower the other, often working in direct opposition to those norms in specific instances without threatening the system as a whole. Workers often tailored their work to the gender of their clientele and promoted their own power by accentuating or selling solutions to problems that clients often may have viewed as insurmountable due to their sex. Thus, workers made themselves the last hope against the seemingly inescapable pressures of fate and biology.

Central to the decision to work for or against someone or to seek out a worker to help in conflicts with the opposite sex was the perception that the potential target had some advantage in power that rendered the use of magic necessary or beneficial. Thus, professional Voodoo practitioners worked both sides of the gender divide, both subverting and reinforcing traditional gender norms. A man who could control his wife through economic and social pressure or threat of physical violence had little need to seek out a worker. Similarly, a woman in control of her own finances or whose husband was faithful did not need to call on a Voodoo doctor. The perception of being at a disadvantage relative to the opposite sex because of one's gender was frequently the motivation for seeking out the workers of New Orleans.

Saint Rita

By the beginning of the twentieth century, Saint Rita, a Catholic saint, had been adopted by workers and associated spiritual practitioners as a patron to be solicited for assistance with problems peculiar to women. According to Catholic tradition, Saint Rita of Cascia was born in Italy in the fourteenth century. Despite begging her elderly parents to allow her to enter a convent to become a nun, they arranged her marriage at twelve to a man with a propensity for violence who mistreated Rita and corrupted their children. After eighteen years of marriage, her husband died in a violent confrontation with a third party, and her two sons died soon thereafter. Later, she entered the convent of the Augustinian nuns at Cascia, in Umbria. She is said to have been miraculously struck on her forehead while praying by one of the thorns from a devotional crucifix so that she might more closely identify with Jesus by suffering as he had. The wound, reportedly resembling the crown of thorns worn by Jesus during what Christians refer to as the Passion, supposedly never healed and was frequently depicted in devotional images of Rita used by Catholics as a miraculous symbol of her piety and closeness to Jesus.[4]

When asked about Saint Rita, an informant interviewed in connection with the practice of Voodoo recounted a story illuminating women's precarious economic situation in relation to the men in their lives in the early twentieth century and the power Saint Rita could exert against those who apparently stood between them and material security. The woman said that she had been helpless when another woman had stolen her husband from her. She said that her husband had all but abandoned his home and his financial obligations, refusing to pay rent or support her or their children. She was desperate because she believed that she "didn't have no cause to go to the white folks" to legally force her husband to contribute economically to the household. While it is unclear why the informant believed she had no legal recourse, in order to deal with what seemed to be a dire situation she needed access to some power outside the kind of influence signified here by "the white folks."

The woman reported visiting Saint Rita, probably at a Catholic church or shrine, where she prayed. She told her interviewer that she burned incense and candles to the saint, acquired an image of her, and created a small altar in her home dedicated to Saint Rita. She sprinkled and scrubbed her house with holy water, wrote her husband's name on a piece of paper nine times forward and nine times backward, as commonly prescribed by workers, and burned a candle on him at the base of the saint's image.[5] The woman maintained that within three days of her performing this rite, her husband returned and paid the rent for the three weeks he had been gone, to the tune of nine dollars. Convinced of Saint Rita's power, the woman left a Methodist church, began praying at a Catholic church, and kept the light to Saint Rita burning for the three years between her husband's return and being interviewed by the ethnographer Harry Hyatt regarding the incident.[6]

The aforementioned informant was at the mercy of her husband socially and economically, a difficult situation exacerbated by the fact that the couple had children. Whether or not her perception was accurate, she also believed that she could not get aid through legal channels. In the face of these material woes, the gross power imbalance, and the lack of alternatives, she reached out to Saint Rita. In this account in particular, Saint Rita was the embodiment of tools Voodoo practitioners in New Orleans used to deal with gender-based power imbalances, in this case economic dependence in the context of a marriage. In addition to performing their own rites for men and women, workers solicited the power of the saints to help them. Workers and their clients called on saints because they felt at a disadvantage with reference to members of the opposite sex, just as they did when they felt disadvantaged by their racial caste or economic situation. Further, as workers developed alternative hagiographies for many saints, they often read the gendered notions regarding the power and roles of each gender into the stories they constructed around saints' lives. Thus they often read the saints as gender biased and called on certain saints on the basis of the gender of the clients seeking help.

Workers understood their world in gendered terms and thus read the saints, their motivations, and their behaviors in similarly gendered terms. Voodoo practitioners often thought of saints as Roman Catholics did: as individuals who lived extraordinary lives, or in the case of Voodoo saints, as people who had exhibited some extraordinary ability or power during their lifetime. After death they became patrons of certain groups and causes, to be entreated for aid, and practitioners frequently described prayers and ceremonies used to entreat them as *novenas*, a term used by Roman Catholics to refer to a period of prayer lasting nine consecutive days. Unrestricted by the official hierarchy or slowly changing dogma of the church, however, practitioners adjusted characteristics ascribed to the saints by the church and added new details to the saints' lives that made them sympathetic to individuals and causes for which they were being entreated.[7] While the background stories for saints often shifted depending on what use workers were attempting to make of their power and how, it was widely believed that saints carried the gendered perceptions of the corporeal world into the afterlife and continued to act on gender biases in their dealings with the living.

This perception of saints being entreated to help in dealings with the opposite sex or even seeking vengeance on members of a particular gender was not restricted to Saint Rita and her aiding of women but extended to both genders and other saints. Some ideas about saints' gender biases may have been picked up from Catholic lore. For example, among Catholics, Saint Raymond is patron saint of infants, expectant mothers, and midwives because of his own birth in the thirteenth century by caesarean section, during which his mother died from complications. There are several Catholic traditions specifically about women who prayed to Saint Anthony and in return for his help promised to give bread or some other kind of food or donation to the poor. Despite what might be implied by Voodoo practitioners' use of Saint Rita, the importance of male saints to causes close to women demonstrates the complexity of gender's role in the lives of saints among both male and female Voodoo practitioners, a complexity familiar, perhaps, to the Catholics from whom they borrowed many of these saints.

Often Voodoo practitioners seemed to attribute more extreme behavior to the saints than did their Catholic counterparts. This sometimes meant reading saints not only as identifying with one particular group or gender but as having pronounced animosity toward the opposite sex. This comparatively extreme reading of gender bias into the lives and activities of the saints may have made gender a less negotiable determinant of ritual practice for Voodoo practitioners. This tendency reflects workers reading the inflexibility of early twentieth-century gender roles into ritual practice. It also demonstrates their use of the certainty of gendered animosity among their clients to make the saints' behavior familiar and thus perhaps more appealing. Boy-Girl, a worker interviewed by Hyatt, said that Saint Expedite did not like women and that he could be called on to ruin a woman who did not love the client, making her life miserable by making her luck bad and doing away with both "her past and future."[8] Saint Peter, one informant claimed, favored women specifically. Thus while men burned candles to the Virgin Mary for help, women burned them to Saint Peter. This informant suggested that if a man burned candles to Saint Peter, the saint might burn down his home rather than help him.[9] The Candle Diviner, a worker in New Orleans, claimed that Saint Raymond favored women and had little to do with men, while Saint Christopher did not like women, because he was supposedly a eunuch, thus reading a pseudosexual motivation into the behavior of the saint. In all these examples, which gender had access to the power of these saints was non-negotiable, and there was implicit or explicit animosity toward members of the other sex.

Of all the gender biases attributed to Voodoo saints, perhaps the most intriguing were those attributed to Saint Rita. A number of Voodoo practitioners interviewed about Saint Rita believed that the saint not only favored women but hated men. Workers and other practitioners of Voodoo in New Orleans constructed a hagiography of Saint Rita recounting a life in which she was plagued by failed relationships with men, so that as a saint she empathized with women and ignored or even assaulted men or even women romantically involved with men. Because workers and believers transmitted these stories by word of mouth, the details about Saint Rita's life changed almost as often as the informants who told the stories.

One informant recounted that Saint Rita had had a number of husbands who were cruel and physically abusive to her, the last of whom was so abusive that he turned her against all men. This was the reason, according to this particular informant, why Saint Rita would not help any man and why an image of Rita in the house of a married woman brought bad luck. Saint Rita, she explained , aided single women.[10] Another informant added that not only did Saint Rita hate men due to her husband's abuse but her sons had died because she prayed to God to "take'em out of dis world" before they grew to be men.[11] Another informant said that in life Saint Rita had been a "sporting woman" and that "every night she would lay with . . . different mens." According to this account, her lone son was shot by one of these men when he mistook the child for another suitor calling at Rita's door. Making no specific mention of her becoming a nun, this informant believed that Rita then moved to the forest and began praying and afterward dedicated her life to helping the poor. This informant claimed that Saint Rita would aid men as long as they were "poor people, bad people," thereby altering Rita's constituency along with her hagiography.[12]

According to all these varied accounts, Rita's own difficulties with men during her life made her especially adept at helping women, particularly with their problems with men. The idea that she could also help women with their children probably derives from the needs of mothers in difficult relationships with men. These adjustments to her hagiography reflect a number of anxieties among women, including concerns about spousal abuse and dangers for sex workers connected to feelings of helplessness in the face of unequal power relations with men that Rita, and thus workers who entreated her, were especially well equipped to deal with.

Even though Rita was most consistently associated with aiding women, there was some ambiguity about her relationship to the opposite sex. A worker in New Orleans who was identified as the Gifted Medium said that when women prayed to Saint Rita because of problems with husbands, most often their husbands died. In contrast, Boy-Girl, a worker with a unique perspective on gender given her own self-identification as a hermaphrodite, described Rita as a household saint who would keep one's wife and children happy and successful and bring general good luck to the household. Boy-Girl said that she had no knowledge of Rita's distaste for men but had heard that she did not like women.[13]

Some believed that Saint Rita's contempt centered not on either sex but on romantic relationships and the institution of marriage. A worker named Ida Bates described Rita as a good saint who would aid a man but would not help a woman get or please a man because despite great effort and affection on her part, her husband had never been contented with her in life.[14] A worker from Algiers who had a number of noteworthy rites in which offerings were made to the saints warned that while Rita could provide work and bread for women, if there was a man present in the woman's life Rita would "make a big disturbance an' dis man'll cut chew, or he'll beat chew tuh death or he might shoot chew." She combined the notion of the saint's hostility to husbands with the notion that she was connected to spousal abuse, causing rather than preventing it in this case. Undoubtedly interpreting depictions of Saint Rita with the scar on her head made to simulate the crown of thorns, the worker said that because Rita's first lover had deceived her and cut her head, she did not like men.[15] The worker said that Rita had worked for her when she and her husband were separated but that when she took him back he assaulted her.[16] It is unclear whether the worker was blaming Rita or sharing in her disdain for the marital relationship. Whatever the case, she read Rita's actions as proof of her violent opposition to the relationship, and we can read this more generally as a projection onto Saint Rita of an implicit anxiety about the inherent danger of the marital relationship for women.

Another informant, in contrast to those who saw Rita as a sympathetic patroness for either gender, believed that the saint would take a cherished family member in exchange for getting rid of a woman's husband.[17] Similarly, Doctor Cafrey, a male worker, described Rita as an "evil force" who had killed both males and females of his family when he kept her image at his place of business.[18] This worker regarded Rita as a completely negative influence. There was no positive association, even for women, further complicating perceptions of her and her relationship to gender and increasing or, in this example, decreasing the number of workers and clients who could make use of her.

Despite their wide variety, the accounts, preferences, and biographies attributed to Saint Rita were consistent in stating that the gender of the client, the target, or both was significant to her. By molding and using Saint Rita to attend to the gender-specific concerns of their clients, workers could market specifically to those with gendered anxieties. Whether a woman wanted to improve her romantic situation or simply dispense with a troublesome man, the notion that Saint Rita, because of her own hardship, understood the situation of women in need may have reassured female clientele of workers who entreated the saint that they had found the right worker to deal with their specific needs and that they, like Rita, could be empowered.

Women's anxiety about the gender biases of the other saints mentioned, from Peter to Anthony and Joseph, may point to a similar anxiety that the gender bias women perceived was universal. By appealing to women's and men's understandings of the power and limitations ascribed to their respective genders, workers could also market themselves as advisers keenly aware not only of the supernatural but also of the social order of the natural world, thereby boosting their business by raising their clients' faith in Voodoo's ability to navigate the cleavages in New Orleans's social order.

Spouses of Workers

Between 1937 and 1940, LWP researchers met several times with Laura Hopkins, or Lala, at her downtown residence in New Orleans. At five foot one and weighing approximately eighty-five pounds, Hopkins was slight in build but bold in demeanor. Unlike many of her contemporaries who obscured their connections to Voodoo, Lala explicitly identified herself to interviewers as a worker. More in line with the secrecy expected of workers, interviewers recalled that when they met with Lala, she got abnormally close to them and spoke as if all the information she imparted about hoodoo was confidential. While this and similarly eccentric behavior undoubtedly made Lala the center of attention during these interviews, her husband, Louis, was also conspicuous.

In contrast to his eccentric partner, Louis was described by researchers as docile and servile; reports asserting that he executed "every whim of Lala's." They recounted that at a meeting with Lala, it was Louis who greeted them and offered them chairs, but after making a place for them at a table with the Voodoo queen, her husband was left to sit on a nearby trunk. Researchers wrote that Lala flaunted her power over Louis and her dominance in their domestic life by boasting in his presence that she had previously put him out of their home. Lala explained to her guests that despite the humiliation of being exiled by his wife, Louis had returned, because he could not "help himself," and in what would seem a final humiliation Louis reportedly confirmed Lala's version of these events. The researcher Robert McKinney could only explain the complete power imbalance between spouses by surmising in his report that "Louis definitely fears Lala and is completely 'hoodooed.'"[19] There may be a more pedestrian explanation for the odd dynamic between Lala and Louis, however.

Lala's control of Louis may have been predicated on professional and economic power as much as on any supernatural influence. Louis seemed to serve as a kind of assistant to Lala in her work. At one of these meetings Lala brought out a small cigar box that Louis had fashioned into a model coffin, a common prop in a number of different rites regularly employed by workers in the early twentieth century. When LWP researchers, under the pretense of becoming Voodoo practitioners themselves, hired Lala to perform a black cat Opening, an initiation rite that would prepare them to perform some of the darker Voodoo rituals, Louis was also present even though this ceremony was held at the home of another worker. Further, Lala reported that her teacher had also worked with a male companion, supporting the observation that her relationship with Louis was both personal and professional. Lala explained that she had begun her training in Voodoo under a worker named Marie Comtesse, whose husband also had also worked with her on occasion. Lala's accounts suggest that Comtesse's husband may not have had another job, so that he was seemingly dependent on his wife for remuneration.[20] Louis too may have been economically dependent on his wife, giving her substantial sway in their domestic relationship.

By presenting herself as the dominant personality in her relationship with her husband and as both her own and her husband's boss professionally, Lala could be seen as effectively making a gender-based sales pitch for her practice in Voodoo. For a potential female client, the image of Lala's power over both her husband and her own finances despite both her gender and her slight physical stature screamed power in a way that her speaking about it may not have. It also suggested the possibility that she could garner similar power for women who could pay her fee.

The ability of Hopkins and her predecessor Marie Comtesse to make a living and provide for their husbands undoubtedly would have increased their influence in their marital relationships as well. This advantage may have been even more pronounced for Hopkins, who operated her business during the Great Depression. In a time when American women routinely contributed less income to their families, creating a business that not only produced substantial profits but also employed their significant others doubtlessly contributed to the personal and economic power of these female workers both in their homes and in their businesses. Her power might also have worked as a selling point for potential clients of the opposite sex. For some men, Lala's portrayal of her own power with reference to her husband might have inspired fear of losing the privileges of patriarchy. However, for a man with ambitions of employing a worker to aid him in his own life, it might have suggested the tantalizing question, If she can dominate her husband, what could she do for me?

An examination of the Crescent City's professional spiritual practitioners, and more specifically their marital relationships, suggests that there was a discernable correlation between Voodoo, economic independence, and power in the context of relationships between men and women. In November 1939, Mother Kate Francis, a successful Spiritual Church mother and a protégé of Leafy Anderson's,[21] died in her church, St. Michael's Temple No. 1, in downtown New Orleans, while leading her congregation in prayer. Journalists from all over the city were attracted to the services held at her brother's church, at St. Michael's No. 2, uptown on Melpomene Street. Though she fancied herself a leader in the Spiritual Church movement and not a worker, she employed a number of rites common among professional Voodoo practitioners, and her church was regularly associated with the practice of Voodoo. After her death, leadership of her temple was assumed by her protégé Ellen Fairwell, who spoke in detail to LWP interviewer Robert McKinney. She explained that she had not yet adopted the title "mother" because she had to be crowned with roses by thirteen of Mother Kate's co-workers and Father Louis Francis, Kate's husband, before she could be called "Mother" Ellen Fairwell.[22] Father Louis had apparently followed Mother Kate into her work after she was called by God to begin working as a healer some fifteen years earlier. Father Louis told a *New Orleans Item* reporter that he had been skeptical when his wife quit her job as a washerwoman for whites uptown for $1.50 a day, largely because he could not support them both on the $2.40 a day he earned as a street paver.[23] Father Louis said that he had become convinced of Kate's call when, just a week after expressing his concerns to his wife, he was promoted to foreman and his salary increased to $6 a day, allowing him to support them both as Kate began her ministry healing infirmed individuals in her neighborhood.[24] Implicit in Father Louis's account, however, was that Kate's financial dependence had previously allowed her husband to determine the family's future.

According to Father Louis, when she died, Mother Kate's flock included twenty-eight temples with Black and white participants both inside and outside New Orleans, an empire that Louis said she knew she was beginning when she opened her first church, labeling it from its inception St. Michael's No. 1, suggesting that there would be others.[25] Ellen Fairwell said of Father Louis that he "kept his eye on Kate. He used to be a street paver, that woman had so much power, yes and money too, he gave up his job and married her. Fo' another turn was made he was being made into a Father, but he was made into a good one."[26] In addition to bringing her husband into the Spiritual Church, she also included her brother Daniel, who headed St. Michael's No. 2, where funeral services for Mother Kate were held, and her sister Virginia Francis, who apparently worked for the church as a secretary and bookkeeper.[27]

The success of Mother Kate's organization allowed her to employ and thereby economically support her immediate family. Her work as a church mother had given her not only a great deal of spiritual power but temporal influence as well, much of it undoubtedly related to the economic success of her ministry. She expanded her own network by training co-workers to start their own churches, charging them a fee to open up in her name—fifteen dollars for her three-month course in spiritualism and five dollars for their charters. Mother Kate also supplied her students with the blessed oil, candles, and other paraphernalia they used in their own churches. This undoubtedly allowed Kate to amass a substantial income, as well as to create positions for her husband and her brother.

Mother Louise Bowers, a co-worker of Mother Kate's since 1930, said that in order to establish her own church she had paid Mother Kate upwards of fifty dollars, an exchange with which she was content because she believed it had contributed to her own success. Her faith that a career as a spiritual mother would improve her circumstances was buttressed by her understanding that Mother Kate's influence had contributed to the success of her own family.[28] Mother Kate's followers remembered her as an extraordinary spiritual leader and a formidable entrepreneur whose economic success allowed her to control not only her own destiny but the livelihood of the men in her immediate family as well. Mother Kate's story was evidence that women need not be economically dependent on the men in their lives. Ellen Fairwell's and Louise Bowers's accounts suggest that they understood from Mother Kate's example that operating as a Spiritual Church mother was an effective means of avoiding a life as economic dependents. As Father Louis's account of the negotiation with Mother Kate about entering a spiritual calling may suggest, neither Lala nor Kate seems to have questioned gender norms in general, just their own power with reference to them.

In 1937 researchers interviewed the Reverend Alice Mancuso, a stout, apparently uneducated Italian woman in her early thirties who headed St. Rita's Spiritual Church. As with the patroness of her church, Alice's relationship with her husband demonstrated a complete refusal to yield to the power of patriarchy. Like Kate, Alice profited from her spiritual classes for co-workers and from the charters she sold them upon the classes' conclusion, which allowed them to found their own churches. Alice also trained as a nurse and a midwife before she became a Spiritual Church mother, ten years prior to the interview, and her husband worked as a police officer. Though he did not approve of her work as a spiritual mother, she apparently ignored his concerns, to her material benefit.

She told interviewers that she preached to an interracial congregation that had just given her a brand-new 1937 Pontiac.[29] Her ability to assert her own will in her family was undoubtedly related to her ability to earn a living first as a nurse and then as a spiritual mother.

By 1941 Reverend Alice had apparently performed the ultimate act of resistance to the uneven power relations present in most marriages of the time by stabbing her husband to death in their home. Rumors researchers picked up from the attendants at her husband's funeral suggested that Alice had killed her husband because their marriage was deteriorating and he planned to take their daughters and leave her when he retired from the police force. She had apparently been absolved of the crime, however, when her teenage daughters told authorities, not that their mother was uninvolved, but that their father had said, with the knife in his chest, that he and not their mother was responsible. It is possible that these rumors were less than accurate, but they may tell us something about how the community viewed Alice's work as a spiritual mother.

Whether or not Reverend Alice was responsible for her husband's death, the accusations to that affect imply that people believed she had the force of will to kill her husband and that she refused to allow her husband to abandon her and take their children. It also suggests that she could, or at least she believed she could, support herself and her children. Though there was also the sinister perception that she would be capable of murder, a perception probably connected to her work as a professional spiritual practitioner, it was apparently accompanied by the perception that her profession had made her self-sufficient and powerful enough to kill her husband and escape prosecution.

These women, especially those that had plugged into Mother Leafy Anderson's model of entrepreneurship in the Spiritual Churches, had created institutions that functioned not only as churches but as businesses. In uncertain economic times this independence and business savvy undoubtedly contributed to their apparent freedom in their marital relationships. Some of the associations made between women and Voodoo were undoubtedly negative. However, the power Voodoo brought to female workers, which was not only spiritual but also temporal and economic, probably added to its appeal. Accidents of birth led to gender roles that were difficult to overcome. Workers proved that it was not impossible, however, and they offered to sell that freedom to clients and co-workers so that even if these roles did not change generally, their spiritual work might provide relief for them and their clients.

Attracting a Mate

Rites to cope with gender-based power imbalances were commonly sold by workers to their clients. In the collective imagination of writers of history and fiction about New Orleans and journalists in and around the city in the early twentieth century, there was a repeated association between Voodoo and human sexuality. This association was most commonly embodied, if not by the ceremonial orgy, then by the Voodoo-derived love "potion." Folklore about practitioners featured lurid tales of women who sought out workers in order to procure a gentleman's heart against his will. At their center these tales, like many of the stories told about workers, were in essence about power. In this case it was the power of the solicitor of the love potion to control the affections of a would-be paramour. Compared with other rites prescribed to deal with romantic relationships, gris-gris used to actually attract a mate was relatively uncommon. More frequently the rites described by early twentieth-century workers were used to hold the interest of a lover or to keep the lover from leaving a relationship in which he or she was already involved. Most salient were rites prescribed for both men and women aimed at controlling a spouse or significant other in some way.[30]

Some rites that at a glance might be construed as functioning like traditional love potions actually seemed to be more about control and stability in romantic relationships than about love. For example, Nahnee, the Boss of Algiers, had a pair of rites that she said were used to put a couple together that only required the client to know the other person's name, which would be written in a particular sequence and combined with various secondary ingredients. These rites could be performed by an admirer on a subject they did not necessarily know well and therefore might be used to attract a mate. However, when Nahnee described an occasion conducive to the performance of these rites, she also said that they were effective for bringing together two people who previously had been separated. She described the procedures as if she were bringing together a couple who had a history rather than bringing two people into a new relationship.[31] Other rites she described required the use of the subject's picture (which in an era before instant flash photography would have required a great deal more effort than today) or dirty socks, a sample of a woman's hair, or some other personal item, all necessitating more contact between the client and the intended subject than a passing relationship would have allowed. [32] The point is that while the love potions did exist in some form, workers' formulas seemed to be focused most often on controlling subjects with whom clients already had a romantic relationship. Thus, attracting a mate was most frequently about control of one's own domestic relations, particularly with members of the opposite sex.

Rites centered on intimacy were usually about power and control. Some rituals required a person to obtain a sample of his or her partner's sexual discharge in order to control that partner's behavior, implying that they would only be useful in preexisting intimate relationships. One such rite was described as a man's solution to keeping a woman who he thought might leave him. Both the rite itself and the circumstances for which it was prescribed explicitly indicate an attempt to control one's partner rather than to cause someone to fall in love. A seventeen-year-old worker who maintained a private shrine had a rite for which she suggested obtaining a man's black sock, a piece of his underwear, and hair from his underarm, his head, and "down below" (his pubic hair), combining them with pins, boiling them with black pepper, and burying them in a place that the man had to pass on a regular basis. [33] The rite would draw a man to a client and keep him focused only on her, diverting his attention from other women and thereby preventing him from ever leaving her. Again, the concern here was with a woman's ability to stabilize her living situation and her relationship in the face of competition from other women.

Simply "jumping town" to escape a relationship was a strategy for maintaining or regaining control in a relationship that could often be employed despite disparities in power. However, the possibility of losing a partner in this way might make the person left behind feel helpless. If the individual leaving did so without warning and could not be found, there would be little the scorned party could do. Many rites dealt with retrieving a departing partner, undoubtedly because a worker might be the last resort for someone who felt helpless to control his or her own life under such circumstances.

Contrary to the love and romance we might associate with the concept of the Voodoo love potion, these rites were almost invariably about manipulating and controlling the actions of a partner and, by consequence, one's own existence. Workers' prescriptions implied that they were most often attempting to help a client maintain control over a romantic relationship by controlling the emotional state of a partner. Workers had formulas that could help clients, male or female, control elements in a relationship that were not easily manipulated physically or fiscally, namely, the feelings and desires of a significant other. What is more, the desire to exert such control was hardly gender specific, so workers had formulas that could alleviate a client's sense that he or she was at the mercy of someone of the opposite sex.

Keeping a Mate

Workers interviewed in New Orleans provided a number of rites to assist clients in maintaining relationships, often in the face of normal social or financial hardships or competition from another suitor. Some of these rites closely resembled formulas used to attract someone of the opposite sex. In these rites, especially those that employed parched or powdered skin from the bottom of a client's feet or parched pieces of their fingernails added to a subject's food or drink, workers were explicitly attempting to keep a man or woman attached to the client rather than to attract someone new. The Gifted Medium of New Orleans graphically explained that if the subject ingested the doctored substance, the clients "feet shall hold yo' an' mah nails shall clutch yo'."[34] Often, though, the formulas for getting and keeping mates were virtually identical.[35] These similarities imply that rites originally intended to acquire companionship were shifted to keep a current partner, further suggesting that keeping a mate was more important to workers and their clients than attracting one.

Two people could be kept together not only by getting a subject to ingest the substance of a client's body. Sometimes it could be achieved by combining material belonging to the client and the subject outside the body. To keep a significant other, the Mind Reader of New Orleans suggested a rite in which she would deposit the subject's hair into an oil lamp along with three drops of her client's blood as well as oil of cinnamon and honey. She would place something that the subject liked to eat nearby and then light the lamp. As long as the lamp burned, the subject would be tied to the client.[36] Again, using hair implied access to the subject, and the language of tying people together, as opposed to language pertaining to acquisition, also suggests a preexisting relationship, as does knowledge of the subject's favorite food.

Perhaps the ultimate rite employed to stabilize a romantic relationship and thus other aspects of the client's living situation involved inducing marriage. An example of such a rite entailed baking a white cake on which one would write the subject's name in white icing and place three lights, or candles—

white, blue, and pink—around the name, with the white in the center. One would stick three straws into the cake, reciting, "Nuthin' kin part me—as these three straws stand together, we stand; divided, we fall."[37] Blue and pink candles were often associated with love, and white candles with luck. The white cake, of course, is traditionally associated with a wedding ceremony. Through this rite a client not only maintained an existing romantic relationship but possibly intensified one to the point of inducing marriage, socially and economically tying himself or herself to the intended subject.

There were certain items that were commonly used to keep a significant other around. The association with feet and keeping a man stable, or at home, was common. Some rites required female clients to measure the length of a man's footsteps with a cord and then knot it nine times.[38] Some employed a shoe or sock, to which magical powder or other ingredients were introduced.[39] Others simply called for placing the subject's name in a bottle with other ingredients, like their urine, and keeping it somewhere in the house to which the client wanted to attach him or her, for example, over a doorframe, under the stairs, or in a mattress.[40] Different ingredients could be employed according to the style of the worker and the need of the client. The common pattern seemed to be the placing of a charm in or near the home to attract the subject and keep him or her there. Again, the implied concern was with the stability of the home as much as with love.

This idea of using the body's substance to control an individual was combined with the notion of keeping someone stationary in a rite employed by the Black Cat Lucky Bone Maker. It required a female client attempting to stop her mate from leaving town to take a bottle of his urine out to a crossroads, conceivably one that had to be crossed to leave town, and pour some of it out there for nine mornings a month for nine months.[41] Often this rite was employed to impede a subject's bodily functions, thereby making the subject ill. Here, however, it was used to stop the entire individual from leaving rather than, for instance, stopping some excretion from leaving the subject's body. The worker explained that by burying a man's filth, that is, samples of his urine or sweat, at a crossroads, a woman could weaken a man's will, forcing him to stay at home with her: "Lak dey got some dinka men, yo' see, hangin' in de house wit dere wife. Dey call dem hen-pecked men. Dey cain't he'p deyself. . . . See, dey bury dat out at de fo'k of de road an' den dey eatin' filth from dis woman."[42]

Even though this explanation employs a euphemism about proverbial "shit eating," using a substance produced by an individual's body to control that person and, further, rooting that substance to a place by burial implies an understanding that is not explicitly explained by workers but seems consistent with similar gris-gris and persists in their deployment of these rituals. There is also an implication that there was something intrinsically wrong with a man sitting home with a woman. Undoubtedly springing from gendered perceptions that the man's place was out working and the woman's was in the home, it seems to suggest anxiety among male workers and clients about gender roles, perhaps more specifically loss of male authority in the home.

Owing to women's perceived connection to children and the ability of men to earn more money than women in a highly gender-biased early twentieth-century labor market, the most common abandonment scenario in the public imagination may have been of a man leaving a woman. However, there is evidence that abandonment was also a concern for which men sought out workers. The Undercover Man, for example, specified that many of his customers sought success in gambling and employment, but most were men seeking the return of wives who had left them.[43] Thus, while many of the examples above specify female clients working on male subjects, this statement explicitly marks this kind of work as relatively common for members of both genders. Workers made use of gender, but gender bias does not appear to have been an issue for many of them.

What may be proof positive that workers did not seek to alter gender norms that placed women at a substantial disadvantage to men both socially and economically and instead aided members of both genders was the use by female workers of controlling rites that targeted female subjects. Likewise, male workers often employed rites targeting troublesome male subjects. Both did so with no apparent regard for how it would help the opposite sex or hurt members of their own gender. Rather, they dealt with the specific issues brought to them by clients of either sex.

Some female workers helped men to dominate women both emotionally and sexually. In his work with the Voodoo queen Madame Ducoyielle, Robert McKinney was provided with a rite for using John the Conqueror root to control a woman. His teacher told him that if his woman was not "treating him right," he should mix the root with cayenne pepper and sugar and deposit it under her bed. Madame assured him that his significant other would love him and "function" at night from then on.[44] As workers often did, she then recounted a case in which she had used the root effectively to separate a man's daughter from a boyfriend he did not approve of and attach her to the man she eventually married. Madame Ducoyielle boasted, "If ya hav any trouble wid ya women see me, Ise er fix'em. Yes Ise a women fixer."[45]

Clearly, Madame Ducoyielle was unconcerned with the young girl's right to choose in this instance or in any instance in which women might fall under the influence of her would-be student. Despite the authority wielded over women by the men in their lives in the early twentieth century, there was obviously money to be made by helping men control the women in their lives, especially in the precarious and fickle circumstances surrounding romantic relationships. This may have been because while social norms allowed fathers and husbands to control women's behavior, Voodoo offered men the opportunity to control women's thoughts and feelings.[46]

A spouse's fleeing had both emotional and financial repercussions for a family left behind, who would have very little recourse for reordering their existence in the face of the lost support. Workers provided an alternative in these and other seemingly helpless situations. Even if one could not locate a lost lover or persuade him or her to return, workers in the city had rites that could restore relationships or families and thus restore clients' control over their own lives.[47] More often than not, the rites that seemed to be about love were more about stability and the power to control one's domestic arrangements. Keeping a mate was often instrumental in keeping a home, supporting children, and maintaining a standard of living. Maintaining relationships could be daunting for both men and women. Women could not leave children, but a man might. A man was supposed to support his family. If he did not, gender biases in hiring or pay might make it hard for a woman to do so. Workers offered the promise of stability in relationships to men and women faced with these issues.

Economic Control and Romantic Relationships

An informant who spoke to one Harry Hyatt in 1940 did so wearing a disguise and was therefore identified only as "Dark Glasses, Dark Lady, Dark Deeds." She recognized that while maintaining a domestic partnership might be paramount to clients, it was also necessary that they be able to manipulate their significant others if they really wanted to control their own fate. She prescribed a specific rite for returning a male partner who had abandoned his female counterpart. She followed this rite with a prescription for a second that required the client to write the man's name nine times and put it in her left shoe along with steel dust, three raisins, salt, and sugar. The Dark Lady said of the compound rite, "An' as fo' me, anywhere ah walk, anywhere ah leave him, ah'm goin' tuh be de rulah. Ah'll control him cause he's undah mah feet. . . . Dat's drawin' him to me. An' now, when he gits dere, ah'm de rulah cause ah got him dere."[48] The worker offered her female client the power to shore up a deteriorating domestic partnership and presumably invert the power dynamic that put her at her significant other's mercy. Whereas in earlier examples the need to control a significant other seems implicit, the Dark Lady is clear about her intent.

Whether the exchange between a worker and a client was inter- or intragender, what was being sold was an escape from a situation in which one individual felt powerless in reference to an individual of the opposite sex. A great many variations of these rites allowed women to control their male partners.[49] A significant number of rites described by workers aimed at maintaining domestic tranquility that did not specify dominance of a spouse as the aim simply sought to keep the home peaceful by keeping the client's partner pleasant.[50] Before there were many protections against spousal abuse or even spousal rape the law could provide little protection to a woman under the thumb of a violent husband. Legally, women in a marriage were at a severe disadvantage because of the perception that a woman's role was to obey her husband and that a husband was within his rights to exert that control physically.

Harry Hyatt's first informant in New Orleans had a number of rites for manipulating emotional states in a relationship, which he prescribed for both men and women. She had a rite using the man's underarm and pubic hair, a red flannel bag kept in a pillow, and a control powder–based scrub specifically for making a husband be nicer to his wife. On the other hand, she also had a formula to keep a female subject focused on one man that required that a bottle containing the woman's urine and cornmeal be buried under her back steps, presumably for use by a male client.[51] In this case, women seemed to be attempting to control the behavior of men in order to better control their own lives. Men in turn seemed to be attempting to exert control over women's emotions, one of the few areas in which they could not dominate them via more quotidian methods. Anyone, regardless of gender, could apparently feel helpless in reference to a significant other. Workers offered men access to power that neither physical strength nor legal regulation could provide, and they offered women what the law and threat of physical violence deprived them of, a sense of security.

A great deal of what workers did was aimed at helping their clients deal with circumstances seemingly beyond their control. At a service held at St. Michael's Temple No. 2, the pastor called on one of his congregation to testify to his success in helping him with her problems. The woman said that she had come to Father Dupont's church the previous Friday because her husband had lost his job. She was starving, behind in her rent, and about to be evicted from her home. While she did not specify that her husband found work, the witness said that in the following days her husband's mood had improved drastically and her landlord had given her an extension to pay her rent. Father Dupont claimed responsibility for her good fortune and cited it as proof that he could hoodoo her enemies. He said that she would not have to worry as long as she continued attending his church.[52] The story here is that the female congregant at St. Michael's was confronted by a number of forces seemingly beyond her control, from which Father Dupont's hoodoo offered her relief. She obviously had no control over her husband's employer and could not control his employment status. Despite her helplessness, her fate, specifically her housing dilemma, would have been directly related to her dependence on her husband's income. Further, her husband's mood, undoubtedly lifted by the willingness of the landlord to await payment of rent, also would have had a direct effect on her domestic situation. Many clients of workers found themselves attempting to deal with similar issues. By having this woman testify to her experience, Father Dupont was marketing himself and marking his hoodoo as a solution to the kinds of complicated relationships between gender, power, and economic security that could make anyone feel unable to extricate themselves from such a scenario.

In many cases, the central concern for women attempting to control the men in their lives was economic. One worker specified that a rite she concluded by burying a bottle containing a man's used bathwater would make him remain home, "right from work on."[53] The implication was that while her clients wanted to keep their spouses, what they wanted most was that their spouses be working and economically viable. A husband's value as far as workers were concerned was measured at least in part by his role as a financial provider or contributor to his household. Keeping him was only partially about affection. It is likely that the multitude of informants who offered rites that helped clients stop men from drinking may have been concerned not only with the correlation between alcohol and domestic abuse but also with the economic ramifications for a woman whose partner spent significant portions of his income on alcohol, or on other things that detracted from his ability to contribute to his family's economic maintenance.[54]

Some workers offered female clients an even more direct method for exerting economic influence in their homes. Madam Lindsey had a rite that she claimed would result in a kind of wealth redistribution in the home. She suggested that if a man did not want to give money to his wife, she take a half dollar from his pocket and file three notches into it. She would then use an unbleached cotton string to measure his height and the circumference around his body while he was asleep. The woman would mark the length of his body by knotting the string first at the top and then at the bottom. In between, she would knot it three times at the point in the string that marked the distance around his body from the top. She would wrap the coin in this string so that it passed through all the notches in the coin and then place both in a bag, also made of unbleached cotton, and pin the bag to her pants, over her genitals, leaving it there for nine days. After the woman removed the coin and spent all of it at any store, she would bring the merchandise into the house and return the string to the bag, wearing it for an indefinite period. The result, according to Madam Lindsey, was that "dat man will bring yo' his money home an' yo' got him so dere's no way fo' him tuh git undah dat. Yo've got him dis way an' *tied down* so he cain't do nuthin but bring dat money home—but he'll bring yo' de best po'tion to it. De least part will be—he'll keep dat, but one-third of his money will always come tuh yo'!"[55]

Some female workers and Spiritual Church mothers managed to control their husbands' incomes by employing them. While difficult, this may have been achievable by other means. Workers offered a woman a rite for controlling a man's finances regardless of whether she could control his employment. This rite had the potential to alleviate the worry of any female client concerned about a husband's predilections for gambling, drinking, or spending his income on any number of things that might create a problem for economic dependents, be they women or children.

This concern with the income of a significant other seems to have been fairly common. One worker in New Orleans reported that she was visited by the spirit of her grandmother when a man she was seeing ended their relationship. Her grandmother gave her a rite that forced the man to return to her after he had been paid at his job. He brought her six dollars, money she apparently had been trying to get from him before the trouble began between them.[56] The same informant described a rite that had achieved a similar result. She claimed that the rite had caused her client's significant other to return home on payday, surrender his entire pay of twenty-five dollars, and then stay home with the woman.[57] Economic dependence on a partner of the opposite sex was a significant problem, and workers could market their services as a solution for women in these cases or even for men who saw their economic stability tied to a significant other.[58] There was a consistent conflation between intimate relationships and economic dependency, a dynamic often manipulated by workers.

Rites employed by workers often implied that even formulas employed to ensure sexual fidelity might have been tied to economic motivations. Ida Bates, of New Orleans, prescribed two rites for a male to use to prevent his significant other from even considering another man, one of which allowed him to affect the woman by simply crossing over her when crawling into or out of bed. Proof positive of the effectiveness of this rite, according to Bates, was that the woman would be so unable to consider another man as a mate that "a man kin put money in her hand and she won't accept it."[59] Perhaps at issue here is workers' ability to market themselves to male clients whose role as a provider might be challenged by someone with deeper pockets. A man could feel unable to compete with a wealthier suitor for his wife if his income was modest. This economic disadvantage with reference to another man, mitigated by the gender-specific role as a provider and the assumption that infidelity could be economically motivated, could be overcome even in the absence of comparable financial means through the use of Voodoo.

Workers apparently also drew a correlation between the physical prowess of a man and control of his money. In her description of one control rite, a worker from Algiers made this connection explicit:

Den ag'in, if yo' wan'a man an' lak 'im tuh be so by yo' an' bring all de money tuh yo'—don' wan' 'im tuh bend tuh nobody else—all yo' do ketch 'im when he's 'sleep, an' take one his stockin's an' piece of one his undaweahs, one his shirts, an' clip a piece off 'is hat, an' den yo' put it undahnet' dere. See, yo' got 'is strength an' he haven't got any mo' his strength. All 'is strength is gone ovah tuh yo'. Now when he go out fo' his money an' anybody ast 'im, say, "Well, treat." Well, he say, "Ah got tuh hurry up an' bring it tuh mah wife," An' whatevah she give 'im he take it. See. Well, his hair done made 'im so dat she got all 'is strength. She drawin' 'im tuh 'er.[60]

Perhaps one of the most extreme instances of equating strength with economic power and sexual potency was given by a doctor called the Black Cat Lucky Bone Maker. Here a woman uses her "filth" to control a man:

She can take her inf'mation rag. An' she take 'er inf'mation rag an' she puts dat undah de part of de bed where he sleep at. Dat'll wit'drew strength outa his back an' keep 'is back weak an' he won' bothah 'er too much, havin' contact wit 'er ovahnight. She's perhaps one of dose kinda women whut chew call a freak woman. See, she jis' got dis man mos'ly fo' convenience. She haven't dis man, say, jis' if she love 'im. She keeps 'im weak whilst so she kin have de money tuh be 'sociate wit de kina people whut she 'sociated wit, lak whu' chew call bulldraggin' women.[61]

This equating of economic control and physical strength seems to have been specific to men in the formulations of workers. Again, most likely tied to the perception that his gender made earning a living and supporting dependents prerequisites for his masculinity, the idea was that only a man who was weak, not just mentally but physically, would allow a woman to control his finances. There were similar implications for the weakness of a man who would allow his woman to get away with infidelity or compromising his material well-being, especially in favor of another man. These gender-specific concerns, while not making a man feel powerless per se, might lead him to seek aid from a worker. These concerns could provide opportunities for workers to market themselves to men's gender-specific concerns.

These kinds of rites also reflect other anxieties about intimate relationships. The first and most nonspecific was men's fear that women were scheming to control them when they were most vulnerable, that is, when they were asleep or during sex. Second was the fear that women's only interest in an intimate relationship was to buttress their own economic security at the expense of their male counterparts. This fear was exaggerated in the previously related instance by the assertion of the possibility that such a woman was uninterested not only in her mate but in men generally, since the informant used a number of derogatory adjectives for homosexual women, including *freak* and *bulldraggin'*, to denote her disinterest.[62]

In addition to not being gender biased, workers seem not to have had much of a moral imperative in deciding which rites to perform. Many workers recounted similar rites that had a female client put her male partner's shoe upside down under their bed so that he would not awake during the night, allowing the woman to leave the house while he slept.[63] This and similar rites frequently carried an implicit, if not explicit, sexual connotation. This suggests that workers were concerned not with issues of justice for men or women but rather with domestic power for their clients, the spiritual power that allowed them as spiritual practitioners to grant it, and the economic benefits that could result for both them and their clients.

Controlling Sexuality

Where the relationship between money and Voodoo practitioners' attempts to control a romantic partner points to economics as the central justification for many of the relationship rites, the means for exerting that control apparently varied greatly. Workers attempted to dominate both the behavior and the emotions of clients' significant others in order to allow those clients to assert control over their domestic lives. A recurring means of exerting influence over relationships revolved around attempts to limit, accentuate, or otherwise control the sexuality of a client's partner. For many men and women, sexual promiscuity or infidelity was at the root of a great many relationship woes. The rituals employed to control sexuality demonstrated similar tendencies by workers to allow difference, in this case gender, to influence or determine the form of their rites, while ignoring these same differences in determining for whom they worked.

One informant described formulas for keeping a significant other faithful, one specifically for men and another for women. The prescription for the man to keep his wife from "going around" with a man while he was at work required him to dress one of her socks or stockings with some of her hair and a number of other ingredients and wear this charm in his coat pocket or sew it into the lining. If he did this, the worker claimed, he would not have to worry about his wife cheating. Conversely, another rite required the wife to use pubic hair from her man combined with alcohol and ammonia and burn a candle on it.

The result, however, would be that not only would he stay away from other women but "he won't have no *nature*" for them, a common euphemism for impotence in a man. In this case, the same worker, while not favoring men or women in terms of prescribing Voodoo, did employ a gender-specific attack on the male victim. The worker was willing to bind a woman sexually as well, but her methodology was drawn distinctly along gender lines.

Most workers for whom sexuality was the chosen means for controlling relationships aimed their rites at manipulating a man's ability to perform sexually. A worker named Rosa prescribed a rite that would keep a husband and make certain that he had "good passion," implying that the intent was to increase sexual prowess.[64] More often than not, however, workers sought to help wives control the sexuality of their husbands by inducing impotence in the man.

While some workers' attention to gender difference led them to induce impotence to control men in the context of a romantic relationship, others specialized in helping men deal with sexual dysfunction. The prophet Joseph Lyons, of the Emperor Haile Selassi Nu-Way Ethiopia Mystic Light Baptist and Spiritual and Kingdom Church, apparently decorated his modest establishment (economically modest at least) not with saints' images but with "many suggestive pictures of women at leisure, the kind that are synonymous with certain places for men only." The Prophet explained: "Many men come in to see me who have had no contact and what they need is to be worked up."[65] Unlike the majority of workers who dealt in sexual manipulation, then, Joseph Lyons dealt in curative rather than malicious work.

Rites inducing impotence were not necessarily about the man's infidelity but might also concern the woman's. In March 1938 the *New Orleans Item* published a story about Cuffie Cash, a forty-five-year-old African American male convicted of killing his wife, Carrie, after a marital spat in Caddo Parish, in northern Louisiana. According to Cuffie, seven years earlier, suspicious that his wife might be involved in an extramarital affair, he had visited a worker named Lennie Henderson, who told him that a salve his wife had apparently rubbed on him was supernatural and had "reduced him to impotence." Henderson made Cash a "magic toby," for which he paid ten dollars. "Dazed, Cuffie wandered back to his home," where he accused his wife of infidelity, and the confrontation apparently ended with him fatally shooting her.[66]

Again, most rites performed in association with impotence involved inducing rather than relieving the condition. Perhaps the most frightening of these rites was one prescribed by Rosa, described as a hoodoo woman from New Orleans, that could be permanent. A number of workers used snails or snail by-products in rites designed to induce sexual dysfunction. To "take a man's nature," Rosa suggested sewing two or three live snails into his underwear, which would prevent him from being aroused by another woman. Because the snails were not intended to be removed, however, and presumably died sewn into the garment, the rite was described as permanent, as the man's sexual function would die with the snails. The inability to be sexually stimulated by any other partner for the rest of one's life could be quite a motivator to men to perpetuate their current relationship indefinitely.[67]

It was not always the case that female workers helped female clients with unfaithful males. Madam Lindsey, of Algiers, described a number of prescriptions for controlling a man's sexuality that resulted in the man's inability to perform with other women. However, she also described a rite to counter this kind of dysfunction, and while her description of the original rite presumed a female target and a male client, in her description of the cure she specified that it could work on either a man or a woman:

> And you take that handkerchief and you fold it coming to you, and you say, "In the Name of the Father and the Son and the Holy Ghost, take this feeling off of me, and let me come to be a real man or real wo-man." Whatsomever or whosomever it is *fixed* like that, say, "Let me come to be, so I can use my body once more in life, In the Name of the Father and the Son and the Holy Ghost." . . . It kills her *hand* or his *hand*—whatsomeever it is, it kills it.[68]

In addition to demonstrating the willingness of workers to perform sexual rites for both genders, the phrases "real wo-man" and "real man" imply that sexual behavior was constitutive of gender identity for workers. What is also clear here is that workers apparently had the will and the occasion to institute control over female targets as well, presumably for male clients.

Lindsey also described a rite she used that was intended specifically to stop a woman from having "feelin' to worry with" anyone but her significant other. The formulas she used for men and for women were distinct. The version of the rite that targeted females employed the woman's urine as the active ingredient, while the man's semen was the active ingredient in the version targeting males. In addition, the word "worry" implies disinterest rather than sexual dysfunction on the part of the woman as the result of the rite.[69] Thus Lindsey demonstrated both the service of clientele of both genders and gender specificity in formulas.

Another worker interviewed in Algiers suggested that there might be an economic motive for outside relationships and that it might represent either the cause of these infidelities or a means for containing them. A worker describing the effects of one rite that supposedly stopped either a man or a woman from having sexual feelings for anyone outside their relationship warned that the intended target "might take all dere money an' throw it away, but dey cain't have no feelin'—cain't have no pleasure no mo'. Dey throwin' dey money away."[70] This suggests an awareness of the economic entanglements that often accompany romantic relationships. It also suggests that money might be not only a motivating factor in perpetuating a sexual relationship but *the* means of perpetuating such a relationship. Thus, the ability to forcibly discontinue the relationship might contribute to the financial control or well-being of the client seeking to control the subject's sexuality.

An analysis of workers' assaults on male sexuality reveals both a willingness to serve clients across gender lines and a keen reading of norms about gender difference. Rites centered on the inherent differences between men and women demonstrate the importance of gender difference to workers. The use of this awareness to serve both male and female clientele demonstrates a concomitant unwillingness among workers to let those differences dictate either their clientele or the subjects of their magical rites.

Reproductive Control

While inducing impotence in a subject may seem particularly vicious, frightening gender-specific attacks by workers were not limited to males. Some workers also had magic specific to unborn children and their mothers. One worker from Algiers described a number of seemingly related rites that she used. She recounted a case in which an older pregnant woman unable to deliver her child used a rite in which she had to catch a specific breed of chicken and place it live in a "slop jar." The woman then poured boiling water over the chicken, presumably to kill it, then removed the chicken's feathers and discarded it. She then sat over the jar of boiling water, and the steam induced the birth of her child. In contrast, to stop a woman from delivering her child naturally, the same worker suggested tying nine knots in a new rope and depositing it under the sill of the pregnant woman's steps or porch so that she would unknowingly pass over it. Unable to deliver her child naturally, she would have to have a doctor "take" the child.[71] Workers used rites to both aid and assault pregnant women. Further, they might employ these rites in the service of both men and women. Thus, even in the case of childbirth, one of the most gender-specific experiences in life, workers found ways to market their skills in accordance with gender difference, but in the service of both genders.

While workers could offer female clients services related to childbirth perhaps similar to those of a midwife, rites that targeted pregnant subjects and their children were disturbingly violent and could be employed by both male and female clients. Pregnant women were particularly vulnerable, and workers took advantage of their vulnerability to both help and assault women and their unborn offspring.

The most disturbing rites involving pregnancy were those designed to negatively impact the child's gestation. Ida Bates, a worker from New Orleans, described a rite in which a worker would tie a new rope around a mare's neck and leave it there for a week or so. Then the worker would retrieve the rope and tie nine knots in the rope, symbolizing the nine months of pregnancy. The worker would then tie off both ends of the rope, so that there were eleven knots, and deposit the rope under a pregnant woman's steps so that she would pass over it. The informant explained that because a mare carries its offspring for nearly a year, longer than a human mother, the rite would cause the woman to carry her baby as long as a mare if it were not taken from her by a doctor.[72]

In some of these rites it was unclear whether the mother or the child was the primary target. The Undercover Man, of New Orleans, said that if a potential subject were carrying a child and one could obtain used menstrual rags from before she ceased menstruation, one could put a knot in the rag, bury it, put salt and pepper on the burial spot, and leave it for nine days. Then the rag was to be exhumed and reburied in a different location. The result was the death of the intended target.[73] Mind Reader prescribed a similar rite that involved tying knots in a pregnant woman's slip worn next to her skin and burying it under her doorstep along with her left shoe. The worker guaranteed that the woman would never deliver the child and that both she and her baby would die.[74] In both of these cases, the death of both mother and child makes it unclear which was the target.

In other cases it was clear that the child was the intended target of the rites.

During his interview, Unkus Man, so named because he made use of a spirit he called Uncle, supposedly the brother of Jesus Christ, who was an apparent father figure, also described a spirit he called Crown Prince. Unkus Man described Crown Prince as "a prince of the world" and "the father of Lucifer." He claimed that Crown Prince could cause pregnant women to lose children. Crown Prince, according to the informant, knew how to make a substance called "bitter apple," a drink given to pregnant women that apparently killed their unborn children.[75] The explicit mention of the child's death and not the mother's makes it clear that the child was the intended target of the rite.

Often workers who recounted formulas for attacking pregnant women did not address the motivations of clients who solicited such services. An Algiers worker identified as Man to the Manner Born suggested that they might have been motivated by concern about control of economic power:

> Fo' a man fo' tuh keep his wife from havin' a chile from him or anybody else, yo' understan', yo' take dose scissors. Take de plain sscissors yo' understan', de scissors dat chew use in de hosue an' if yo' kin git close enough tuh her tuh cut a little piece of her hair off her place, anywhere roun' heah.
> (Down below?)
> . . . Cut Jes' a little piece of hair from rith out de center . . . take dat . . . an' wear dat to mah left side, anywhere; jes' make it small as ah could jes' sew it an; she nevah see it. Den ah rule her. Den ah take de scissors an' break de scissors. . . an' throw 'em away. . . . Dat's dead evil, though. . . .
> Yo' rule her and she cain't get no chile by yo' nor nobody. She migh have plenty property or somethin' othah an' ah might have plenty property an' she wanta have a chile from me on accounta, yo' understan', so she kin own a chile, yo' know, an' mah property. Or if she goin' wit somebody else she nevah have no chle from me.[76]

Here the worker suggested that male clients might seek to prevent pregnancy in order to maintain control of their property. Therefore, preventing pregnancy would be a method of control in the context of a marriage for a man with few options for controlling this aspect of his economic future.

Boy-Girl, who may have been particularly sensitive to gender-specific issues, described a rite used to cause stillbirths. The rite required mixing an herb called "ammonia herb" into a tea or food and feeding it to the pregnant woman without her knowledge. While the clandestine nature of this prescription im-plies malice, this kind of work could also point to some overlap between health practitioners who dealt in pregnancy and Voodoo practitioners who supplied abortifacients to pregnant women.

In the eighteenth and nineteenth centuries women commonly ingested herbs to induce early abortions and restore menstruation, the cessation of which was often viewed as an imbalance in the body. These herbs included juniper, pennyroyal, tansy, ergot, and seneca snakeroot.[77] While the clandestine use of abortifacients as a weapon against pregnant women is alarming, it is also possible that workers with this kind of expertise might have been solicited to help women.

By contrast, some worker assaults on pregnant women may have been the result of competition for a man or vengeance among women. A male worker from New Orleans described a rite used on his own sister-in-law that caused her to have multiple stillborn children. He said that the assailant must have been a woman, because he had never known a man to undertake this rite.[78] While it is unlikely that no male ever employed this rite, this reading of intra-gender conflict implies that women's understanding of the vulnerability that accompanied this period may have contributed to soliciting this vicious brand of magic, as well as attempts to ease the burden of pregnancy.

Whatever the gender of the client, the attack on females in a manner so specific to their gender exhibits a willingness of workers to exploit gender as a weapon against women. Men's and women's perceived loss of control over their and their families' future with regard to reproduction gave workers an avenue to exploit that insecurity. Likewise, the hardship and expense associated with childbirth could make pregnancy a difficult situation. Thus, pregnancy and the reproductive capacity of women led both men and women to seek out workers.

Hustlin' and Sportin' Women

By marketing their services to sex workers, professional Voodoo practitioners attempted to market to a gender-specific customer base that could not expect a great deal of aid from any other source. Both their gender and their profession made sex workers a particularly vulnerable group. Most frequently referred to in early twentieth-century New Orleans as "hustlin'" or "sportin'" women, prostitutes were particularly vulnerable not only to the judgments of a sexist society that perpetuated the sex trade while condemning sex workers but also with reference to law enforcement. First and foremost, for most of the early twentieth century prostitution was illegal in New Orleans, so that sex workers were vulnerable to arrest and prosecution by police. What is more, their livelihood depended on payment from men engaged in illicit activities who could not be forced by the law to pay for the services sex workers provided. The Voodoo rites employed by sex workers that spiritual practitioners in New Orleans most frequently described were rites to protect themselves from the law and draw well-paying customers, implying that these were the paramount concerns of "sportin'" women who sought their aid. The need for that aid was invariably tied to the power male clients wielded over sex workers because of both the physical disadvantage implicit in most intergender exchanges and the patriarchal legal proscriptions against sex work enforced by police.

Despite the seeming demand for vice-related industries in New Orleans suggested by the existence of Storyville, a legally sanctioned vice district downtown that operated until the First World War, perhaps the most frequent rites described by workers specifically for hustlin' women were to ensure they could attract clients. The Voodoo queen Madame Ducoyielle described a rite for sportin' houses:

> Take a pot, put some onion peel or garlic (garlic is better) and water in it, let it boil good, strain and add oil of geranium, verbenia or bergemon; add a half bucket of water; wipe sill and steps with it well, throw what is left in back yard. This will sho' bring business. You sell a small bottle for $2.15. Use a lot of alcohol, too, as that is good to draw a man. You can also make a water of boilin' parsley, cinnamon, basile, be sho' to use the male leaf, which is the large one and that will bring customers. Oh yes, add plenty mustard seed to those waters, the more the better, as mustard seed sho' draws a men.[79]

This is a variation on a formula for creating scrubs to attract customers to a business made gender specific by service of a house of ill repute. Nahnee, a worker from Algiers, described a similar scrub for drawing "trade" to the "fast-house" that required hustlin' women to scrub themselves rather than their establishments.[80] She suggested that if they wanted to attract a lot of men, they should boil several kinds of tree bark and bathe in the water, to which they should add perfume and sugar.[81] Finally, Boy-Girl suggested steaming the establishment with a mixture of holy water and sugar boiled to a vapor in the oven.[82] The fact that numerous workers had formulas for this purpose suggests that as with the entrepreneurs who employed similar rites to ensure the success of their businesses, making a living was the overwhelming concern for sex workers. Prohibited from advertising or employing other traditional forms of marketing, sex workers needed to find a way to attract customers. Voodoo may have been the next best thing, and workers may have had a unique understanding of selling an illicit service.

An informant in New Orleans said that sex workers burned candles of certain colors to attract a specific class of male clients and others to repel "enemy mens . . . dat's lika a man whut would come aroun' an' ain't got much money tuh spend." The informant added that the police were also enemies of women in the "hustlin' racket" and that in addition to keeping police away by burning black candles, they also burned candles to Saint Raymond and to the Mother of Perpetual Help daily, the result being that "all dose mens comin'—white men an' othah wealthy men with money—dese mens goin' come, but de policeman nevah come tuh her do'."[83] The implication here is that sex workers were concerned with not only the quantity but also the quality of customers. If they only attracted poor men, they might have as much of a problem making a living as if they attracted none at all. The equating of race with economic status may be problematic, but it still speaks to the point that the central concern of hustlin' women engaged by Voodoo workers was remuneration. Further, economic problems and those involving law enforcement seem to have been closely related. Not only were arrests and police raids a hardship in and of themselves, but while they were in jail sex workers earned no income. Of course this would have been more of a problem if they had had children or other dependents or if they had been serving an extended sentence, in which case money for immediate support might not have been the greatest concern.

There may have been instances in which sex workers sought out Voodoo workers to deal with moral as opposed to economic issues. In an attempt to demonstrate the power of Mother Kate Francis over those who had been hoodooed, one of her followers described an incident involving a supposed sex worker aided by Mother Kate. In what appears to be a conversion story, Ellen Fairwell, one of Mother Kate's followers and her would-be successor, described an incident in which "A young sportin' class woman" had come to

Mother Kate. Fairwell described the woman as "a woman of the streets" who "had her money, stacks of it." She said that the woman had proclaimed that she believed in the faith of Mother Kate and wanted to be rid of her sins. Mother Kate reportedly stooped over the woman and comforted her. Then, after declaring that she would take away all the woman's sins with "one pull," Mother Kate yanked "a ten-inch rattle snake from under that woman's arm. She flipped that snake around her fingers and chunked it out of the window."[84] This seems to be a Christian-style conversion story with a Voodoo twist, told to demonstrate Mother Francis's power. The woman in the story is most likely identified as a sex worker to mark her as amoral and point out that Mother Kate, as a Christian leader, was attempting to save her from her sins. What is interesting is the combination of the spiritual healing common in this kind of Christian conversion story and the imagery of the spiritual mother countering hoodoo by pulling an undesirable animal, such as a snake or a frog, from the body of the afflicted individual. In this case the sex worker, the very archetype of the redeemable sinner, was cured of her transgressions by being de-hoodooed. Just the equating of Christian notions of sin and the indwelling beasts of hoodoo is an intriguing case of members of one tradition co-opting imagery from the other. The implication for sex workers was that Voodoo practitioners could help them cope with both their material and their spiritual needs. Workers thereby made themselves a conduit to economic and spiritual power for a gender-specific population in a particularly vulnerable position.

Workers were aware that race, class, and gender divided the city of New Orleans. In order to increase their own power, they marketed their spiritual power as a solution to the problems related to the social and economic disadvantages associated with certain racial and gender identities. Accidents of birth, these identities could seem unyielding constraints on behavior and opportunity. In the case of gender, both males and females experienced the limitations on their behavior and authority related to their sex. Workers recognized this and marketed their services to both men and women.

Workers' rites seem to have been shaped by a culture of domestic conflict that was significant in the early twentieth century. Rather than using rites from the distant past, workers in the early twentieth century used rites concerning gender and sexuality that, like the rites that drew on contemporary racial norms for their form and purpose, read contemporary domestic and sexual conflicts from the immediate cultural context into their rites. Because their clients were concerned about domestic stability, especially economic stability tied to intimate relationships, it became the concern of workers and helped to determine aspects of Voodoo in New Orleans. Further, by reading the needs of both male and female clients and using Voodoo to meet them all, workers made gender-based, but not specific or exclusive, appeals to clients. Addressing the conflicts and anxieties of a broad base of clients, workers brought the outside culture into Voodoo, allowing it to dynamically adjust to the needs of New Orleanians, male and female alike. What united them all was the perception of vulnerability and attempts to use Voodoo and the power it promised to counter that vulnerability.

5

THE "BISNESS"

The Centrality of Economics and Local Culture
to Business Models in New Orleans Voodoo

n the late 1930s, researchers with the Louisiana Writers' Project sought out Lala Hopkins, a woman referred to them and identified by other practitioners in the city as a well-known Voodoo queen. In addition to her own reputation in the city, part of Lala's claim to fame was her impressive spiritual lineage. She identified her mentor in the work as a queen called Marie Comtesse, a worker whose ability Lala praised and who Lala boasted had learned her trade from the infamous nineteenth-century Voodoo queen Marie Laveau. Some workers thought of themselves as connected to Laveau by blood ties, whereas Lala saw Laveau as the source of her power through a professional lineage. Lala claimed to be the best worker in town. She bragged to interviewers that because she had trained with Comtesse, and Comtesse had trained with Laveau, she knew what Marie Laveau knew, and what she did not know was not to be known. Lala proudly proclaimed that she had learned everything she knew from Comtesse, and she thought it only natural that she would use her mentor's techniques. Despite her pride in practicing the Voodoo of Laveau and Comtesse, however, Lala did assert that the rites she performed were not identical to those of her predecessors. She told interviewers that she had altered and "streamlined" the Voodoo she had learned in order to better serve her clientele, explaining, "Ya know ya got to fix dis bisness lak de people wants it. Dis makes it different."[1]

For Lala as for her mentors before her, Voodoo was a business. Use of the term *worker* for professional practitioners and references to their professional religious and magical services as "the work" implied the centrality of the economic exchange for professional practitioners of Voodoo.[2] Tracing her professional lineage back to Laveau, Lala positioned herself within a culture and history as specific to the social and economic milieu of early twentieth-century New Orleans as the mythohistorical accounts of the iconic Voodoo queen were to the nineteenth-century Crescent City. The rituals performed by Lala and other workers in this period were heavily influenced by the socioeconomic circumstances under which they were conducted. As Lala so eloquently explained, professional practitioners had to ascertain the needs of local clientele and then adapt their services to meet those needs, thereby making innovation as much a part of their profession as tradition. Most salient, especially by the 1930s, was the shift of workers to meet the economic needs of clients, who, like a large segment of the U.S. population at the time, were suffering in the grips of the Great Depression.

Employment and money were scarce, and professional practitioners devoted a great deal of their effort and power to obtaining jobs for clients and attempting to help them improve their economic circumstances. In addition to dealing with the influence exerted by clients, workers had to reshape their rites so that they could practice within the constrictions of city ordinances and state and federal law enforcement. Rather than deal with the complications that might result from prosecuting Voodoo practitioners for their religious practices, authorities specifically targeted the economic aspects of workers' spiritual practices as various types of fraud. Further, because of the push of consumerism and the triumph of a cash-based economy that began at the end of the nineteenth century and continued into the early twentieth century, practitioners in New Orleans, like most other Americans, began to understand U.S. currency as powerful in its own right. Practitioners in New Orleans came to believe that U.S. currency actually held metaphysical power, as they included money as components in magical rites. Rather than simply offering food or alcohol to the saints and spirits they entreated for assistance, they often began to offer cash in addition to these offerings or in place of them. All these influences on workers point to the extraordinary impact of money on Voodoo in early twentieth-century New Orleans.

The dynamic adjustments to the needs of customers, the legal restrictions, and the rise of consumerism demonstrate the fluidity and the malleability of Voodoo in early twentieth-century New Orleans. The ways in which practitioners bent and shaped the work illuminate the importance of indigenous American cultural exchanges, the social and economic vagaries of life in New Orleans, and the centrality of economics to Voodoo in the Crescent City.

A World of Money

At a ceremony to mourn the passing of the spiritual mother and known Voodoo practitioner Kate Francis, Mother Louise Bowers was interviewed by researchers from the Works Progress Administration's Federal Writers' Project. Offering her services to the interviewer who had come to speak to her about Mother Kate, she told him, "Fo' a quarter, I could stimulate yo' luck with her blessings direct." Then in no uncertain terms she let the interviewer know that she required compensation for her services: "What could I do fo' nothing? Nothing." Even in the midst of honoring her co-worker, Mother Louise did not forget the bottom line. "What the people don't know," she explained, "is that the saints want money too. Brother, I guess this is a world of money."[3]

In her statement Mother Louise hit on two key points: first, that she lived in a society preoccupied with the pecuniary value of goods and services; and second, that the spiritual realm was not exempt from the consuming concern with money. In the early twentieth century many workers managed to monetize and often institutionalize their spiritual work, and similar changes were occurring throughout the United States.

Between 1880 and 1930 American society was transformed by corporate business. The new reigning culture was preoccupied with consumption, comfort, and bodily well-being, and the predominant measure of all values in society became economic. Establishment of a relatively stable currency-based economy in the second half of the nineteenth century led to a new standard by the beginning of the twentieth in which pecuniary or market values became the base measure for all other values, including beauty, friendship, and even spirituality. The value of anything was determined by the price it could fetch in the market. Voodoo practitioners, as privy to these changes as most Americans, embraced them in order to meet the needs of their clientele, which by the twentieth century were overwhelmingly economic.[4] The services most frequently requested of workers dealt with relieving the financial burdens on those who came to them for help. In exchange, both workers and the saints they enlisted for aid often demanded monetary compensation for that aid.

By the early twentieth century, Voodoo practitioners in New Orleans were establishing a model of practice that would allow them to turn a profit and earn a living. Reports of Voodoo-related gatherings or ceremonies in the nineteenth century suggest that rather than finding legal ways to practice Voodoo, practitioners simply practiced clandestinely. If this was true, it would have severely limit the activities of practitioners and effectively made practice of Voodoo unsustainable, which was undoubtedly the goal of the arrests and legal proscriptions. In line with the push of consumer culture and the increasingly cash-based economy, workers sought ways to operate within the law in order to make a living or profit by practicing Voodoo. Similarly, the extreme privation coinciding with economic downturns in the late nineteenth and early twentieth centuries also made economic well-being an overwhelming concern of workers' clientele. The argument here is that workers internalized larger American ideological trends concerning currency, work, and consumerism, and those trends were reflected in their rituals.

During the Great Depression, basic expenses seemed unmanageable for many Americans. Economic downturns in the 1890s, 1920s, and 1930s increased the attractiveness of participating in marginal economies despite the many social stigmas attached to traditions like Voodoo, which were frequently racialized by outsiders. Harry Middleton Hyatt defined *hoodoo*, a more common term among his informants than *Voodoo*, as the eruption of modern commercialism in the field of magic.[5] Workers in this period, consistent with the wider trend toward consumerism and the financial hardships that accompanied the aforementioned economic downturns, focused on rites that could be marketed for both their own and their clients' economic gain. Hyatt believed that in any given locale there was a direct correlation between the abundance of good informants, many of whom came to him seeking employment, and the economic privation of the people.[6] Despite the stories of enormous wealth being earned by workers, stories told both by outsiders and by workers themselves in interviews seemed to indicate that many of them were in a precarious financial state. This might imply that their services as workers were supplementing other relatively meager sources of income rather than making them wealthy.

In this economic climate workers were most commonly solicited to improve the material lives of their clients by aiding their businesses or job searches, helping clients acquire and maintain a place to live, and increasing their chances in gambling. By looking at the variety of rites consistently aimed at creating or increasing profits for their clients, I seek to establish the centrality of economics for these clients and the professional practitioners of Voodoo who served them.

Work by Workers

Perhaps the most common aid sought by clients of workers was for finding employment or prosperity in business. Most workers had rites they used to influence employers to hire or keep on employees. The number and diversity of these rites implies a preoccupation among clients with supporting themselves that aligns with the economic difficulties throughout the country during the 1930s, when many of these men and women were interviewed about their work as practitioners of Voodoo. The difficulty many Americans had finding employment during this period suggests that Voodoo workers may have been adjusting to the employment market to better serve their clients. One of the ways they did so was to direct a large number of formulas toward finding or sustaining employment.

In the early stages of the Great Depression, Louisiana's unemployed population was concentrated in New Orleans. In 1930 the U.S. Department of Commerce and the Bureau of the Census collected detailed figures on unemployment in Louisiana. The Census Bureau reported 2,101,593 individuals living in the state, 1,622,868 of whom it classified as employable, that is, older than ten years of age and able to work. The cutoff age of ten may tell us something about child labor in this period. That being noted, of the more than 1.6 million employable people in the state, some 39,396 were unemployed or receiving no income in 1930. Of the more than 2 million people in the state, 1,268,061 were classified as living in rural areas. Of the 833,532 living in urban areas, 535,417 lived in the state's two largest cities, Shreveport (76,655) and New Orleans (458,762). Of the state's 39,396 unemployed workers, only 2,121 lived in Shreveport, with a full 19,782 concentrated in New Orleans. Thus, with 9.6 percent of the employable population of New Orleans unemployed, even though the city's residents only made up 22 percent of the state's population, the city's unemployed accounted for more than 50 percent of the unemployed population of the state.[7] This is undoubtedly why employment rites became so important to professional Voodoo practitioners and their clients in New Orleans during this period.

One indication of the importance of employment to the clients of professional Voodoo practitioners may be that rites formerly used for reasons other than finding or maintaining employment were now being used to get or keep jobs. Havana Man, a worker who claimed to be from Havana, Cuba, used a rite that required his client to wear his underclothes inside out and bathe his feet in sugar and cinnamon bark, after which he was to seek employment wearing no socks. The instruction to wear one's underclothes inside out is similar to instructions in rites used by some workers to get clients accused of crimes acquitted in court cases. Another worker described a ritual used simply to make one man favor another. Rather than changing the use of the ritual, he suggested that if used on an employer, this same rite was effective for getting a job.[8] The use of rites initially employed for other purposes to help clients get work suggests how important jobs were to those seeking the aid of professional Voodoo practitioners.

Candle rites were often used to exert control over lovers or to harm someone in conflict with a worker's client, but by the Depression these ceremonies were also performed to control employers. One candle rite described in the 1930s was supposedly effective even if an employer had already turned down a person seeking a job. If conducted properly, the candle rite was supposed to ensure that the client would be rehired eight days after its completion.[9] One worker even claimed that he could use a candle rite not only to get clients hired but also to influence the salary they would receive.[10]

Workers also had formulas to "sweeten" employers' disposition toward their clients. To get an employer to select a worker's client from a group of applicants, one worker suggested reading the twenty-seventh psalm of David, a common prescription among workers, and rubbing "pecone [pecan] oil" on one's hands, which would draw the employer to the person. Another worker suggested shaking a honeycomb toward oneself to achieve a similar result.[11] Madam Lindsey, a worker from Algiers, Louisiana, had one of the more interesting prescriptions for swaying an employer. It required a client to drink water sweetened with a particular sugar, then spit it onto the ground and walk across it just before seeing an employer about a job. Finally, the client would bite into a "wishing bean" while talking to the interviewer, who would then hire him.[12]

The hope was obviously to curry favor with someone who might provide a job by using something sweet to attract him, a formulation common among workers who dealt in romantic relationships.

This wide variety of rites suggests an extraordinary need to secure employment among those seeking out Voodoo practitioners. Finding and holding a job when unemployment soared throughout the nation, reaching an estimated 25 percent at points in the 1930s, was the most urgent concern of a great many Americans when both Hyatt and LWP members interviewed Voodoo practitioners in New Orleans. Rites aimed at aiding laborers were common. Perhaps just as common, or more so, were rites for aiding clients who were attempting to earn a living as entrepreneurs.

Workers listed dozens of formulas for "scrubs" peddled to entrepreneurs to improve the state of their businesses. It is not clear from testimony whether this was because workers were sought out by a larger number of business owners during this period or because workers, often in business for themselves, had a bias toward entrepreneurs. It is also possible that the difficulty in getting work inspired individuals to strike out on their own in hopes of supporting themselves. Whatever the case, the most common prescriptions for business owners were liquid mixtures used to clean or bathe a place of business. The scrubs contained cinnamon, honey, white and brown sugar, filé, soured smartweed, parsley, green onions, John the Conqueror powder or root, syrup, milk, rosewater, garlic, fish, ants, perfume, rainwater, and numerous other components in various combinations and permutations.[13] The thinking behind some of the combinations was obviously to combine pleasant-tasting or pleasant-smelling spices and other substances in hopes of "sweetening" one's business and or customers. Others contained less pleasant components, with a less obvious logic. Nonetheless, all manner of scrubs were suggested by workers for everything from temporary ventures common during this period, like house parties and fish fries, to permanent establishments and underground economic ventures of questionable legal status, like bootlegging and gambling houses. Scrubs used for most businesses were designed to attract large numbers of customers and even make those customers amiable.

It was not only legitimate businesses but more questionable economic ventures needed to attract customers. Formulas used to help businesses tied to underground economies were often aimed at keeping law enforcement away. An informant who admitted to working as a bootlegger before the end of prohibition said that he had managed to keep the law away from his business by simply sprinkling holy water from a Catholic church on his floor on the advice of a local worker. Another worker suggested keeping the law or other enemies away by keeping a Bible opened to Psalm 35 next to a glass of water sweetened with white or brown sugar. One of the most interesting rites required placing a beef tongue, nails, and a number of other items at the entrance to a bootlegging business. The client was to invite in a law officer, who would pass over the charm and afterward not only refrain from taking action against the bootlegger but protect him from his competition in the same illicit business.[14] Rites using beef tongue were often employed to silence individuals who might speak against a worker's clients, especially opposing witnesses in court cases. Here, however, co-opting the power of law enforcement seems a great deal more proactive, and again we see an example of a rite with another purpose being employed to aid in economic advancement. The power of workers was aimed at increasing the profits of entrepreneurs. All these rites described by workers point to their concern with bolstering their clients' economic enterprises, the legal status of which seemed to be of little or no consequence.

In addition to attempting to improve clients' businesses and help them gain employment, workers also attempted to harm clients' enemies. A particularly invidious method was to assault their livelihoods. The custodian of a Spiritualist shrine said that she could get someone fired by using a concoction of mustard, wine, and a number of other components in a glass jar in conjunction with a reading of the 109th psalm.[15] This same practitioner employed another method in which she wrote the boss's name and the name of the intended victim on a piece of paper and fed it to a frog, which was subsequently released.[16] She did not specify whether this was a rite employed out of malice toward the victim or perhaps to commandeer the job of the fired individual. Nahnee, the Boss of Algiers, was from the section of New Orleans on the west bank of the Mississippi River so famous for its workers that it was often referred to as Hoodoo Town. Nahnee described a rite that consisted in simply blowing disturbance, "confusement," and "get-away" powders into someone's place of business.[17] Another worker used a rite that required the intended victim's photo and a lock of that person's hair. She promised that the rite would not only "run," or drive, the victim crazy, a common assault by workers on subjects, but also induce general poverty, perhaps resulting from the insanity.[18] Other workers who sought to drive someone crazy implied that this was an end in itself. Here the worker may have only adjusted how the rite was marketed and not changed the actual formula at all. In an era of widespread unemployment, a person wishing to hurt an enemy or a worker attempting to market his or her services to such an individual could not do much better than to deprive a subject of the ability to bring in adequate income. Given the innumerable rites available to workers to kill, maim, or otherwise harm subjects, the use of rites that specifically targeted jobs demonstrates the preoccupation of workers, their clients, or both with economic matters.

Workers' use of saints to aid clients with their businesses or jobs also demonstrates the centrality of monetary concerns. Nearly every saint commonly used by workers—Saints Anthony, Expedite, Peter, and Raymond—along with Our Mother of Perpetual Help and the Sacred Heart of Jesus, was enlisted by workers to help clients with employment.[19] With a few exceptions, no matter what saints were considered patrons of, most of them were called on to help with money or jobs.

Thus in order to serve the needs of a clientele overwhelmingly preoccupied with earning a living, workers made use of scrubs they had invented for that purpose, along with rites specially adapted to helping clients find work, and they called on almost every saint commonly used by workers. By offering these services, workers could attract Americans out of work and business owners suffering because these and others could not frequent their establishments. Workers thus created a broad base to which they could appeal in a time of severe unemployment by making their clients' overwhelming concern with making a living their own.

Moving and Renting

Housing rites may be among the Voodoo rites performed by workers that best demonstrate clients' diversity. Economic difficulty that precludes an individual's covering the cost of housing adversely affects both his or her ability to secure living space and the landlord's ability to turn a profit. In turn, that may affect a landlord's ability to pay his or her bills. Thus, the clientele seeking workers' aid in connection with housing costs included both tenants and landlords. For tenants, workers performed rites to stop their landlords from evicting them. If they had already been evicted or were seeking a place to live, they might seek a worker's aid to move someone out of a house or to prevent a space from being rented or occupied by a new tenant. Landlords sought aid in moving people out of their own buildings, presumably undesirable tenants, and in finding tenants for rental properties they owned. In the case of housing, professional Voodoo practitioners worked both sides of the class divide. This was possible because the Depression had created a sense of powerlessness and a concomitant preoccupation with money among both renters and landlords.

During the Depression, even with rates as low as three dollars a week, it was often difficult for tenants to pay their rent. In most cases, workers performed rites aimed at influencing or controlling landlords. Many of these rites involved writing the landlord's name on a piece of paper and burning a candle on it, or sweetening it with cinnamon or syrup to gain the landlord's favor or control over him or her. Some of the rites were less directly aimed at the landlord. An Algiers worker interviewed in New Orleans described one of the more interesting rites for resolving rental issues:

> If yo' have a notice to move—if yo' have a notice tuh move an' yo' jes' cannot pay yore rent an' if yo' kin git chew a crawfish. Git chew a live crawfish an' wrap him all ovah three safety matches. Take an' tie him, jes' tie him enough so he cain't back up, backwards an' fo'wards, an' turn him loose into yore house. Yo' understan',' yo' see, an' dat crawfish goin' all roun' an' he kin not git out, he cain't git in no hole or crack. An' if yo' keep dat crawfish in dere until dat crawfish dies, yo'll stay right wit dat landlord. He cain't move yo' . . . take dem matches an' tie 'em undahneat' his belly—wrap 'em, don' tie 'em.[20]

This rite was predicated on a relatively common principle in Voodoo, the animal involved becoming a surrogate for the person the worker or his client intended to affect. In this case, the crawfish remaining in the house until his death represents the client who wanted to remain in the home indefinitely. The landlord seems to have been affected indirectly, as he would not be able to change tenants. But the primary purpose was for the client to gain power over his or her own living situation. Control over the landlord via his property was in this instance collateral. Further, the use of a rite intended to work indefinitely may imply a continual rather than a momentary concern with paying rent, perhaps speaking to perpetual economic insecurity on the part of workers' clientele.

Control over a landlord could also be more direct and often extended to attempting to make his or her property unrentable. The implication was often that the client or the worker targeting the landlord was aiming to settle a vendetta after being evicted by making certain the landlord could not turn a profit from the rental. A worker named Ida went as far as to suggest burning oil of lodestone and sulfur in a house to prevent it from being rented for a period of six months. In that case, the resulting odor might accomplish this goal even absent any metaphysical power.[21] Along with the sense that the punishment here fit the crime, attacks on the ability of the landlord to rent his or her property, like attacks on the livelihood of laborers, may suggest a preoccupation with money on the part of workers and their clients.

In addition to stopping a house from being rented, workers also claimed to be able to move someone out of a home. The reasons clients commissioned these rites were varied and often ambiguous in descriptions of the ceremonies. They could be used to harm the landlord by cutting off income or to make the home available for the worker's client to rent. In the case of a shortage of desirable rental properties, the intended victim might also be the tenant. In one instance a worker called Madam Murray said that it was more difficult to move someone out of a house if he or she actually owned the property. In this case, the sole motivation seems to have been to get rid of the person in the house, not to acquire the space for the client's own use.[22] In at least one instance a rite was even used by a landlord to move one of his own tenants out, presumably not to lower his own income but to replace an undesirable tenant with a better one.[23]

There were also rites used to rent a house, suggesting the use of workers' power to aid landlords, whom we would normally view as dominant in relation to tenants. Frequently, the scrubs used to improve businesses and draw customers were also used by landlords to attract renters to a property. Workers suggested scrubbing homes with cinnamon, sugar, and sweet milk and burning candles. Some even promised that the property would be rented by a specific date or that candles burned to Saint Peter or the Virgin Mary would ensure that tenants paid their rent on time.[24] Here it is not the rites that are new but their use in the service of landlords. Thus, by serving the interests of the renter, workers worked counter to the interests of the landlord; by aiding the landlords in securing tenants and even timely payment of rents, workers also served their interests.

Both landlords and renters sought the aid of workers to improve situations they felt powerless to alter on their own. Tenants who could not produce enough income to cover rent were at the mercy of their landlords, but there was little a landlord could do to extract money tenants did not have. Eviction would not make up for lost rent, and in a period when funds were difficult to come by, the next tenant might not be any more financially stable than the last. These financial obstacles could seem insurmountable. When renters had no money and landlords could not keep renters, both parties might have felt powerless. Arraying their power and that of the saints against such forces was a specialty of New Orleans workers. The rites workers performed concerning housing demonstrate both the preoccupation with economic concerns and the tendency of workers to keep a wide client base by serving diverse, even seemingly contradictory groups of clients. By internalizing, manipulating, and invariably profiting from what was a national culture of privation brought on by the Great Depression, professional practitioners of Voodoo demonstrated their ability to adjust to the socioeconomic milieu in which they operated. In turn, their spiritual practices were marked by this economic culture based in want and need in a way that was unique to the circumstances in the United States in general and New Orleans in particular.

Frog Legs and Black Cat Bones

People also sought out workers to augment their luck in gambling. Workers most frequently prescribed the creation and use of a "hand" to increase the probability of winning these games of chance. These charms varied greatly in composition. The active ingredients in many were components of various small animals. The creation and use of gambling hands illuminates several important concepts of cost and accumulation that characterize the practice of Voodoo in the twentieth century, namely, the centrality of economic concerns to practitioners, the intertwining of the realms of spiritual power and monetary gain, and the exchange of life for profit.

One unique formula was used to create a hand to stop anyone from cheating clients shooting dice. It required one to leave a frog to be eaten by ants in order to extract a particular bone from its leg. The bone in turn was then kept in one's pocket with the dice. Another hand required cutting a hole into a live frog, filling the opening with a mixture of salt, pepper, and other components, and sewing the opening closed. The live but anguished animal would bring luck in gambling. Other hands included the use of a rabbit's foot, a hog's hoof, or a bat's heart, as well as various lodestones, steel dust, and other ingredients commonly used by workers to "draw," or attract, luck.[25] The life and suffering of the animal were indirectly exchanged for economic gain. Unlike in the cases of employment and housing rites, the aim here seems to have been not just securing what was a necessity for the worker's client but the accumulation of wealth. Abstractions like pain and death gained a pecuniary value through their involvement with games of chance in these instances. The equating of these intrinsically negative states with accumulation demonstrates the ambiguous feelings of Voodoo practitioners about accumulation in an era of rising consumerism.[26]

Used in many rites, including those for luck and gambling, the black cat bone was one of the most well-known ingredients used by workers. However, workers often expressed reservations about using it because of the suffering of the animal entailed in extracting it. Madam Lindsey said that she could use the black cat bone to make a charm infallible for gambling that was also good for "general success." The problem was that to obtain the bone the worker had to gruesomely dispatch the cat, dropping it live into a kettle of boiling water and leaving it there until the flesh separated from the bones. After the U-shaped bone was extracted, it was combined with other, more common ingredients available at Voodoo drugstores and sewn into a bag. The charm, according to Lindsey, would bring success in anything, but because of the suffering involved for the animal, she did not perform the rite.[27] Workers who would not work with or extract the black cat bone themselves had decided that the resulting material gain was not worth the suffering of the animal. Madam Lindsey refused to work with the black cat bone at all. The certainty that those negative consequences existed, however, is a clear demonstration of a moral ambiguity surrounding the exchange of an animal's life or an animal's suffering for material benefit.

In general, the black cat bone seems to have been used in what practitioners classified as evil work. The Black Cat Lucky Bone Maker stated that in addition to other uses the bone was good for thieves who specialized in breaking and entering. However, he claimed that in this case wearing the black cat bone amounted to selling one's soul to the devil.[28] Workers believed that great or even unlimited power could be attained by those who performed this kind of magic.[29] But the implication that in this Faustian bargain material gain could result in the loss of what, in Judeo-Christian thinking, is the most precious commodity a man has points to a distinct value judgment of accumulation in a growing culture of consumption. While workers seem to have been generally invested in improving both their own and their clients' material condition, the extreme cost they attached to these rites seems to have placed a limit on how far they were willing to go.

These kinds of exchanges may have been a result of the creation and re-creation of Voodoo in the American context, which combined both the Judeo-Christian influence, which conceived of the soul as a kind of contested moral commodity coveted by both God and the devil, and the influence of living in what Arjun Appadurai classified as a highly commoditized society, a society in which many or most things sometimes pass through the state of being a commodity. While Appadurai was on the whole speaking about the commoditization of goods and services, objects and labor, the "diversion" of a philosophical abstraction like the human soul into what he called a "commodity situation" seems to further accentuate the high level of commoditization in the American context. In Appadurai's estimation even human beings have passed into and out of this commodity situation at various points in history via the institution of various forms of slavery.[30] But in the case of the black cat bone it was not the person as an object or as labor who was passing into the commodity situation but a moral-philosophical construct like the "soul."

One informant recounted what may be an even clearer example of commoditization of the soul in the service of consumerism:

> Well, she tole me dat dere wus a woman by de name of Marie Baptiste. She had two daughters an' she liked fo' her daughters tuh outdress de girls down in de 7th ward. . . . An' she sol' herself to de devil at twelve a'clock at night wit de fire of furnace—a furnace fire, yo' know at de fo'k of de road in the woods . . . an' she sol' herself to him dat she could git anything she wanted so she could go in de sto's an' anything she take dey couldn't see her.[31]

This account seems to combine the ambiguity about accumulation that equates methods of acquisition with crime and evil, and the exchange of the soul to acquire consumer products. The significance of the woman in the story outdressing "de girls down in de 7th ward" is tied to the perception of the Seventh

Ward as an enclave of successful or privileged middle-class African Americans.[32] More specifically, many members of the Afro-Creole community in New Orleans called the Seventh Ward home. Owing to the perception of this community as privileged in comparison with the majority of African Americans in the city, the reference to "de girls down in the 7th ward" in this account would have been a reference to affluence peculiar to New Orleans natives. With the expansion of the consumer economy, the number and appeal of products multiplied, and many retailers and advertisers targeted women.[33] Fashion was integral to the rise of consumer culture in the United States. The fashion industry sought to lift women in particular into a world of pseudoluxury, beyond the drudgery of obligations like bills, by offering them "release through purchase." However, this often led to "anxiety and restlessness in a world where people feared not being able to afford things other people had."[34] The implication that in the privation of the 1930s the affluence embodied by the Seventh Ward in the public imagination could only be maintained by selling one's soul is a powerful statement of both the moral ambiguity of material accumulation and the pull of consumerism.

There were also instances in which the cost of material gain might extend from one's own soul to the lives of family members. A number of informants believed that praying to some saints, whether Peter, Expedite, or Roc, for favors could carry a high cost outside monetary compensation to workers. One informant claimed that if a client did not give Saint Peter the promised offering for services he provided, that person's worldly possessions would be consumed in a fire. Another claimed that the penalty extracted by Saint Expedite for not providing the promised offering of flowers would be the death of a family member.[35] Similarly, Nahnee claimed that Saint Roc was a vengeful saint called upon to maim victims, in exchange for which he took the life of a member of the family of the person who had called on him.[36] Thus in the economy of Voodoo even the lives of family members could be used as a form of currency to purchase power. Further, the inclusion of Catholic saints popular in New Orleans, as well as sites like the Seventh Ward, demonstrates the dependence of Voodoo practitioners on the cultural milieu in which they constructed this economy.

These exchanges again imply a moral judgment that equated malice with material gain. Here again, workers seemed to believe that almost anything might have a pecuniary value, but they maintained a discomfort with some exchanges. These rites may demonstrate what Margaret Radin described as a crystallization of concerns about inappropriate commodification that she associated with the use of market rhetoric, especially when applied to human beings or ideals like love, considered properly inalienable in a market economy.[37] This concern may have been best stated by a worker describing a rite that would kill a victim: "It's a very hard task to go through, it's very cruel to do such of those things; but when we gets paid for it, why we does it."[38]

Workers who were willing to involve themselves in the more morally ambiguous rites functioned very much like brokers, a class that was expanding exponentially in the twentieth century. As intermediaries, brokers were required to repress their own convictions in favor of forging profitable relationships. It has been posited that the vast expansion of this class in corporate business helped to inject a new amoral attitude conducive to the inflation of desire that drove consumerism.[39] As with the gambling hands that included parts of animals, the implication here was that accumulation had a cost and that such accumulation at another's expense did not come without a parallel cost to the benefactor. However, the willingness of some workers to provide these services despite that cost demonstrates an amoral attitude toward this kind of accumulation among a segment of the community of Voodoo practitioners, whereas the employment and housing rites seem to have been more widely accepted.

Some rites performed by workers demonstrated an increase in cost that was not vertical, as in the increase in price from animal to human to family lives, but horizontal, calling for investments to increase in frequency as well as amount. For example, gambling hands were often not a onetime investment, as many required "feeding" to maintain their power.[40] Perhaps the most common substance used to feed a gambling hand was whiskey. An informant Hyatt identified as the Hoodoo Book Man described a gambling hand made of lodestone, steel dust, garlic, and a dime, wrapped in a flannel bag that was kept in one's pocket. To ensure the bag's effectiveness, the user had to pour whiskey onto it while gambling.[41] Paying for the alcohol to regularly feed a gambling hand required a continuing investment on the part of the client.

In some cases money was not only exchanged for power but also used to generate power in a way even more direct than paying for magical services. The charge for a gambling hand ranged from about twenty-five to fifty dollars. The ability of a worker to charge a substantial fee for a hand depended on the supposition that more than the initial fee would be realized in gambling profits. Often, the fee charged for the hand was not the only currency necessary to make it effective, however. U.S. currency, in most cases a dime or a quarter, was often an ingredient in making a hand. In these instances, the buying power of currency was understood as the metaphysical power to create more wealth. In fact, the Hoodoo Book Man described the creation of a hand that came in two sizes, large and small, the larger being more expensive and requiring a larger denomination of currency but supposedly achieving better results: "Dey use de same thin' in both size, but de biggah pieces dey make mo' powah . . . you put a quartah; if you gon'a make a small one, you put a dime. It got to be silvah money."[42] In this instance, more money quite literally translated into more power.[43]

Not only gambling but a number of others rites included currency as a component. One of the most frequent uses of currency in rites was to cure ailments, natural or otherwise. Again, the denomination of the coin seemed to take on some significance. Often workers would grind or shave pieces of a coin and have someone drink or eat the shavings in a solution to cure him or her of poison or to get rid of an animal, namely, a frog or snake, magically put into the person's body, presumably by another worker, to cause harm. While these rites usually specified the coin to be used, none of the rites that required filing or grinding the silver from a coin required filing or grinding the entire coin. One might assume that the denomination of the coin was less important than the composition of the metal used in making it and that workers simply wanted to include silver in their formulas. However, these examples suggest that it was the denomination of the coin, which was determined by the state, that was important. If the point were simply to use the coins as a source of silver, it would never make sense to spend more money by extracting silver from a quarter or half dollar instead of a dime, assuming they were all made of the same metal. But workers specifying the use of more valuable coins implied that the value of the coin had some bearing on the rite and that the currency itself, not just the metal used to create it, held some metaphysical significance.[44] Just as in the instance of a gambling hand, in which both the power of the charm and its cost increased when a quarter rather than a dime was used, the value of the currency was often a factor in the potency of the rite, again suggesting an understanding that more money equated to more spiritual power.

Other formulations also suggested that currency itself held power. Some rites allowed workers to use a coin as a spiritual tool to attack the person attempting to harm their client rather than simply curing the client. One practitioner claimed that by praying to Saint Raymond on the thirteenth of the month and later heating a penny and scratching the word *one* from the penny, a worker could "destroy" the person trying to harm his or her client. Other workers used shavings of silver coins to put harmful creatures into the stomach of a victim rather than to extract them as previously described. There was even an instance in which what the worker seemed to describe was wishing on a silver dollar rather than using it in a specific formula with additional components. Even rites employing other major components, for example, animal parts, also required the inclusion of currency. The implication seemed to be that U.S. currency held power similar to that of the other included spiritual accoutrements used in these rites. The use of currency in so many different instances may speak to workers' confidence in the power of U.S. currency, not necessarily in a world market but rather in their own lives. It suggests that money's importance had been imbibed so fully by workers in New Orleans that it took on metaphysical characteristics in their rites.

There has long been speculation about the power of money in society and the concomitant effect of culture on money. The quantification of quality that Viviana Zelizer labels a "morally dangerous alchemy" is, she says, the quality of all money that allows it to reduce all qualitative distinctions between objects to a system of numbers. Further, she argues that "money turned even intangible objects devoid of utility—such as conscience or honor—into ordinary commodities." At the same time, Zelizer argues that while money corrupts values into numbers, values "reciprocally corrupt money by investing it with moral, social, and religious meaning."[45] In this sense, the money used in these rites attained a quality that made it a source of spiritual or magical power. The moral and philosophical judgments levied on the values being monetized in these transactions might be transferred to money as well.

As workers understood it, even saints and spirits required payment for their help. Saints and spirits were given offerings of flowers, spices, alcohol, cigars, and all manner of material goods. On occasion, though, they were simply paid in U.S. currency. What may have been unique about payment of the saints, however, was that there was no perception that the saints needed money or wanted to accumulate wealth. Workers often left dimes or other currency on graves for spirits when they collected graveyard dirt, a common component in many rites. According to one worker, however, it was only necessary to pay spirits to do something negative; positive work with grave dirt was apparently free.[46] One formulation for burning a candle to Saint Raymond in order to get bread for one's children specified that it had to be burned in church, where one would pay twenty-five cents. It is unclear what happened to the money. Some formulations required that money be left for a saint at the foot of a statue or shrine. Madam Lindsey, of Algiers, specified that when asking Saint Anthony for help finding a job, one had to leave bread for the poor in a church.[47] Another informant reported that he had been instructed to pay Saint Expedite to give someone else bad luck by putting a quarter in a box at a Catholic church when burning a candle to the saint.[48] The custodian of a shrine in Algiers described a similar phenomenon in her use of Saint Rosalie: "She's de money Queen. . . . She's a saint dat she had so much money she didn't know whut tuh do wit it. . . . Yo' always make'em leave a penny or a Nickel . . . an' tell'em dat's fo St. Rosalie an' don't nevah spend dat money . . . jis' give it to de sick an' de blind. . . . Dey goin' Pay yo' fo' whut chew doin' fo' dem separate but dat penny is fo' de poah."[49]

While this hagiography for Saint Rosalie is probably peculiar to Voodoo, the idea of paying for the favor of the saint with an act of charity is not. The donation does, however, present an interesting contrast to the profit motive often expressed by workers. Even though the saints were drawn into the world of monetary exchange, there is no notion that they needed the money. Instead the payments seem to have benefited people in need. Unlike money given to the spirits in some other African diaspora religions, though, the money here became sacrosanct, at least for the practitioner. To give the money to a fellow practitioner, even after it had served its ritual purpose, apparently did not qualify as a sacrifice to the saints. This conception may also represent a value judgment of the money used in rites that involved "bad work" by making it singular and nonfungible.[50] Unlike monetary sacrifices provided to the spirits in some of African diasporic religions throughout the Americas, which was collected and redistributed to members of the community, whether this money was given to the poor via a Catholic donation box, left near a statue of a saint or a grave, the money passed out of the hands of the practitioner. There was an effort, not to pragmatically move the money to other practitioners in an effort to sustain them and their ritual practice, but to actually "sacrifice" the money in the most literal sense, that is, to give it up.[51]

Together the rites that include currency suggest a wide faith in the power of money in the occult economy of Voodoo. The use of currency in gambling hands differed from its inclusion in curative rites or counterspell formulas or the notion of paying saints. The ubiquity and diversity of monetary costs in these exchanges seems to demonstrate the importance of currency, a preoccupation with tangible, material needs, and an understanding of value, even the value of spiritual power, in monetary terms. Workers suggested that pecuniary payments to the saints could result in a great deal of help in meeting material needs. This suggests that practitioners assigned a monetary value not only to the power of workers but also to the power of the saints. While workers' association of soul bartering and loss of goods and life with excessive accumulation suggests a moral ambiguity about the material success that would seem to have been the goal of much of the work performed by Voodoo practitioners, in general spiritual power was used to influence luck, health, and even the saints for the material benefit of both workers and their clients.

It was not only practitioners who were focused on their economic activities and meanings. Rather than targeting workers' religious activities, antagonistic legislators and law-enforcement agencies targeted their economic activities. The adjustments made to the constraints of law in order to create a business model for practicing Voodoo that internalized rising consumer culture and demonstrated the importance of national economic culture and local predecessors exemplify the centrality of indigenous American cultural influences on the practice of Voodoo in New Orleans. The ways in which practitioners bent and shaped rituals illuminates both the importance of economics to the practice of Voodoo and the importance of New Orleans as a site where ritual was constantly being shaped to determine Voodoo's ever-changing character.

Trial and Error

Ironically, some of the most significant influences on Voodoo in New Orleans were the municipal, state, and federal legal apparatuses used to prosecute workers in attempts to curtail or stamp out the practice of Voodoo. Almost none of the legal statutes under which workers were prosecuted were explicitly aimed at the practice of Voodoo. Federal authorities prosecuted workers who communicated with clients and did business through the U.S. Postal Service for fraudulent use of the mails. State officials became involved when suspects were accused of practicing medicine without a license or violating other regulations put in place by the state board of health. Finally, local courts, most frequently the recorder's courts, created in New Orleans to deal with petty offenses, prosecuted workers for violating city ordinances against everything from loitering and vagrancy to malicious mischief and disturbing the peace. The convergence of three overlapping legal spheres created an increasingly constricted space in which workers had to operate if they wanted to avoid fines into the hundreds of dollars and jail time ranging from thirty days to two years. This space was circumscribed by a larger economic culture that informed the business model of workers in New Orleans. In order to understand the ways in which legal authorities helped to shape and define Voodoo in New Orleans, we must examine the charges under which practitioners were arrested and prosecuted and the methods developed by workers to circumvent these limitations.

Practitioners of Voodoo, both professionals and their clients, were arrested and tried between 1883 and 1938 on more than fifteen different criminal charges. In New Orleans these short trials most frequently took place in the recorder's courts. Unfortunately, on the whole, records for the city's recorder's courts have not survived. Therefore, for the purposes of this study I examined forty-one cases as reported in local newspapers in Louisiana. Of these cases, thirty-five were tried New Orleans. Of the remaining cases, one was tried in Gulfport, Mississippi, one was decided in Cedar Grove, St. James Parish, and four were tried in Shreveport, Louisiana. In the reports of six of these cases, the crime supposedly committed is described, but there is no direct mention of the charge levied by the court. Thus, while conjecture based on description of the crime is possible, given the wide variety of charges levied against workers in this period, it is impossible to be certain exactly which crimes individuals were charged with. Further, some defendants were charged with multiple related crimes, such as malicious mischief and disturbing the peace.[52] The analyses that are possible do indicate the range of crimes for which practitioners could be charged. The significant number of cases surveyed suggests a substantial effort on the part of police, federal postal inspectors, and the state medical establishment to stamp out Voodoo in New Orleans by focusing on workers' economic endeavors. It also illustrates how innovative and dynamic workers had to be to avoid prosecution.

The most frequent prosecutions were undertaken for violation of state medical laws. Six of the forty-one cases surveyed, 14.6 percent, indicate that the state medical board or one of its officers or regulations was the driving force behind the prosecution. It has been suggested that at various times in

American history the medical establishment has been an arm of the state, the latter using the former to enforce official policy regarding health care. From the mid-nineteenth to the early twentieth century the medical establishment was actively engaged in a battle to wrest control of healing from medical sects it termed "Irregulars," including practitioners like homeopaths and midwives.[53] The medical establishment's efforts may have led to the prosecution of professional practitioners. In 1913 J. B. Williams and Mattie Matthew were caught in what the *New Orleans Times-Democrat* called "the State Board of Health dragnet." A board of health inspector masquerading as a patient sought treatment from the duo in order to get the evidence required to take them before the state board of medical examiners for legal action.[54] In 1938 the state board of health was obviously still active in this crusade, as a known Voodoo practitioner was arrested for making medicine without a license after one of his out-of-state clients lodged a complaint with the board. An article in the *New Orleans Item* claimed that he was only one of several arrested in this campaign.[55] In both cases, the implication was that the state medical board was actively seeking out cases involving supernatural healers, which may explain the frequency with which workers were prosecuted under prohibitions related to medical practice. Thus, in New Orleans, even if professional practitioners could stay on the right side of the municipal authorities, the statewide medical apparatus was often actively seeking to prosecute them, sending agents to the businesses of practitioners and taking complaints from distant clients.

U.S. Post Office inspectors also often headed active investigations to gather evidence against workers in New Orleans. Among federal prosecutions, those for mail fraud were the second most frequently filed against workers in the cases examined, at 12.2 percent. Like the Louisiana medical establishment, the federal government seems to have continued to pursue cases against workers in New Orleans over the period 1914–34. Federal sentences were often some of the longer sentences imposed on workers. In June 1914 Joseph McKay, known as Dr. Cat, was arrested by federal authorities in Birmingham, Alabama, where he had fled following indictment by a grand jury in May. His arrest was predicated on a letter turned over to U.S. Post Office inspectors by the *New Orleans Item* when it was brought to the paper's attention that he was making bold claims to clients about his power and using the federal mails to conduct business. He pled guilty to charges of using the mails to defraud and was sentenced to two years in a federal penitentiary in Atlanta. In addition, though she was not convicted, his wife was arrested as an accomplice, an illustration of the additional hardships that a federal prosecution might entail.[56]

Unlike the federal and state authorities, the recorder's courts in New Orleans were not focused on one line of prosecution. Most prosecutions of workers in the recorder's courts were for "malicious mischief" or practicing fortune-telling or magnetic healing, each accounting for approximately 10.25 percent of the surveyed cases. Also prosecuted in the recorder's courts were workers charged with disturbing the peace and obtaining money under false pretenses, each accounting for just over 7 percent of the cases. Other charges included loitering, vagrancy, and "being a suspicious character." In general, the cases of malicious mischief and disturbing the peace in the surveyed articles were the result of practitioners being caught in the act of placing gris-gris, or the material ingredients of Voodoo rituals, at someone's home, usually on the front porch or steps. These were often simple combinations of powders and household items left near the person's home to curse them. Charges could be levied separately or simultaneously on the same defendant.[57] The city ordinance against fortune-telling and magnetic healing was passed several times with minor adjustments from 1879 to 1920. It prohibited "fortunetelling, predicting future events, and all the phases of mediumship, clairvoyance, etc."[58] With such a wide array of charges to levy against Voodoo practitioners, it did not give them much room in which to operate legally. The nebulous nature of some of the charges made it difficult to know what exactly constituted malicious mischief, disturbing the peace, or obtaining money under false pretenses.

In order to avoid arrest and prosecution by federal, state, or municipal law enforcement, professional practitioners of Voodoo employed a number of different strategies that reflect their experience and lessons learned. First, many involved in operating mail-order businesses began shipping through private express-mail services to avoid prosecution for defrauding the federal mails. Some workers went so far as to set up a Spiritual Church along the lines of Mother Leafy Anderson's.[59] They began taking donations for services rendered rather than charging a fee and only provided religious or magical services that might be viewed as Voodoo or hoodoo in private or clandestine settings, recruiting clientele in the open with the promise of help but never performing the rituals where anyone but the client could witness the details. There was also a noted move by workers to retain the services of lawyers in order to deal with any legal trouble that might arise despite other precautions. Finally, there is evidence suggesting that many professional practitioners began limiting their clientele to those within a familiar network. Some workers began to refuse to work with or provide services to unknown or unfamiliar individuals. Even the pharmacists and drugstore owners may have sold materials only to those whom they knew or who had been recommended by familiar customers.

Many workers learned to navigate the law in New Orleans through—pardon the pun—trial and error. Dr. A. Rockford Lewis was arrested at least twice in New Orleans. He was first arrested in February 1934 for mail fraud, for which he was sentenced to serve time in a federal prison. Decades after the arrest, the *Louisiana Weekly* reported that Lewis had been arrested after a white client in Texas reported him to federal authorities. The report claimed that in an attempt to solicit payment he was due from the client, Lewis had written to him claiming that he had buried a certain seed in the cemetery that as it rotted would also deteriorate the heart of this delinquent Texan. The client, rather than paying Lewis, had contacted the Federal Bureau of Investigation, resulting in Lewis's arrest.[60] After his release, Lewis was prosecuted again in 1938 for making medicine without a license. Prosecuted first by the federal government, then for violating state medical laws, Lewis was caught on two of the three levels of law enforcement deployed against workers. His arrests may have gone just as far as his business in establishing him as one of the city's most well known workers. A number of workers named Lewis as the person from whose experience they learned to operate within the boundaries of the law. Lewis may also have been a transitional figure, not in period but in technique, a hybrid between the workers who openly practiced Voodoo and operators of Spiritual Churches. LWP workers noted that after his arrests Lewis had toned down what researchers characterized as his opulent surroundings. Further, Lewis had acquired a charter to open a Spiritualist Church and had set up a number of altars in an auditorium he owned next to his home. His arrests may have led him to adopt some of the methods of the Spiritual Churches, which were doing a better job of avoiding legal problems than he was.

Not only did Rockford Lewis learn from his own mistakes but his troubles with the law, publicized in local newspapers, shaped the practice of other workers in the city. During an interview with Lewis after his second arrest, an LWP researcher noted that retaining lawyers had become common among workers and that even those who did not, were known to consult Lewis for advice on their operations. Professor J.,R. Hall, whom LWP researchers interviewed after Lewis's 1938 arrest, said that he ran a successful mail-order business that avoided federal prosecution by employing private express-mail services. Hall had a new drugstore on Rampart Street, which was well known in this period for stores that carried Voodoo paraphernalia. While Hall criticized Lewis during the interview, he repeated Lewis's warning to researchers not to work with women. Both were reluctant to do business with women, implying that Hall's criticism of Lewis did not preclude him from learning from him in this respect or with reference to Lewis's earlier trouble with U.S. Post Office inspectors.

Arrest records suggest that Mother Leafy Anderson, founder of the Spiritual Church movement in New Orleans, was arrested on a number of occasions while learning how to operate her church within the bounds of the law. As noted in chapter 2, reports of Mother Anderson's arrest by local police in June 1921 for fortune-telling and again in April 1925 for disturbing the peace and holding a "Voodoo Meeting" in the Lower Ninth Ward suggest that this model of practice was still evolving in New Orleans.

Father Thomas, a protégé of Mother Anderson's, specifically stated that Mother Anderson had many procedures but employed them in "private healings," so that only the cured knew what they were.[61] The clandestine nature of Anderson's healing rituals protected her from prosecution but also led to rumor and suspicion. Captain Williams, one of the officers who arrested her in 1921, claimed after her death that she had been "operating a confidence game in the back of church," though she was never arrested under such a charge.[62] Many of Anderson's followers also noted that she retained the services of a lawyer. A police captain named Smith, who investigated Anderson in the early days of her church in New Orleans, claimed that her lawyer's name was Stafford and accused both him and Anderson of being "racketeers." Another officer claimed that Stafford was a state senator and could have covered up some of Anderson's early arrests.[63] Whoever this lawyer was and whatever his connections, Anderson used him to navigate the legal pitfalls that workers encountered for decades in New Orleans. Like Lewis, she considered legal advice crucial to running her Spiritual Church in the city.

In addition to serving as an example in the use of lawyers and holding rituals in secret, the Leafy Anderson model may also have been the source of the trend in the Spiritual Church community of taking donations for services rather than charging a fee. Christian churches most often gathered the funds necessary to continue functioning by soliciting donations rather than charging fees for services. The prophet Joseph Lyons, proprietor of a small church that openly admitted to practicing Voodoo, also stated explicitly that in his organization there was no fee to attend services, but participants were expected to donate "small change to the spirits."[64] Similarly, researchers who attended the services of the Reverend Lloyd Thomas, pastor of St. Paul Spiritualist Temple Number 1, in which he healed the sick and invalid, reported that everything at the services was free; not even a collection was taken.[65] In order to keep his organization afloat, Thomas may have needed to solicit funds in private, but not collecting money in view of the public undoubtedly reduced his chances of running into problems with the law. In addition, it is likely that Thomas picked this model up from Leafy Anderson, as he identified himself as one of her students and admitted that she had contributed financially to the opening of his church.[66]

In the end, the business models of workers, whether the legend of Marie Laveau, the Spiritual Church model of Leafy Anderson, or the continued rebounding of A. Rockford Lewis, all served as examples of how to cope with the complex web of federal, state, and municipal laws, and workers drew on the experience of these previous practitioners to create and re-create Voodoo in New Orleans. The business model that evolved was necessary if practitioners, whether they identified as workers or Spiritualists, were to turn a profit from their endeavors. The economic culture of the United States in general, and New Orleans in particular, provided salient influences on Voodoo. Both clients and workers needed money to survive. Professional practitioners molded their services to meet the needs of clients, which included jobs, housing, and luck finding either. As economic concerns became increasingly central to practice, the understanding of both material and metaphysical realities began to reflect the importance of these concerns for workers.

Workers and their associates who were able to monetize their practices gained the means to build economic and religious institutions around their work, which in turn legitimized their practices and allowed them to accumulate wealth and property without fear of legal persecution. In this formulation, the focus on money financed an institutionalization that in turn allowed the accumulation of more money. The incorporation of many rites common among workers into the Spiritual Churches of New Orleans and the selling of Voodoo-related paraphernalia at drugstores created safe spaces for these practices, allowing their continuation and even proliferation.

6

"GREEN MONEY MEANS SUCCESS"

I n 1937 LWP researchers, under the guise of training to become Voodoo practitioners themselves, had a number of meetings with the purported Voodoo queen Lala Hopkins. They formed relationships with a number of workers in the city in order to gather information about their practices. Some of these individuals in turn introduced them to Lala, intending that she participate in their Opening. This ceremony, characterized by the offering of food or drink to the spirits, was necessary for initiates to become workers. Lala, because of her expertise in "evil work," was called in specifically to perform what she called a "black cat opening," which was designed to prepare initiates to practice some of the more foreboding rituals associated with Voodoo. Many practitioners considered these rituals to be exceedingly profitable. To observe and record the Opening, researchers brought in additional personnel whom they identified as members of New York's "underworld" who were starting their own "hoodoo racket."[1]

The relationship between Voodoo, money, and crime was part of a complex relationship between spiritual power, economic success, and legitimacy that is illustrative of the dynamism of New Orleans's Voodoo practitioners during the first four decades of the twentieth century. Everything about Lala's modest appearance suggested that she was of humble means. Researchers described Lala, who was approximately fifty-three at the time, as small in stature, thin, with a brown complexion, decaying teeth, and matted hair. Lala's home between mid-city and downtown New Orleans was a "dilapidated single cottage" with "very old furniture," but she told researchers that there had been a time when she enjoyed material success.[2] Lala's spiritual work, like that of most of the workers interviewed from the late 1920s to the early 1940s, had been performed for pay. The LWP researchers eventually paid Lala for her participation in their

Opening because for her and most other professional practitioners in the city spiritual power and economic success were intimately connected. Boasting for the purposes of marketing and self-promotion, Lala told her would-be clients that not only had her spiritual power allowed her to evade police and a judge by performing Voodoo but it had allowed her to conjure up her own economic prosperity by demanding considerable sums from both clients and students. She explained to researchers that while Voodoo had allowed her to make "plenty good money," her depressed material condition in the late 1930s and early 1940s had come as a result of both her own questionable choices and the intervention of the spirits.[3] Researchers reported that workers spoke about an oppositional relationship to the law and spiritual and economic power all in the same breath.

Workers interviewed in the 1930s often spoke about their spiritual power in economic terms. Workers saw the ability to garner material success as evidence that the spirits were with them and their expertise was sought after. Workers attempting to market themselves to potential clients touted their economic success, suggesting that they believed this would be the most convincing proof of their abilities. Making claims to wealth was not uncomplicated for workers, however. Legal prosecution of workers was often related to services they provided for pay and charges of fraud. What workers' claims to economic affluence tell us is that like the police and judges that persecuted them, workers began to understand their spiritual power in economic terms. Further, the advent of the Spiritual Church movement in New Orleans may suggest that the rest of the city and municipal authorities also understood spiritual power, or perhaps more correctly the legitimacy of spiritual power, in economic and material terms as well.

The relationship between Voodoo, money, and the law was complex. Throughout the first four decades of the twentieth century workers had used their spiritual power to garner economic profits and often thought of their spiritual power in terms of material success. This often put them at odds with legal authorities, however, who viewed payment for services rendered via Voodoo as illegitimate and criminal. With the advent of Spiritual Churches circa 1920, Spiritual Church leaders, who also often viewed their relationship to the law as adversarial, created a structure for spiritual practice that allowed some of them to incorporate practices common to workers and also allowed known workers to legitimize their practices despite their previously troubled relationship to the law. Profit was by no means new to Voodoo in the 1930s. There is evidence that from the end of the nineteenth century through the 1920s, before the creation of the Spiritual Churches, Voodoo practitioners were able to make money from their spiritual practices. However, largely owing to the advent of Spiritual Churches in New Orleans, many practitioners were able to incorporate practices thought of as Voodoo, and thus criminal and illegitimate in the eyes of the law, into a structure that achieved a modicum of stability and legitimacy. The best evidence of this achievement is the granting of the tax-exempt status accorded to religious institutions to a number of Spiritual Churches operating in New Orleans by the late 1930s.

These exemptions represent a stark contrast to the legal prosecutions for fraud of those identified as Voodoo practitioners prior to and after the advent of the Spiritual Church movement. This achievement was due largely to the association of spiritual power with economic success. The garnering of significant profits and the adoption of Christian church–style methods of collecting those profits contributed significantly to many Voodoo practitioners' ability to make use of the structure created by Spiritual Churches. This attention to money allowed practitioners to purchase and rent the infrastructure, the edifices, and the accoutrements that made their businesses look like, or perhaps more accurately, behave like, Christian churches. Ironically, then, the association between money and spiritual power was crucial to both the criminalization and the implicit legitimization of practices regarded as Voodoo in New Orleans.

The importance of the image and infrastructure of a church, in combination with economic success, is further demonstrated by the operation of many of the city drugstores that dealt in Voodoo-related paraphernalia. While the tax exemption of Spiritual Churches denotes a certain degree of legitimacy, the continuation of clandestine methods of selling Voodoo paraphernalia through pharmacies implies that drugstore owners may still have feared legal reprisals. Pharmacists' clandestine operations paralleled similar tactics by workers, indicating that not all legitimate institutions were effective umbrellas for Voodoo and that there was something unique about churches in this regard. I argue that the practice of Voodoo in early twentieth-century New Orleans suggests that religious legitimacy in the United States may have been as much about wealth and aesthetics as it was about practice.

Profit Margin

Monetary compensation often seemed to be the overriding concern for workers in the early twentieth century. Madam Murray, a worker interviewed by Harry Middleton Hyatt, preceded a number of descriptions of her rites with qualifiers like, "Now if a person is paying yo' enough an' yo' wanta be shure of whut chure doin' . . ." The implication was that better compensation was directly related to the effort put into "a piece of work."[4] This formulation equated greater pay with greater, or more effective, forms of spiritual power. The LWP interviews suggest that workers, their clients, and the pharmacies and supply houses that sold them the necessities for Voodoo-related businesses were often attracted to these alternative religious practices by the promise of profits and economic power. It is little wonder, then, that workers began to understand their spiritual power and their economic success as interrelated, associating great power and great profit.

The profit margin for providing such services may have been huge. In 1940 the LWP researcher Robert McKinney, under the advice of his informants and would-be teachers with whom he had undergone an Opening, or initiation, made a list of the supplies he would need in order to practice as a Voodoo doctor. The list he compiled at the Cracker Jack Drug Store, Flash's Pharmacy, and Stolzenthaler Pharmacy, some of the city's most common suppliers of Voodoo paraphernalia, included devil's shoestrings, love powder, dragon's blood, goofer dust, controlling powder, get together drops, sacred sand, black cat oil, and a copy of the *Sixth and Seventh Books of Moses*. The most expensive item on his list, Easy Life Powder, would cost him $2.50. McKinney believed he could acquire all these items for a grand total of $8.50.[5] Further, he believed he could make most of the other items he would need from combinations of these supplies. Thus, researchers believed that one could acquire the accoutrements needed to start a career as a worker for what a hired domestic could make during the Depression in a few weeks of washing and ironing. A modest investment in these supplies by a domestic, for example, could result in independence from the drudgery of domestic work or the need to seek relief from a government agency like the WPA.

In contrast to the relatively low overhead apparently involved in starting a basic business as a worker, the services workers provided often commanded comparatively extravagant fees. One customer willing to spend $25 on a gambling hand could make a return on this initial investment, or even triple it. In *Mules and Men*, Zora Neale Hurston wrote that after her initiation one of her mentors told her how to cast a death spell that he had charged a client $250 to perform, undoubtedly because it not only ensured the intended victim's death but took ninety days to cast and take effect.[6] Many practitioners believed that more sinister and more involved rites were intrinsically more profitable, but the high cost of Voodoo-related services was not limited to malicious activity. Workers told LWP researchers that they could charge $50 to beat a robbery case, $200 to keep a judge and a district attorney from sentencing someone, and $500 to cast a spell and pray for five months to "run a person crazy." According to informants, the charge for murdering someone via Voodoo or curing insanity also could run as high as $500. Less expensive services included making someone sick for $10, separating a couple for $15, or sending someone away for $25.[7]

Workers were not the only entrepreneurs who profited from occult economies in and around New Orleans. Some businesses sold Voodoo paraphernalia via ads in periodicals. One such company, the Dixie Sales Agency, at 2121 Erato Street, which dealt in roots, herbs, and novelties, placed an ad for one of the products on the aforementioned Voodoo shopping list (see fig. 1):

DEVIL'S SHOE STRING

The Root is long and slender and somewhat resembles a Shoe String. An old Colored Mammy explains that this Root, if placed around a baby's neck will drive away Evil Spirits and stop children from crying, especially during teething. Voodoos and Witch Doctors make many claims such as carrying a Devil's Shoe String for Luck in Games, and Money Matters. However, we make no claims to this effect and sell only as Genuine Devil's Shoe String.
ORDER BY No. 11
PRICE ONLY. 25c

By adding the disclaimer, vendors obviously hoped to avoid criminal prosecution for fraud, clearly a continuing concern of Voodoo practitioners. By including instructions, merchants could encourage believers to order products for their own use rather than seeking out an expert worker, whom they would have to pay. This broadened the consumer base for these products from workers to a more general public. The disclaimer also suggests the legal danger involved in such a marketing strategy. Nonetheless, this catalog-style sale of Voodoo paraphernalia was employed by a number of businesses in this period.

Thinking in economic terms undoubtedly helped Voodoo practitioners to market themselves to clients. Some medical remedies, for example, may have been appealing because they were more affordable than seeking out a physician. At twenty-five cents, some devil's shoestrings was undoubtedly more affordable than paying a pediatrician to diagnose a crying or teething infant.[8] What is more, to facilitate sales some drugstore owners allowed purchasers to pay part of the cost of materials initially if their finances were inadequate. Thus, understanding of their clients' economic situations increased salesmen's opportunities to profit by more effectively marketing and selling Voodoo-related services and paraphernalia.

The economic strategies of Voodoo-related businesses were based not only on the experience of workers but on consumer trends among other American businesses. The use of the disclaimer language, for example, was not limited to the sale of Voodoo paraphernalia. Some workers also made the most of their ventures by drawing out services and having clients pay in installments. One such case exemplifies the continuing legal danger for early twentieth-century workers dealing in Voodoo. William Link was arrested in April 1925 by a postal inspector for defrauding the federal mails. Link dealt in "love philters," or love potions, to "restore estranged wives or sweethearts."[9] Link reportedly sold to clients in Florida and Georgia, charging them five dollars down and five dollars monthly. He was arrested for a sale in which the customer had paid him a total of twenty-five dollars by mail. Some clients may have been willing to spend more over a longer period of time than they would have spent if they had had to make a single payment up front.

What is interesting is that workers caught on to sales techniques like installment buying, made popular by department stores as consumer culture flourished in the early twentieth century, and employed them to increase the viability of their own economic enterprises. In very limited use throughout the nineteenth century, credit lending for consumer buying did not begin to become standard until the 1880s. Small-loan businesses were still widely considered illegal until the 1920s owing mostly to the stigma attached to usury. Many major department stores began to expand the number of charge accounts they opened, spreading this business from the upper classes down the socioeconomic ladder in this period. Some major stores, however, obviously skeptical, lagged into the first two decades of the twentieth century without adopting these practices.[10]

One of Hyatt's informants, the Undercover Man, claimed to have made a great deal of money by charging in installments: "They paid me as high as $60 for a toby. The fellow went away with his *luck* and with that *luck* he made sometimes like about $200. And I made him pay me $35.95 down. . . . And when he sent me the balance, he sent me $6 to get to the city. But I didn't guarantee it for no more than six months. See, after six months he'd have to renew it but it cost him $60."[11] Thus the client was able to obtain the charm immediately and pay later, undoubtedly making it an easier purchase if the sixty-dollar price tag was discouraging. Department stores discovered similar patterns and sought to increase their credit business. The Undercover Man might also draw additional business if the client was pleased with the toby and returned in six months to renew it. He had thus tapped into a relatively new kind of credit spending to better market his services.

All these innovations in selling Voodoo undoubtedly increased the potential profit margin for workers and other members of this economic community. Workers stood to gain a great deal from thinking in economic terms and increasing profits. The balance reached by some of the most successful participants in the occult economies connected to Voodoo had a great deal to do not only with the potential of workers to draw in a wide client base by appealing to clients' material needs but also with their marketing of their power by signaling their own material success. Often that material success, especially with reference to the acquisition of property, spoke to not only their spiritual power but also their ability to legitimize their practices. Interestingly, by looking at the property accumulated by workers we can gain some insight into not only their claims to power but also the relationship between profit, institutionalization, and legitimacy.

Accumulated Wealth, Accumulated Power

Despite Voodoo practitioners' claims to economic affluence and extraordinary success, property ownership and values suggest that their economic status varied. The data suggest that those involved with Voodoo in New Orleans who were able to legitimize their practices by incorporating them into less provocative institutions, namely, pharmacies and Spiritual Churches, were able to secure some stability and avoid legal prosecution. Perhaps most salient among the property accumulated by individuals involved in the sale of Voodoo-related products and services were the buildings that housed their businesses. An examination of those properties points to an apparent correlation between economic success and spiritual legitimacy.

Of the 137,165 dwelling units in New Orleans reported by the 1940 U.S. Census, only 31,552, or 23 percent, were owned by the individuals living in them. By looking at home ownership, we can determine, at least to some extent, how practitioners fared in terms of accumulated wealth in comparison with the city's population in general. While we cannot equate home ownership and economic affluence or read a lack thereof as a sign of abject poverty, property ownership does serve as an indicator, albeit a general one, of financial status.

Practitioners often equated wealth with power. As much as they were selling any one service, frequently they were also selling an image of prosperity and escape from economic hardship. Claims of exorbitant prices charged for rites most often were meant to illustrate workers' prowess and effectiveness. The ability to overcome the hardships of the Depression had become the ultimate expression of power by the late 1930s. One informant told a story about a New Orleans worker named Sarah Pugh, who "charged people $350, $375, or fo' or five hundred dollahs apiece—fo' work."[12] In this particular instance, not the best but the only support for her claim of Sarah's efficacy as a worker was Sarah's ability to command high pay for her work.

One of the most infamous members of New Orleans's nineteenth-century Voodoo community was Dr. Jim Alexandre. Dr. Jim, a supposed contemporary of Marie Laveau, New Orleans's most notorious Voodoo queen, died at age fifty-four at his home in the heart of the French Quarter around the turn of the century. One informant told LWP researchers that Dr. Jim had owned all the land from Spanish Fort to Gentilly, a stretch of territory covering more than two square miles.[13] This was undoubtedly an exaggeration. However, in 1900 his widow was trying to gain title to the property he did own.[14] According to the succession filed with the civil district court, Charles Lafontaine, also known as Dr. Jim Alexandre, owned a four-room cottage at 2105 Orleans Street and property on that block valued at nearly five thousand dollars. The succession also indicated that Dr. Jim may also have had three thousand dollars in other real estate that was still in dispute in 1902. It is difficult to know whether

Dr. Jim was the exception or the rule for late nineteenth-century practitioners, as few firsthand accounts that identify workers are available from the period. This level of success was certainly not the rule for the first two decades of the twentieth century, however. The property Dr. Jim amassed contributed to his reputation as a powerful Voodoo doctor. His economic and spiritual power were intertwined in the legends surrounding his work.

Often, wealth amassed via Voodoo was accompanied by legal woes. "Doctor" Julius P. Caesar was arrested in October 1902 at his home in New Orleans.[15] According to coverage of his trial, Caesar was operating as a "magnetic healer" in New Orleans, with a diploma in the art from an unnamed college in Missouri. He reportedly received letters from across the country requesting his aid. Despite the interstate nature of Caesar's practice though, there is no indication that he attained the kind of economic success enjoyed by Dr. Jim. The home he lived in uptown was owned by a gentleman with a great deal of property on the block. However, the dimensions of the building Caesar lived in suggest that it was the largest on the street, so that he may have paid substantially more rent than his neighbors.[16] A man identifying himself as Caesar's cousin who in the late 1930s had moved to New Orleans from Richmond, Virginia, claimed that he had learned his work from Caesar and that similarly to Caesar, he had a diploma from a "so-called palace in Calcutta," which "was surely one of the many diploma mills issuing a paper stating that you are qualified by the institute, brotherhood, fellowship . . . to practice or teach . . ." Caesar's supposed cousin claimed that in his day Caesar had been the "top Hoodoo in New Orleans" and that Caesar had "left nearly $150,000 worth of real estate when he died," clearly equating property ownership and spiritual power.[17] Even if we question this latter informant's claim that he was related to Caesar, the fact that he attempted to use Caesar's reputation to legitimize himself as a worker again speaks to the effectiveness of Caesar's self-marketing. The implication is that Caesar's projected image of his own prosperity, and thus his power, was convincing enough that another worker attempted to use Caesar's reputation to bolster his own.

In February 1937 LWP researchers sought out Madame Ducoyielle, a woman famed in New Orleans's alternative religious community as a powerful Voodoo queen. Madame Ducoyielle, an elderly Black woman who admitted to the researchers that her real name was Robinson, lived in the home of her protégé, Mrs. Dereco, an aged white woman, less than a mile from the French

Quarter. During one of the researchers' earliest meetings with her, Madame Ducoyielle touted her expertise in hoodoo by equating it with economic success, boasting that in her youth she had made thousands of dollars as a worker, though neither Madame Ducoyielle nor Mrs. Dereco was listed as the owner of their home on St. Phillip Street.[18] We can infer that their boasts were a means of marketing themselves to potential clients, one that obviously had some success, as they were sought out by LWP researchers looking for successful workers.

In some instances an affluent lifestyle may have buttressed claims made by workers to both material wealth and spiritual power. In 1937 LWP researchers also interviewed Professor J. R. Hall. Representatives of the LWP had been familiar with Hall since the onset of the Depression, likely because he had a reputation for flash and flair. Researchers claimed that Hall bought a new car every year, and in 1937 they noted that he drove a new LaSalle, a luxury automobile produced by General Motors with a price tag of nearly $2,000.[19] Hall was known to spend extravagantly on acquaintances and claimed to live in a "white neighborhood" where he owned "half of the block" and rented only to whites.[20] The city's property-tax records make no mention of anyone named Hall owning a home in the 3100 block of Toulouse Street, where Hall told LWP interviewers he lived. In 1937 the homes on the block ranged in value from $2,700 to $4,900, with the home at the address Hall provided being assessed at $4,200, the second most costly home on the block. If Hall did live here, it suggests some financial success, though not quite what he claimed.[21]

It is also interesting that Hall expressed his power in terms of economic influence over whites. Of the more than 31,552 homeowners listed in the city in 1940, 27,030, or 85 percent, identified themselves as white. The census classified 4,494, or 14 percent, of homeowners as Negro, and 28, less than 1 percent, as neither white nor Black. It was a point of pride for Hall that he supposedly rented property to whites. In his view, participation in Voodoo gave him influence over individuals over whom he might otherwise have been unable to exert influence because of racial restrictions. The implication was that economic power could allow one to overcome the disadvantages implicit in racial segregation. While it is unlikely that Hall owned a home in the neighborhood, the U.S. Census tract for 1940 encompassing 3100 Toulouse Street supports Hall's claim about the racial demographics of the area. The neighborhood was in fact 87.8 percent white and only 12.2 percent non-white, as Hall asserted.[22] If we at least assumed that Hall lived here, despite the apparent fabrication about owning the home, and we also assume that majority white neighborhoods were on the whole more affluent than majority Black ones, as was suggested by the worker in his interview, Hall's address may still indicate a modicum of material success that matched the image he projected.

During the Great Depression, New Orleans saw the coming of one of its most notorious and perhaps most prosperous workers: A. Rockford Lewis. Lewis, who moved to New Orleans from Thibodaux, Louisiana, seemed to do well in his Voodoo-related business.[23] LWP researchers who interacted with Lewis throughout the 1930s knew Lewis to drive a number of expensive automobiles, including a Pierce Arrow, a luxury car worth upwards of $4,000 in this period, and later a less costly Ford V-8 (also known as a Model 18), which ranged in cost from $460 to $650. In addition, when Lewis was arrested twice in 1934 for defrauding the federal mails and in 1938 for violating regulations of the state board of health, he had the economic resources to fight both suits, the latter successfully. Lewis told interviewers: "Mah lawyer told me dat Ah'm going to have to give one of dem politicians some money, er bout $15,000. Dat suits me 'cause Ah remember de last time Ah was in trouble and it cost me much more dan dat. Dat trial cost me close to $8,000 er more."[24]

Lewis's statement suggests that not only did he have the funds to make the $1,000 bond that he posted after being arrested in 1938 but he had the funds to pay for an affluent lawyer with offices in the Maison Blanche Department Store building on Canal Street, in what was long New Orleans's central business and premier shopping district, as well as the money to bribe local officials. The aforementioned costs came to some $24,000, a great deal of money during the Depression. What is apparent from Lewis's experience is the economic detriment of Voodoo-related legal troubles. Further, whether or not the interviewer's assertion that "the noteworthy queens and doctors . . . practices net them over $50,000 yearly" was accurate, it is evident that the monetizing of his religious practices managed to net Lewis a substantial income in the midst of the worst economic crisis in American history. He was then able to translate that economic power into politics by retaining a lawyer to manipulate the legal system and bribing local politicians to purchase their favor.

This economic success may have resulted largely from the expansion of Lewis's clientele beyond the bounds of the city of New Orleans. His federal prosecution for defrauding the U.S. Postal Service is evidence that his client base extended beyond state lines. To keep his business thriving prior to this arrest, Lewis employed two registered pharmacists and a stenographer, who testified at his trial that "as far as she knew . . . the mail order business 'Dr.' Lewis operated was entirely concerned with shipments of 'Save Your Life Rheumatic Oil.'"[25]

Some informants suggested that geography affected their ability to make a living as a worker. Too many practitioners operating in and around New Orleans created an apparent glut on the market. The presence of so many unreliable practitioners apparently made it difficult for genuine workers and increased the viability of markets outside of the city. One worker supposed that there might be greater profits to be had in places like Arkansas, Texas, and northern Louisiana, for instance, where there was less competition.[26] This may have been an impetus for workers to establish mail-order businesses and court interstate clientele.

In addition, creating and marketing cures for rheumatism was big business at the beginning of the twentieth century, and it had been the purview of patent-medicine men in the nineteenth. *Rheumatism* is a non-specific term that was commonly used to refer to a number of painful conditions affecting joints, connective tissue, and muscles. A dozen different conditions are covered by the term, with different symptoms and treatments. Patent-medicine men had sold clients on self-transformation through a kind of magical intervention that reflected the persistence of magical thinking throughout the United States.[27] It is not surprising that the treatment of such a complex disorder would have fallen into the realm of Voodoo practitioners, and profiting from the marketing of an effective panacea for rheumatism situates Lewis in the wider American tradition of makers of patent medicine, distinctly connected to a kind of curative magic.

A. Rockford Lewis's material success was undoubtedly related to the diversity of his economic activities. In addition, Lewis's business may speak to a different kind of diversity, a conceptual innovation that may be related to his success. He may have been a transitional figure, not in period but in technique, a hybrid between the workers who openly practiced Voodoo and the operators of Spiritual Churches. By the mid-1930s Lewis owned a sizeable piece of property in the 5100 block of Royal Street, in what is today the Lower Ninth Ward. The land, on the outskirts of the city, was valued at $600 in 1937 but had some $2,000 in improvements, which included not only Lewis's home but also a building identified as an auditorium by LWP researchers and identified as a dancehall by Lewis, where he did much of his business.[28] Lewis was one of the only workers surveyed who did not explicitly self-identify as a Spiritual Church head but can be shown to have owned his home. LWP researchers noted that after his arrests Lewis had toned down what researchers characterized as opulent surroundings. In August 1960 Lewis was killed as the result of a gun-related accident at his home in which he apparently shot himself. His reputation and fame as a "voodoo doctor" was recounted by the journalist who covered his shooting, who wrote that "Oldtimers" remembered Lewis "standing on So. Rampart corners displaying a two headed cat in a bottle" in "colorful garments including a ten gallon hat," which "attracted a large crowd."[29] Further, even though he had been trained by Lala Hopkins, a Voodoo queen and self-proclaimed worker, Lewis had acquired a charter to open a Spiritual Church and had set up a number of altars in the auditorium next to his home.[30] Echoing descriptions of Leafy Anderson's more private visits with clients, the site was also said to contain a small room that "was always locked and was visited by only Lewis and a one-legged assistant during the 'thirties."[31] His arrests may have persuaded him to adopt some of the methods of the Spiritual Churches, which were doing a better job of avoiding legal problems than he was.

Voodoo and Church

The Spiritual Church mothers who founded Christian-based churches in New Orleans often incorporated practices similar or identical to those described by workers as part of their own repertoires. It is uncertain whether the Spiritual Church movement that took root in the early twentieth century was founded in the Crescent City or transplanted from Chicago.[32] However, we do know that in 1920 Mother Leafy Anderson, of Chicago, founded the first of a group of churches in New Orleans and trained associates who referred to themselves as co-workers. They in turn founded their own churches, which seemed to be autonomous in terms of the rituals they employed. This autonomy would have allowed many of the practices associated with Voodoo to become common in Spiritual Churches, and some workers looked to the Spiritual Church movement as a vehicle for merging Christianity and Voodoo in a form less likely than the Laveau method to attract legal attention or the ire of Christians.

Legitimacy, especially with reference to the state's treatment of Spiritual

Churches, was an issue central to the culture of these churches. By the late 1930s, ten years after Leafy Anderson's death and almost twenty years after the establishment of her first church in New Orleans, some of her followers still recounted stories about the difficulty she had had in obtaining a charter to found her church in 1920. They recounted instances of police harassment and repeated visits to city hall in which Mother Anderson was allegedly denied a charter.[33] The charter was undoubtedly denied because of the perception that Spiritual Church leaders practiced Voodoo. Like workers before them, Spiritual Church heads operated under the suspicion of fraud associated with these practices. In fact, even workers outside the Spiritual Church movement recounted stories about Anderson's connection to "the work" and her having to bribe local law-enforcement officers in order to secure a place for her organization in the city.[34] LWP researchers questioned the veracity of these accounts because of the lack of evidence in files at city hall or the city attorney's office that Anderson experienced any difficulty in obtaining a charter.[35] Nonetheless, in the collective memory of the institutions created by Anderson's students, the perception that Spiritual Churches had a precarious relationship with legal authorities persisted.

The history of connections between Anderson's co-workers, practitioners of Voodoo, and the prevailing perception that the Laveau legacy was part and parcel of the rituals of the Spiritual Churches is at least partly responsible for the notion among Spiritual Church leaders that their organization existed in opposition to the law. This is particularly intriguing in light of the fact that the structure employed by Spiritual Churches could create a legitimate space for Voodoo practitioners in the city's legal landscape. A number of articles of Anderson's original charter allowed her church to receive donations and buy and sell property, both real and personal, within the bounds of the law.[36] As long as she and her successors conducted their business within the bounds of these charters, they could accumulate significant assets. In turn, those assets allowed them to conduct business much as other Christian churches did, by establishing edifices in which they conducted services in view of the public, unlike the workers operating in the city before them. Finally, the according of tax-exempt status to those edifices, a status granted by local authorities to religious institutions, represented recognition by the state that individuals operating these organizations, despite the stigma of Voodoo, which remained a part of the churches' collective image, were legitimate religious institutions.

The establishment of churches was integral to this accomplishment. As we will see, other Voodoo-related businesses, namely pharmacies, were apparently licensed to do business in the city, as the owners and operators were frequently identified by workers as "registered" pharmacists. While informants did not go into detail about what becoming registered entailed, the implication was certainly that pharmacists had the sanction of law. However, they, like workers, continued to fear legal reprisals. Like workers and members of the Spiritual Churches, they viewed themselves as operating counter to legal authorities. Spiritual Church heads, however, seemed not to live in fear of legal reprisal. Even though conflicts with law enforcement were a part of their history, weaved into accounts of Anderson's establishment of her first church. In contrast, pharmacists conducted their sales of Voodoo-related paraphernalia clandestinely, in fear of fraud-related legal prosecutions. Thus, the key triumph was not in the legal sanction for the establishment represented by the charters granted to Spiritual Churches. This is demonstrated by the aforementioned workers Julius P. Caesar and his cousin, who had charters or certificates that did not exempt Caesar from legal prosecution. But the status of "church" accorded to Spiritual Churches, combined with the legal sanction implied by tax exemption, seems to have provided a more stable space for spiritual practice than did pharmacies or charters.

Mother Catherine Seals, a famed healer and a student and co-worker of Mother Leafy Anderson's, founded the Church of Innocent Blood. She owned both the building that housed the church and an adjoining structure that she and her followers called "the Manger," which seated some three hundred people. The property was valuable enough that Mother Catherine thought it necessary to see to its disposal after her death by completing a will, which, apparently because she was illiterate, she signed with an X. She wrote: "Now if its colored in here at the time I pass out the building shall be run by them. The taxes shall be kept by them you will have no trouble to run them away. . . . I leaves all I got to them what stands in here with me."[37]

Despite Mother Catherine's explicit instructions leaving her property to her congregation, the state disputed the validity of her will after her death in 1930. The will was disputed from 1931 to 1933, when it was validated by the state supreme court, whereupon her estate, valued at four thousand dollars, was passed to her congregation in the person of her chosen successor, Mother Rita.[38] It is not a stretch to interpret the racially specific language of the will as an attempt by Catherine to pass on her power, both economic and spiritual, via her church to the Black community. Logistically, owning the church would have made it easier to carry on her spiritual legacy. Though she was known to boast an interracial congregation, another accomplishment she and her followers touted as a mark of her power, the need to secure this material benefit for her African American followers specifically, suggests an understanding that economic power was tied to the spiritual power that would be passed to her congregation. The racial specificity may also imply that she believed her Black successors would have particular need for the economic power implicit in control of one's own institutions that accompanied property ownership. The phrase "if its colored in here" tells us not only that Innocent Blood had an interracial congregation but that there were enough white members that Mother Catherine had to consider the possibility that the church might be white by numerical majority or dominant influence by the time she died. It also suggests that Mother Catherine was aware of the importance of the church edifice for maintaining both the physical space and the conceptual space created by working in a "church."

Just as many Voodoo practitioners and Spiritual Church heads understood the relationship between their own spiritual power and the economic power it could help them garner, some evidence suggests that spiritual and economic power may have created still other avenues and opportunities for socioeconomic advancement. Mother Maude Shannon was head of the Daniel Helping Hand Spiritual Church, located just outside Treme, one of New Orleans's oldest neighborhoods. The building that housed Mother Shannon's church was valued at $2,900, making it the most costly building on the block. The owner of the property was listed as Mrs. May Smith Sanders, who was also listed in the New Orleans city directory as a resident of the property in 1937. It is possible that Shannon was a pseudonym employed by May Smith. If that was the case, then Shannon owned the most valuable property on the block. If not, notations in the city directory suggest that the owner lived in the church. If Smith and Shannon were different women, then even though she was not affiliated with the church, Smith lived in the building that housed it, although there is no suggestion in the records of multiple residences at the address. Even if this unlikely scenario proved accurate, it would still mean that Mother Shannon had the financial wherewithal and congregation to warrant renting the most expensive property on the block.[39]

When LWP researchers visited Mother Shannon's church, they encountered her daughter, a coed studying to be a dietician at the University of Chicago, whom they described as an educated and comely woman. Mother Shannon's material success via the Spiritual Church may have created opportunities for her daughter to pursue an education at a distant, well-endowed university. The same savvy that allowed those who practiced Voodoo and related traditions to understand power in both spiritual and economic terms may also have made it possible for Mother Shannon to understand that her daughter's success might lie in higher education and a career field seemingly unrelated to her own, increasing the ways in which she and her family might advance in society. On the same day, LWP researchers also encountered Bishop Thomas B. Watson, who was serving as a guest official. Bishop Watson, who had an undergraduate degree from Xavier University, the United States' only historically Black Catholic university, where he was also working on a master's degree, reportedly also worked as a teacher at an institution he identified as Sylvians Williams, again pointing to the marriage of higher education and spiritual power as a strategy for socioeconomic success. Thus, like many of the city's alternative religious practitioners, members of this church were pursuing corporeal and spiritual advancement simultaneously.

Not far from Mother Shannon's church was Mother Mamie Reason's Helping Hand Spiritualist Church of Christian Love, which may point to yet another connection between spiritual power and economic savvy. The listed owners of Mother Reason's church were Mr. and Mrs. Hy Reason. What is interesting here is that Mother Reason had the business acumen to have her church, a building assessors valued at $4,200, declared tax-exempt as a religious institution.[40] The only building on the block more valuable than Mother Reason's church was the Sacred Heart Spiritualist Church, valued at $4,400. Tax records did not list a single owner for Sacred Heart; rather, an unnamed "society" was listed as owner. However, it may have had some connection to an uptown Spiritual Church also bearing the name Sacred Heart, run by Mother Lena Scovotto. Tax records list the owner as Lena Gondolfi, but the identical given names suggest that this is likely the same woman, who also had the wherewithal to have Sacred Heart, valued at $9,000, made tax-exempt. The city directory listed Sacred Heart's address as 1734 Amelia Street and Mother Lena's residence as 1738. The directory also contains a notation indicating that Mother Lena listed herself as the owner of her residence, a noticeably larger edifice than the church on the corner of Amelia and Baronne.[41] Outside of the Sacred Heart location on Amelia, property values on that block ranged from $3,200 to $8,000, making the property owned by Mother Lena the most valuable on the block. This suggests that she enjoyed significant economic success.[42]

LWP researchers described Sacred Heart as an "exact replica" of a Roman Catholic church. Researchers also wrote that "this church is undoubtedly the most expensive and best constructed Spiritualist church in the city, at present," and they confirmed that Mother Lena had "missions all over the city and some in the parishes,"[43] which supports the presumption that both this Sacred Heart Spiritualist Church and the aforementioned location were in fact connected. It is also not surprising, given the prevalence and influence of the Catholic Church in New Orleans, that the church would have adopted that expensive, but for New Orleans normative, aesthetic.

By adopting the appearance of not just any Christian church but a Catholic church, Mother Scovotto may have attracted less of the kind of attention attracted by her counterparts with less conventional churches. The status as an official religious organization that protected the spiritual mothers from prosecution was likely related to the apparent economic success suggested by the grand "Roman Catholic" appearance of churches like Sacred Heart. The material accoutrements of religion suggested by the infrastructure of the church may have detracted from the scrutiny commonly incurred by self-identified workers, traditional practitioners of Voodoo who did not run "churches" per se, but often operated out of their homes and the homes of colleagues. The resulting stability undoubtedly allowed Spiritual Churches to continue soliciting donations and fees unmolested by police. In turn the additional fees added to the ability to create and maintain the rather impressive but normalizing aesthetic associated with Christian churches.

While most of the aforementioned Spiritual Churches had little identifiable connection to Voodoo, the Spiritual Church movement may have represented a chance at legitimacy for those select Spiritual Church owners like Mother Kate Francis and the prophet Joseph Lyons, who were known to incorporate Voodoo in their churches, as well as known workers like A. Rockford Lewis, reportedly trained by the self-proclaimed worker Lala Hopkins. It was one thing to understand that the accumulation of spiritual power and one's resulting success as a worker would allow for the building of an institution such as the business established by A. Rockford Lewis, which in turn resulted in a degree of material success, represented by Mr. Lewis's significant real and personal property. However, the declaring of one's property as tax exempt suggests an evolution in that thinking. Unlike many of their predecessors who practiced openly as workers, the more Christianized and therefore seemingly orthodox Spiritual Churches gained an air of legitimacy in the eyes not only of other practitioners but of the state, which, by declaring their property tax exempt, explicitly acknowledged them as legitimate religious institutions.

Tax exemption granted to religious institutions embodies the commitment of the national culture in the United States to freedom of religion as best expressed by the Establishment Clause of the First Amendment to the U.S. Constitution. While not included in the Constitution, the Bill of Rights, or federal statutes, tax exemptions granted to religious institutions are state policy in all fifty states and a result of policies that predate the Constitution and "continued uninterrupted" into the twentieth century. They are thus an integral part of the American understanding of what protections are granted to religious organizations to ensure freedom of religious practice in the United States. The understanding of the U.S. Supreme Court on this issue is that exemption prevents the "excessive government entanglement" between church and state that is impermissible in light of the First Amendment, as taxation would give the state the power to financially destroy religious institutions. Exemptions are granted based on the assumption that churches exist "in a harmonious relationship to the community at large," and "foster its 'moral or mental' improvement." By granting tax exemption to Spiritual Churches in New Orleans, the state explicitly put them into this category. Tax exemption allowed Spiritual Churches to avoid the pitfalls faced by workers who were afflicted by what the Supreme Court defined as the "official and continuing surveillance leading to an impermissible degree of entanglement."[44] Those involved in practices that we might classify as Voodoo who created Spiritual Churches or Spiritual Church heads who incorporated similar practices in their organizations altered the relationship between the state and the practice of Voodoo.

Further, religious legitimacy in this case seemed to be predicated on, or at the very least buttressed by, material success. Since Leafy Anderson's establishment of her Spiritual Church in New Orleans, hers and related institutions had occupied a liminal space in terms of spiritual and legal legitimacy. This is demonstrated by association of the Spiritual Churches with Voodoo and fraud, as well as stories about the difficulty Anderson had in obtaining a charter.

The move by practitioners of Voodoo-style rituals into the framework of the Spiritual Church, while still contested and debated both by practitioners and outsiders, may have represented the most open practice of what many called Voodoo by the 1930s. In turn, the acquisition of churches by practitioners led to a degree of property ownership and stability. The establishment of churches, specifically the infrastructure that made it apparent that these groups of spiritual practitioners constituted congregations or "churches," also saw these spiritual workers gaining the state sanction implied by tax exemption. Thus, the declaration of these churches as legitimate religious institutions worthy of tax exemption represents the use of economic power, embodied in property ownership, to create spiritual power in the form of religious legitimacy. In this formulation there is a cycle in which spiritual power creates economic prosperity, which in turn creates religious legitimacy, itself a form of spiritual power, which, because it can be practiced in the open, in turn leads to the opportunity for economic growth or prosperity.

A great deal of this economic success may have resulted from the fact that Spiritual Churches, in order to escape the prosecution of the law, often took donations as described in Leafy Anderson's original charter rather than soliciting money for their services, even at the risk of not being paid at all. A number of informants described this policy. One woman, who recounting her visit to what was described as a public shrine said that the woman who had helped her there called herself a Spiritualist and accepted donations rather than charging a fee.[45] Another informant, the Gifted Medium, stated: "Well, undah de spiritual form, there is no attachment of pay, yo' understan'. Aftah the work is completed then they give yo' whut they wants. Some don't give yo' anything—dey jes' let cher go tuh de wind. Then othahs will give yo' something, but the law does not allow you to put any charges. Well yo' go somewhere there are charges, that is people that is jes' doin' volumes of *ism*."[46]

The Gifted Medium identified herself as Catholic and said that her work was done mostly with the help of Sacred Heart (a popular Catholic incarnation of Jesus), Saint Anthony, and the Blessed Mother (Mary, mother of Jesus). She described this work as spiritualism, however, and set up a kind of dichotomy between that kind of work and what she called *ism*, probably short for *hoodooism*, a common term used to refer to workers and their practice of Voodoo. The informant equated hoodooism with both evil work and charging money for services, perhaps an indicator of the moral ambiguity that surfaced among workers with reference to pecuniary remuneration for services. The medium saw no contradiction between her self-identification as a Catholic and her association with spiritualism. The Spiritual Church–style collection of donations was a legal way to collect for her work, and the statement that "the law" did not allow for a direct charge to be applied to services was an indication of the importance of the law in directing the practice of spiritual practitioners in the city. It is not certain whether those who were interested in becoming workers but instead became Spiritual Church mothers and fathers did so to legitimize their practices. It may have been that rites common among workers survived or were adopted by the Spiritual Churches because they operated more freely. Whatever the case, there was some relationship between proponents of the Laveau Legacy and the Anderson model. Property records show that a significant number of Spiritual Church heads moved themselves into that privileged minority of the city's property owners, again demonstrating a relationship between material success, legal legitimacy, and spiritual power.

The legitimation of alternative religious practices suggested by the chartering and recognition of a Spiritual Church, which would have been necessary in order for it to be acknowledged as a tax-exempt religious institution, went hand in hand with property ownership. The Reverend Thomas Lloyd, head of St. Paul Spiritualist Temple No. 1 in uptown New Orleans, had a church large enough to accommodate some two hundred individual chairs and fifty benches. Reverend Thomas, like many of his peers among the Spiritual Church heads, conflated the ideas of education and economic and spiritual power, though he had a rather unique take on the connections between them: "Da hoodoo people deys is educated too. . . . Dem hoodooes are always tellin's ya how to make money an' git what ya wants. Dey is poor as church mice. . . . Look at me, I neber has to beg, ya all knows dat. If ya walks in da way of da Lord ya will never go hungry." Reverend Thomas seems to have been attempting to demonize education by associating it with both hoodoo and material poverty. While his conclusions may seem odd, tax assessors' records suggest that he owned his church, which was valued at $2,500 in a block in which the property ranged in value from $800 to $3,000, supporting his claim to financial security. The property was also listed as tax exempt, suggesting that his economic station may have owed as much to his business acumen as to his spiritual power. The distinction that he drew between his own church and the work of "hoodoos" suggests that he attributed his economic success to his status as head of a "legitimate" church. [47]

It would be misleading to suggest that all Spiritual Churches attained the kind of success that Reverend Thomas, Mother Reason, and Mother Scovotto enjoyed. For example, the prophet Joseph Lyons did not have as much good fortune as some of his peers. Although he ran his own church, the Emperor Haile Selassi Nu-Way Ethiopia Mystic Light Baptist and Spiritual and Kingdom Church, in mid-city New Orleans, there is little evidence that he enjoyed material success. A LWP interviewer described his home as "a three room very shabby double cottage whose window panes are broken, and whose exterior needs painting badly. The prophet lives in his church, sleeping on a cast-off cot."[48] The interviewer noted that Lyons's church had a rat infestation (which did not bother the Prophet, because "they is r'ligious rats") and wires hanging from the ceiling (which he claimed brought electricity from the spirits).[49]

While there was some confusion about what classification best suited Lyons's church, he was clear about its purpose: "I don't know exactly what kind of church this is but it is one that is established. I'm teaching all of the religions and giving all my customers anything they want, from baptism to voodoo paraphernalia. . . . A satisfied soul will not only come back but will recommend high class customers."[50] While Lyons's statements undoubtedly contributed to LWP researchers' skepticism about his claims to spiritual power, Lyons's unofficial statement of purpose for his church may have hit on the central advantage of integrating alternative religious beliefs into a Christian-style structure. Being "established," as he put it, protected him from persecution from authorities and gave his project an air of legitimacy. He boasted about his evasion of the law, saying, "They'll never get me like they got Rockford Lewis because my work is legitimate. . . . The police will not stop me. . . . They can't do [me] anything for helping people. Can they?"[51] Lyons did not own the rather modest, perhaps very un-churchlike building out of which he worked, which may further support the notion of a connection between the ownership of church-style infrastructure and economic success.[52]

By the early twentieth century, workers had come to understand how the acquisition of physical space could create an ideological space in which to operate. By owning a church, they could erect within a physical edifice designed to shield one from the elements a conceptual space that shielded practitioners from the persecution of law enforcement in the city. The bans against fortune-telling and obtaining money under false pretenses under which Voodoo practitioners were prosecuted were rarely, if ever, the concern of Christian churches.

By pushing the practices that had defined Voodoo in New Orleans into the spaces of Christian worship, some workers legitimized their businesses in the eyes of the state. Contrary to the view of Voodoo practitioners like Betsy Toledano that these practices had been a religion since the nineteenth century, it was the acquisition of both the physical and the ideological space of "church" that moved them into the protected space granted to religions in the United States. Alternative religious practitioners in New Orleans came to understand that claiming to be a religion was not as effective as behaving like one, especially with reference to acquisitions and the material possessions of churches.

Winnifred Fallers Sullivan argues in her book *The Impossibility of Religious Freedom* that it is impossible to have religious freedom in the United States, because in order to exercise that freedom, practices and practitioners must first qualify as religious in the eyes of the state. Those that most easily fit the criteria are those that have a structure, a hierarchy, infrastructures, and an organizational body that identify their religion and what they believe. Sullivan's argument centers on the injustice of requiring the clearly spiritual, that is, religious, practices of individuals to be specifically identified as sanctioned practices of official or recognized churches in order for them to be accorded the status of religion. In other words, when freedom of worship is at issue, the U.S. legal establishment generally turns to sanctioned religious organizations to determine which practices are legitimately religious and which are individual idiosyncrasies. Therefore, in order to be accorded First Amendment protection, religious communities or individuals must first be recognized as members of a legitimate religious organization. However, simply by adopting the outward trappings of the most recognizable legitimized religious institutions in the United States, Spiritual Churches in New Orleans became a religion almost overnight. The creed and practice of these institutions were not as relevant for avoiding legal trouble as their institutionalization.

It is natural to associate dogma and theology with the practice of religion. Out of necessity, religious institutions distinguish themselves from one another by their different creeds and their disparate practices. However, religions are often identified by other markers, such as the institutionalized hierarchies that control them, the buildings out of which they operate, or, in the case of workers, the lack thereof. By adopting the aesthetic, infrastructural, and funding practices of Christian religion, some Voodoo practitioners were able to create for themselves a legal and ideological space in which to operate.

This shift in ideological orientation was largely made possible by the monetization and commercialization of Voodoo in the early twentieth century. It was perhaps always a necessity for workers who provided services to others to profit from their efforts in order to sustain themselves, especially if they wished to subsist off of the work. However, in the early twentieth century, business savvy and the influence of capitalism on American culture (if nothing else, the influence of the failure of capitalism represented by the Great Depression), which made money the first priority in the eyes of so many, along with the introduction of a new, malleable religious model in the form of Spiritual Churches, contributed to workers' creating the requisite air of religion around their practices.[53]

It is important to note that while the Spiritual Churches created a structure that integrated alternative religious practices well, this was not the case with all institutions. After Leafy Anderson was arrested in the Lower Ninth Ward in April 1925, the city's recorder's court required her associate Antonio Vega to pay a fine of ten dollars or serve thirty days in jail. Mr. and Mrs. Vega had applied for and received a permit from the city for a "fish fry" that was subsequently raided by the police when neighbors complained of strange noises coming from the home. Police concluded that they had stumbled on a Voodoo meeting when they raided the home and found "Twenty negroes, the Vegas and several white men," with a large Black woman "raving around." Outside the walls of her church, Anderson and her congregation were as susceptible as her predecessors in the city who had operated as workers out of their homes. Neither her status as a spiritual mother, the church's charter, nor the Vegas' fish-fry permit prevented her arrest.[54] The use of the permit to cover up the meeting suggests that Anderson understood that her practices needed shielding from the law, which were best provided, I argue here, by the walls of a church.

Stashing the Voodoo behind the Drugs

As important as the elements of spiritual and economic power that combined to allow Spiritual Church leaders to acquire the infrastructure that enhanced religious legitimacy was the status of church. There were other businesses and organizations that enjoyed success in connection with workers and their practices, namely, drugstores and pharmacies. By selling Voodoo paraphernalia clandestinely, they were able to bolster their own profits and economic success.

During the 1934 trial of A. Rockford Lewis, authorities identified two registered pharmacists in his employ. Later, when researchers attempted to ascertain Lewis's whereabouts, they got information from Mr. J. C. Coleman, the proprietor of Ideal Drugstore. Both Lewis's employment of registered pharmacists and Mr. Colman's knowledge of Lewis's situation and location suggest a relationship between drugstore owners and practitioners of Voodoo that was more than a relationship between suppliers and clients. It was undoubtedly good for businesses to know and keep tabs on their best customers. What was unique about the relationship between the pharmacists and drugstores that dealt in Voodoo paraphernalia was that they were linked together in a clandestine community. That linkage speaks both to the necessary connections formed between workers and drugstores dealing in Voodoo-related paraphernalia and to drugstores' inability to legitimize their sales of such products. This further suggests that Spiritual Churches' designation as legitimate religious institutions was what helped them escape legal sanction in connection, or perceived connection, with Voodoo practitioners or practices. It was not simply the incorporation of aspects of Voodoo into a legal or legitimate structure that relieved the pressure on practitioners. If it had been, pharmacists operating legitimate drugstores would not have felt the need to hide their sales of Voodoo-related products.

J. C. Coleman's multiple investments in the Voodoo community, along with his apparent knowledge of what was happening to one of the city's most disreputable practitioners, suggest how deeply entangled some of the city's pharmacists and Voodoo practitioners were, undoubtedly owing to the profits to be garnered by both. Coleman did not own the building that housed Ideal Drugstore, but he did pay a substantial rent of $250 per month for the use of a the building, whose value increased from $3,400 in 1936 to $3,600 in 1937.[55] Coleman was also the likely proprietor of the Dixie Sales Agency, a mail-order supplier of Voodoo paraphernalia, as it was operated from his home on Erato Street.[56] Coleman also indicated to interviewers that he had once been employed at the Cracker Jack Drug Store, one of the most well known suppliers of Voodoo paraphernalia in the city. Thus, Coleman was obviously entrenched with this segment of his clientele, working with or operating one Voodoo-related business after another.

Some pharmacists who dealt in Voodoo-related paraphernalia in New Orleans seem to have been ambivalent about their dealings with this segment of their clientele. At one drugstore on Canal Street, in the heart of New Orleans's business district, LWP researchers who inquired about some Voodoo-related paraphernalia listened to the owner vent his frustrations on the matter. He claimed that he sold herbs that he characterized as "voodoo stuff," but he said that he did not think the customers who inquired about such items could discern between the mystical powders and roots. He said that he sold them whatever he had in order to supplement his income until a medicine he had patented to treat corns could become more successful. His objection to selling the Voodoo-related herbs he carried did not seem to stem from a concern about their effectiveness, however. He told interviewers: "Them powder people worry you to death. They pester you day and night, like a bunch of dope fiends. If I can get my Corn Knockers to go like I want it I'm going to give up all that stuff. . . . It takes more than hoodoo to kill corns. It takes good medicine . . . if someone insists that I give them some hoodoo stuff for their corns I will give them some herbs. They work as good as anything else."[57]

Property values suggest that drugstore owners connected to workers and Spiritual Churches enjoyed a great deal of material success. When LWP researchers were planning their Opening with Lala Hopkins, she sent them to Stolzenthaler's Pharmacy for the supplies they would need, suggesting that she had been there before or had some relationship with that establishment.[58] The store's listed owner was a Michael Stolzenthaler, and the building, valued at $8,800, was located in a block in which the property ranged in value from $2,900 to $12,500. Only the Shell filling station, on the opposite corner, was listed as more valuable property, suggesting that pharmacists who dealt in Voodoo may have profited a great deal from their relationship with workers. This was undoubtedly a great motivation for their investment in this kind of merchandise, despite the legal and social stigmas attached to Voodoo.

Most of the pharmacies that catered to this kind of clientele did not do so exclusively. In general, registered pharmacists who carried the Voodoo-related goods in addition to their normal stock did so because of the potential for increased profits. When educating LWP researchers on the varieties and uses of one of the most popular components of many Voodoo formulas, John the Conqueror root, the Voodoo queen Madame Ducoyielle told researchers: "Neber go in a drug store and ask for johnny conqueror root, always ask fo something else furst. De drug store man gits suspicious quick and thinks dat ya is de gove'ment man or sumpin'. Let me introduce you to all of them. C'on go wid me." She then took her would-be apprentice to Guichard's Pharmacy and instructed him to wait outside while she arranged for an introduction. The building that housed the pharmacy was the most valuable on the block, suggesting the profitability of Guichard's business. This incident also suggests, however, that that profitability may have been predicated on his ability to keep his Voodoo-related income hidden. That need in turn suggests that the pharmacies, while having successfully found a way to incorporate Voodoo practitioners into their businesses, were not able to do so in the open for fear of the legal and social stigmas associated with Voodoo.

In addition to being known by workers, the proprietor of Guichard's Pharmacy, like Coleman, apparently maintained connections with workers in the city. When they wanted to interview Voodoo practitioners in the city, Dr. Guichard referred LWP interviewers to Mrs. Mary Washington, a seventy-five-year-old worker who claimed to have trained directly under Marie Laveau. As the abovementioned accounts make clear, these pharmacists often had relationships with local workers who patronized their establishments and kept tabs on those patrons. This was undoubtedly necessary to distinguish between legitimate clients and law enforcement.

The Cracker Jack Drug Store may have been one of the most profitable providers of Voodoo-related paraphernalia in the city. Located in what by the late twentieth century was the central business district, it was apparently successful enough to pay rent or purchase property in a high-rent neighborhood. Values on the block ranged from $4,500 to $15,000, with the building housing the Cracker Jack valued at $9,200, a middling value here but at the higher end for buildings inhabited by alternative religious practitioners in the city and surveyed thus far.[59] The implication is that businesses that did trade in Voodoo-related goods and services were very profitable. It would be presumptuous to assume that dealing in Voodoo paraphernalia was the only reason for the success suggested by the property values of these drugstores. It may be that shrewd druggists saw an open market and that the same business sense that had led them to deal in these products kept their businesses solvent even in the midst of the Depression. That same shrewd business sense told these pharmacists that it was necessary to keep their clients close so as not to have to openly advertise their Voodoo-related products, suggesting that the legitimacy of operating a drugstore, unlike that of operating a church, was not enough to offset the practice of Voodoo.

▼ ▼ ▼

This alternative religious community was a complex and diverse group of individuals tied together by the promise of power suggested by the practice of Voodoo. Not the least of the ways they sought to augment that power was through economic gain. Some of the workers were independent entrepreneurs practicing and operating mail-order businesses out of their homes. Others were established pharmacists grasping at the opportunity suggested by the increased sales to a hungry alternative religious community. Some, called workers, asserted the power of Voodoo. Others, who labeled themselves Spiritual Church leaders, often claimed to be battling against Voodoo, employing rituals similar to those used by workers to do so. The pharmacists who supplied them all often eschewed any knowledge of Voodoo outside of their knowledge of the products they carried. What unified all of these groups was their participation in a group of religious practices, either directly or peripherally, that promised to improve their material circumstances. All were drawn, at least in part, by the promise of economic power and profit.

The relationship between economic and spiritual power drawn by workers demonstrates their awareness of both their own needs and those of their clients. It also suggests an inculcation of the wider American consumer culture that measured value, even spiritual value, in monetary terms. By embracing those values and growing economically, many accumulated the resources necessary to create the structure and infrastructure of "church" around their practices. By adopting the aesthetic of churches, many of these spiritual practitioners altered their relationship to the state. Spiritual Church heads who incorporated aspects of Voodoo were protected in a way that their predecessors who had gathered clandestinely and operated out of their homes had not been. However, this ability to change the form of one's practice most frequently required some investment in infrastructure, which inherently bound the legitimacy represented by tax exemption to economic success. When it could be achieved, though, this shift in the form of practice may have represented an attempt by workers to conform their practices to the wider American cultural norms regarding religious practice, at least as expressed by the laws of the state. Like the inculcation of racial and economic norms, workers here exhibited the dynamism of Voodoo and its interdependence with and contributions to the culture of the rest of New Orleans and the state.

"THE WORST KIND OF RELIGION"

n January 1940 St. Bernard Parish, just outside the city limits of New Orleans, played host to a number of "séances" conducted by practitioners of Voodoo. Practitioners came together to seek retribution against William Stander, a deputy sheriff in the parish. Stander claimed that an African American suspect had physically threatened him, necessitating his use of deadly force in retaliation. Others in the city believed that Stander had wantonly murdered Oscar Smith, a Black dice dealer in a St. Bernard gambling house and a rumored fellow traveler among the city's most notable Voodoo practitioners. Though those rumored to have participated in the St. Bernard ceremonies categorically denied that such rites ever occurred, witnesses and known practitioners of Voodoo in the community reported that the "séances" had called on the power of the Voodoo gods to "run Stander crazy." Shortly thereafter, Stander was found confined in the Hôtel-Dieu, suffering from a mental disorder. Stander eventually recovered enough to be removed from the hospital but never returned to normal health. In January 1941, a year after the rumored St. Bernard séances, Stander died in New Orleans at the age of forty-seven.[1]

Some of New Orleans's most prominent Voodoo personalities and spiritual leaders rumored to support Voodoo practices clandestinely in their churches were among those cited at the ceremonies in St. Bernard. Despite the friction between Voodoo practitioners in the city and Christian religious leaders, many shared a common opinion about the Stander séances. Professor Hall, an admitted practitioner of Voodoo, said of the "voodoo people": "They have taken up where the courts left off. If the white folks ain't goin' to do nothin' the queens sure are. . . . It's a strange case of voodooism. . . . It done struck down a mighty man, a man nobody could touch." The Reverend Sam Jackson, pastor of a local Baptist church, made a similar statement: "It's a tribute to the worst kind of religion, but we don't mind it at all. Let'em fight and run down them evil white folks who is makin' trouble fo' niggers, I say. I wasn't a bit sorry and I'm not a bit sorry. It's mighty fine that we have some of us whose powers is strong enough to do the things them folks downtown is doin', indeed. It's something we need, let'em work, let'em."

The statements by Hall and Jackson are indicative of the promise of power that was at the heart of Voodoo's success in stamping itself on the culture of New Orleans. The ability of workers to strike at an individual out of their reach because of both his position in law enforcement and his racial identity spoke volumes about Voodoo's power to overcome commonplace social divisions and empower the disempowered. The approval of a Baptist minister, despite the obvious conflict Voodoo presented for a Christian religious leader, demonstrates Voodoo's ability to cross even the hardest ideological boundaries to appeal to the city's population. A more subtle indication of intercultural penetration is Jackson's reference to the practitioners as "them folks downtown." Technically, the séances occurred in St. Bernard Parish, outside the New Orleans city limits. But like the followers of Mother Kate who spoke about Catholics downtown (see chapter 3), specifically those at Corpus Christi Catholic Church, and as in the story of Marie Baptiste selling her soul to compete with the girls of the Seventh Ward (chapter 5), Jackson's use of this geographic marker in New Orleans is loaded. It signals his identification of Voodoo with the indigenous Creole or Afro-Creole culture in the city and the importance of an understanding of the local historical and cultural context in New Orleans to comprehending Voodoo. His identity as a Protestant Christian situates him on the American side of a cultural paradigm that juxtaposed Catholic Creoles (downtown) with American Protestants (uptown). Despite this apparent urban-cultural-geographic divide, Jackson's reference to Voodoo as "something we need" suggests a limited acceptance of and camaraderie with the city's practitioners based on shared racial disempowerment.

In addition to suggesting the impact of the culture of Voodoo on other residents of New Orleans, this anecdote also demonstrates how residents impacted Voodoo. By providing for their immediate spiritual, social, and economic needs, Voodoo allowed practitioners to constantly shape and reshape the rites and practice of Voodoo. By using their power against a man protected by the social conventions of law enforcement, racism, and segregation, workers were reading the cultural needs of the disempowered in the city. Consistently responding to these kinds of needs and shaping and reshaping the rites to meet these needs allowed Voodoo practitioners to read and respond to the culture in New Orleans. Thus, Voodoo was constantly impacting and being impacted by the culture of the Crescent City.

In effect, this book is an account of cultural exchange and the dynamism of cultural production viewed through the lens of religious practices. My discussion of the impact of historical New Orleans figures like Marie Laveau and Leafy Anderson on the practice of Voodoo is meant to demonstrate the impact of the city's unique population and their culture on the practice of Voodoo. Further, the discussions of the racial politics of Jim Crow segregation and folklore studies are meant to demonstrate the impact of the wider culture of the American South, and perhaps more broadly U.S. racial culture, on Voodoo. Similarly, the frequently gendered domestic conflicts that informed Voodoo speak to practitioners' ability to meet the complex, specific needs of practitioners and clients. They also speak to the cultural impact of even the most ordinary struggles between individuals by reading the frequently economically and romantically motivated strife of the domestic sphere into the rituals of Voodoo.

This is a story of cultural exchange, and Voodoo's relationship to culture in New Orleans is hardly one-way. Input from the practitioners, who constantly created and re-created Voodoo by altering its rituals, allowed those practitioners to impact the culture of New Orleans. In meeting the economic needs of the population by helping clients find jobs and increase profits during a notoriously lean period in the city's and the country's history, Voodoo undoubtedly broadened its appeal in the city. In response, a community of workers, pharmacists, and Spiritual Church leaders arose to create institutions intimately involved with and arguably dependent on the practice of Voodoo. Their economic successes allowed these individuals to surround their socially and legally suspect spiritual practices with the material infrastructure of legitimacy—lawyers, businesses, and churches. This legitimacy altered the racialized and criminalized perception of the work of late nineteenth- and early twentieth-century workers on the part of the state in general and law enforcement in particular, making it easier for workers and their successors to make a cultural impact on the city of New Orleans. Now, in the early twenty-first century, undoubtedly owing to the space these individuals created in the city's cultural landscape, the French Quarter, the city's cultural and tourist center, is home to Voodoo temples, museums, and cultural centers, in addition to the myriad souvenir shops and secular business that deploy Voodoo's image for profit.

The overwhelming dynamism of this cultural exchange between what is most frequently viewed as a distinct, relatively sectarian spiritual subculture and the larger community in one of America's most important and unique cities demonstrates the fluidity with which cultural productions move across social boundaries. The story of Voodoo in New Orleans is one of culture shared— between Black and white, rich and poor, men and women. By virtue of this exchange, Voodoo's practitioners have made it simultaneously and indistinguishably African American culture, New Orleans culture, and American culture.

To the extent that African Americans share a history and material circumstances, they share a culture. To the extent that they share history and material circumstances with other ethnic or racial communities, Black and white, they are more properly viewed as participating in a broader New Orleanian, southern, or even American culture. I have argued here that in order to understand early twentieth-century Voodoo in New Orleans, it is important to move the discussion away from one of African origins to examine the influence of local Creole culture, Jim Crow segregation in the South, and American racial ideology, all of which mark Voodoo as a product of its historical context. The material circumstances shared across the boundaries of race, gender, and class, characterized by economic privation, materialism, and consumerism, also affected a large portion of New Orleanians, southerners, and Americans more generally. The inculcation of these concerns in the rituals and ideology of Voodoo practitioners attracted a cross section of practitioners, drawn by the promise of overcoming whatever power disparities hindered their lives.

I do not mean to imply here that there is no such thing as African American religion. But Voodoo as practiced in New Orleans in the early twentieth century does not properly belong to that category. Rastafarians, the Nation of Islam, and the Moorish Science Temple were all African American religions in that African American identity was intrinsic to inclusion in these communities. Their theologies make explicit statements about that identity and speak to a history and future that is peculiar to people of African descent, or Black people as defined by those traditions. Voodoo practitioners in New Orleans seem to have made no such claims in the early twentieth century.

Whites participated as clients and professional practitioners. Even the earliest recorded claims to African origins for ritual practice of Voodoo in the nineteenth century were made by a woman, Betsy Toledano, who apparently included whites in her community of practitioners. While American racial ideology was crucial to many rites performed by Voodoo practitioners, the evidence seems to belie racial exclusivity among them. Rather, what united workers and their clients was Voodoo's promise of power. All New Orleanians participated in the creation of Voodoo as cocreators of the city's culture, from the early French Roman Catholics, whose veneration of the saints had such a substantial impact on practitioners of Voodoo; to the slaves who danced in pre–Louisiana Purchase Congo Square; to the white women who not only validated practitioners by attending their rituals and financing their continuation by paying for ritual performances and the paraphernalia used in the production of gris-gris but also became professional practitioners in their own right; to the cemetery officials and sextons who cordoned off the Black sections of cemeteries, inadvertently hiding them from the prying eyes of the majority of white visitors and making them perfect for the practice of "Black magic"; to the white pharmacists who facilitated the perpetuation of Voodoo by acting as suppliers; to the African American workers who claimed that Voodoo gave them the power to affect whites across the color line. These people were not outliers but cocreators of New Orleans Voodoo. Black clients and workers and even their white counterparts created rituals and practices that spoke to and of all these influences in the quest for power—the power to accumulate wealth and control one's own home and one's own life. When we remove the ill-fitted classification of folk culture from Voodoo as practiced in early twentieth-century New Orleans, it becomes apparent that what united practitioners was not gender or race but that pursuit of power.

NOTES

Introduction

1. Gayraud S. Wilmore, *Black Religion and Black Radicalism: An Interpretation of the Religious History of Afro-American People* (Maryknoll, NY: Orbis Books, 1998), p. 5.

2. Ibid.

3. Dain Borges, "Healing Mischief: Witchcraft in Brazilian Law and Literature, 1890–1922," in *Crime and Punishment in Latin America*, edited by Ricardo D. Salvatore, Carlos Aguirre, and Gilbert M. Joseph (Durham, NC: Duke University Press, 2001), p. 190. Borges tells us that in 1930s Brazil one of the strategies for defending religious centers was to argue for the respectability and tradition of "pure African" religions such as Candomblé.

Chapter One

1. Lewis Flannery, "Watch Doorstep For Voodoo," *New Orleans Item*, 23 September 1947.

2. Ibid.

3. Carolyn Morrow Long, *A New Orleans Voudou Priestess: The Legend and Reality of Marie Laveau* (Gainesville: University of Florida Press, 2006).

4. Bennet H. Wall, ed., *Louisiana: A History* (Wheeling IL: Harlan Davidson, 2002), pp. 26, 51–52.

5. Ibid.

6. Stephan Palmié, "Conventionalization, Distortion and Plagiarism in the Historiography of Afro-Caribbean Religion in New Orleans," in *Creoles and Cajuns*, edited by W. Binder (Frankfurt: Peter Lang, 1998), p. 316.

7. Ina J. Fandrich, *The Mysterious Voodoo Queen, Marie Laveaux: A Study of Powerful Female Leadership in Nineteenth Century New Orleans* (New York: Routledge, 2005); Martha Ward, *Voodoo Queen: The Spirited Lives of Marie Laveau* (Jackson: University Press of Mississippi, 2004); Carolyn Morrow Long, *Spiritual Merchants: Religion, Magic and Commerce* (Knoxville: University of Tennessee Press, 2001); C. Long, *New Orleans Voudou Priestess*.

8. See Palmié, "Conventionalization, Distortion and Plagiarism," p. 333. It is important to

note the work of Blake Touchstone and Gwendolyn Midlo Hall as exceptions to many of these critiques.

9. Laura Porteous, "The Gri-Gri Case: A Criminal Trial in Louisiana during the Spanish Regime, 1773," *Louisiana Historical Quarterly* 17 (1934): 48–63, as cited by Carolyn Morrow Long in *Spiritual Merchants*, p. 39.

10. C. Long, *Spiritual Merchants*, p. 42.

11. C. Long, *New Orleans Voudou Priestess*, pp. 102–16.

12. My interpretation here privileges accounts by witnesses who claimed to be practitioners of Voodoo or those who had known Marie Laveau in their youth over those who eschewed participation or personal experience with Voodoo. For accounts of Congo Square as a site of Voodoo practice, see Louisiana Writers' Project (hereafter LWP), Works Progress Administration, Federal Writers' Project, Cammie G. Henry Research Center, Eugene P. Watson Memorial Library, Northwestern State University, Natchitoches, Louisiana, folder 44, p. 81; folder 44 (pt. 2 of 2), pp. 22, 77, 90; folder 587, pp. 10, 27, 37; folder 588, pp. 7, 16, 25; and Robert Tallant Papers, 1938–1957 (hereafter Tallant Papers), Louisiana Division, New Orleans Public Library, reel 6, p. 62, interview with Theresa Kavanaugh; reel 8, p. 616, interview with Joseph Morris; reel 8, p. 668, interview with Raymond Rivares; reel 8, p. 669, interview with James St. Ann; reel 8, p. 709, interview with Marie Brown; reel 8, p. 786, interview with Eugene Fritz. For accounts maintaining the clandestine nature of Voodoo rituals and disputing Congo Square as a site for these practices, see LWP, folders 587, pp. 54–55, and 588, p. 2; and Tallant Papers, reel 8, pp. 313–27, untitled; p. 629, interview with Mrs. Marie Dede; p. 741, interview with Oscar Felix; p. 764, interview with Alexandre Augustin. Documents contained in the LWP folders and in the Tallant Papers often are not paginated. Page numbers given here correspond to the pages in my own digitized collection of the documents.

13. C. Long, *New Orleans Voudou Priestess*, p. 105.

14. Ibid.

15. See Joseph G. Tregle Jr., "Creoles and Americans," in *Creole New Orleans: Race and Americanization*, edited by Arnold Hirsch and Joseph Logsdon (Baton Rouge: Louisiana State University Press, 1992).

16. Interview with Gloria Jones, LWP, folder 587, pp. 7–8.

17. Interview with Joseph Morris, ibid., pp. 9–10.

18. Ibid. It is interesting that while Morris claimed no knowledge of Voodoo, he did mention the use of a snake at the dances and people leaving offerings that included food, liquor, and money in fifteen-cent multiples in a large hollow tree in Congo Square. Such offerings are commonly reported in Voodoo rites, and multiples of fifteen cents added to the cost of services provided by workers are offered to the spirits.

19. Ibid.

20. Interview with Oscar Felix, ibid., pp. 48–49. Laveau is also described as brown skinned in an interview with Camille Harrison, LWP, folder 540, pp. 21–22.

21. See Rodolphe Lucien Desdunes, *Our People and Our History: A Tribute to the Creole People of Color in Memory of the Great Men They Have Given Us and of the Good Works They Have Accomplished*, translated and edited by Sister Dorothea Olga McCants (Baton Rouge: Louisiana State University Press, 1973).

22. Interview with Oscar Felix, LWP, folder 587, pp. 48–50.

23. See ibid.; and interviews with Alberta Jefferson and Mrs. Fortune, ibid., p. 13.

24. Interview with Alberta Jefferson, p. 13.

25. C. Long, *New Orleans Voudou Priestess*, pp. 20–21.

26. Tallant Papers, reel 7, pp. 73–74.

27. *New Orleans Item Tribune*, 5 August 1928, ibid., reel 8, pp. 233–40.

28. *New Orleans Times-Picayune*, 19 November 1922, ibid., pp. 184–91. The use of *below* here probably does not refer to a compass direction, which is notoriously difficult to ascertain in New Orleans due to the city's orientation toward both the Mississippi River and Lake Pontchatrain, but rather to the area north of Canal Street as downtown and the area south of Canal as uptown.

29. "Death of Marie Laveau," *New Orleans Daily Picayune*, 17 April 1881, ibid., p. 17.

30. "Death of the Queen of the Voudous Just Before St. John's Eve." *New Orleans Democrat*, 17 June 1881, ibid., p. 13.

31. Interview with Raymond Rivaros, LWP, folder 587, p. 28. As late as the end of the nineteenth century, local newspapers covered the celebration by believers in Voodoo of a holiday on 23 June called St. John's Eve on the shores of Lake Pontchartrain, which until the twentieth century also marked the edge of the city. The holiday is apparently associated with the Catholic feast day that marks the nativity of Saint John the Baptist, an important figure in Christian theology. A similar ceremony on the eve of this feast day has also been noted by practitioners of Voudou in Haiti.

32. "Where is Marie Buried?—Posey," ibid., pp. 37–38. Another witness said that he had always been told by "old folks" that Laveau could pass for white but chose to associate mostly with Negroes. See also "A Few Facts about Marie Laveau," ibid., folder 588, p. 2, where in a set of notes researchers described Laveau as a majestic figure and asserted that she wore a red tignon as a "badge of her authority." Laveau is described as mulatto in interview with Mrs. Jones, Tallant Papers, reel 8, p. 782, and she is described as fair or light skinned in interview with Mary Douglass, ibid., p. 788, and interview with Mathilda Mendosa, ibid., p. 726.

33. Jerah Johnson, *Congo Square in New Orleans* (New Orleans: Louisiana Landmarks Society, 1995).

34. Interview with Miss Delavigne, LWP, folder 587, pp. 11–12. Another witness recalled a story about Malvina being darker because her father was.

35. Ward, *Voodoo Queen*.

36. Interview with Theresa Kavanaugh, LWP, folder 588, pp. 16–17. See also "Interview on Marie Laveau, 1913 Royal St.," Tallant Papers, reel 8, pp. 795–96, 672–79, 629–39. The story about one of Marie Laveau's daughters passing as white or marrying a white man is recounted with various amounts of detail. Most only recalled that one of her daughters passed for white. One witness claimed that that daughter's name was Loise Legendre, and another said that the white man she married was from New York.

37. Interview with Emile Labat, LWP, folder 588, pp. 19–20.

38. Interview with John Paul Smith, ibid., folder 587, pp. 16–19. Interviewers sometimes, as here, included a parenthetical racial notation when informants were not African Americans, suggesting that the majority of people they sought out for interviews were Black.

39. Ibid., pp. 16–20.

40. C. Long, *Spiritual Merchants*, p. 123. Long notes the existence of a booklet called *The Life and Works of Marie Laveau*, most likely published in the early twentieth century, though her description of the text suggests that it had very little connection to Laveau herself.

41. Interview with Charles Raphael, by Villere and Hazel Breaux, LWP, folder 587, pp. 21–24.

42. Interview with Charles Raphael, ibid., p. 31.

43. Interview with Charles Raphael, by Villere and Breaux, ibid., p. 21. Here I am referring specifically to Raphael's claim to own a '*Tit Albert*, a magic manual commonly mentioned in connection with Voodoo in the 1930s.

44. The Picayune *The Picayune Creole Cookbook* (Dover, 2002), p. 1901. Alternatively known as *estomac mulatre*, "mulatto's stomach," these were gingerbread cakes supposedly common in New Orleans in the early twentieth century. www.gumbopages.com/food/breakfast/estomac -mulatre.html.

45. Interview with Marie Dede, Tallant Papers, reel 8, pp. 629–39.

46. Interviews with Mrs. Mary Washington, ibid., pp. 672–79, and Marie Dede, 629–39. Dede recalled that "they would dance in her [Laveau's] front room and sing just like the spiritualist do today. I believe the spiritualist got that idea from Marie Laveau."

47. Interviews with James St. Ann (Indian), LWP, folder 588, pp. 3–4, and Mrs. Dauphine, ibid., pp. 7–8. Sometimes clients of Laveau won court cases because of her help; at other times she got them out of prison or helped them to avoid jail altogether.

48. "About Marie Laveau," ibid., p. 9.

49. Ibid.; interview with Edward Ashley, Tallant Papers, reel 8, pp. 772–73. Ashley claimed that he too attended Laveau's Friday night meetings.

50. Excerpt from life story of Anita Fonvergne, LWP, folder 587, p. 5.

51. Interview with Raymond Rivaros, ibid., pp. 27–28.

52. Interview with Oscar Felix, ibid., pp. 48–56.

53. Interview with Theresa Kavanaugh, ibid., folder 588, p. 16; interview with Aileen Eugene, Tallant Papers, reel 8, p. 619. Theresa Kavanaugh said that she did not know anything about Laveau's funeral but that people flocked to her grave after her death. Interview with Marie Laveau, ibid., p. 622. One informant related a story about knocking on Laveau's grave and promising her offerings in connection with saying a novena at Our Lady of Guadeloupe, a Catholic church on the edge of the French Quarter.

54. Interview with Sophie Rey, LWP, folder 588, p. 21.

55. Interview with Mary Louise Butler, ibid., p. 12.

56. C. Long, *New Orleans Voudou Priestess*. Long questions the historicity of many of these accounts, maintaining that historical records demonstrate the modesty of Laveau's property holdings.

57. Interview with Marie Brown, LWP, folder 588, p. 26. Brown suggested that racial proscriptions that excluded African Americans from the infamous quadroon balls, where white men met their mixed-race partners, may have offered Laveau a unique opportunity. On the quadroon balls, see Monique Guillory, "Some Enchanted Evening on the Auction Block: The Cultural Legacy of the New Orleans Quadroon Balls" (PhD diss., New York University, 1999).

58. Interview with Oscar Felix, LWP, folder 587, p. 55.

59. Interviews with Mrs. Dauphine, ibid., folder 588, p. 7; Raymond Rivaros, ibid., folder 587, pp. 27–29; Louis Laveaux, ibid., pp. 43–45; and Miss Dede, ibid., folder 539, pp. 1–3. For instances of twentieth-century workers emulating Laveau's supposed dedication to helping the poor, see LWP researchers' comments on donating items from their initiation ceremony to the poor in Robert McKinney, "A Description of a Hoodoo Opening Ceremony," ibid., folder 44, p. 46.

60. Interviews with Joseph Morris, LWP, folder 587, p. 10; Raymond Rivaros, ibid., p. 29; and Theresa Kavanaugh, ibid., folder 588, p. 16. An exception was Sophie Rey, who believed that Laveau's husband was a Black chief of police. Interview with Sophie Rey, ibid., p. 22.

Chapter Two

1. Claude F. Jacobs and Andrew J. Kaslow, *The Spiritual Churches of New Orleans: Origins, Beliefs, and Rituals of an African American Religion* (Knoxville: University of Tennessee Press, 2001), pp. 33–34.

2. Interviews with Mary Johnson, LWP, folder 44 (pt. 2 of 2), pp. 79–84, and Catherine Dillon, insert on Mother Anderson, ibid., folder 91 (folder 1 of 3, pt. 2 of 2), p. 22. The context suggests that *some* here is part of a colloquialism that means "very" or "really."

3. Catherine Dillon, "Voodoo" (unpublished manuscript), ibid., folder 118, sec. D, p. 13.

4. Ibid., p. 30.

5. C. Long, *Spiritual Merchants*, p. 131.

6. Zora Neale Hurston, "Hoodoo in America," *Journal of American Folklore* 44, no. 174 (October–December 1931): 319–20.

7. Interview with Mary Johnson, LWP, folder 44 (pt. 2 of 2), pp. 79–81.

8. Hurston, "Hoodoo in America," 319.

9. "Italian Homestead Ass'n, Legendre Building, 12/10/37," in LWP, folder 591, p. 51. The agent actually refers to Price as Alberta Bennett. Alberta was married for some time to a man named Samuel Bennett, which is probably the reason for the different family name. She filed to be declared administratrix of Anderson's estate only four days after her death. A later document asserts that Price's contention that she was Anderson's niece was false. "Succession note 12/16/27," ibid., pp. 63–64. See also "Petition by Alberta Price" ibid., p. 58; "Succession of Mrs. Leafy Williams Anderson," ibid., p. 59; interview with Mother Keller, ibid., p. 82; and interview with Ophelia Bennett, ibid., pp. 86–88.

10. "Father Thomas on Black Hawk," ibid., pp. 135–39.

11. Ibid.

12. Hurston, "Hoodoo in America," pp. 319–20.

13. Interviews with Pauline Smith, LWP, folder 591, p. 85, and Ms. Alice, ibid., pp. 117–18.

14. Catherine Dillon manuscript, ibid., folder 91, p. 47. The Eternal Life Christian Spiritual Church appeared in 1934 at 2308 S. Liberty Street, with "Elias (Eli) Williams" listed as pastor.

15. "Insert, description of Eli (Elias) Williams," ibid., p. 49.

16. Charter for Mother Anderson's church, ibid., folder 591, p. 3.

17. Ibid.

18. "Death Notice: Anderson," *New Orleans Times Picayune*, 13 December 1927, LWP, folder 591, p. 62.

19. Mother Leafy Anderson, 15 December 1927, ibid., p. 62; interview with Dora Tyson, ibid., p. 89; Daniel Wendling Papers, ibid., pp. 46–49.

20. Interview with Dora Tyson, ibid., p. 89.

21. Interview with Mary Johnson, ibid., folder 44 (pt. 2 of 2).

22. Catherine Dillon manuscript, ibid., folder 91, pp. 46–47.

23. Alberta B[ennett], list of Anderson property, ibid., folder 591, pp. 56–57.

24. See LWP, folder 591, p. 72.

25. "Eternal Life Spiritualist Church," *Louisiana Weekly*, 19 April 1930, ibid., folder 91, p. 48.

26. Arrest record on Mother Anderson, ibid., folder 591, pp. 9–10.

27. Interview with Captain Williams, of the Detective Bureau, ibid., p. 128.

28. Interviews with Daniel Wendling, ibid., pp. 46–47, and Father Thomas, by Robert McKinney, ibid., p. 99; follow-up calls to police, ibid., p. 120; interview with Captain Williams, of the Detective Bureau, ibid., pp. 128, 130, and folder 91, p. 43. Father Thomas also confirmed that Anderson had a prominent lawyer. There is no record, however, of a Louisiana state senator or a state representative from Orleans Parish named Stafford.

29. It is possible that members of Anderson's Spiritual Church movement may have borrowed the term *worker* from Voodoo practitioners.

30. Father Thomas, interview by McKinney, LWP, folder 591, p. 101.

31. Interview with Ms. Alice, ibid., p. 117.

32. Interview with Dora Tyson, ibid., pp. 91–92.

33. Ibid.

34. Interview with Ms. Alice, ibid., p. 117.

35. Interview with Dora Tyson, ibid., pp. 91–92.

36. Father Thomas, interview by McKinney, ibid., p. 101.

37. Interview with Dora Tyson, ibid., p. 93; Catherine Dillon, "Mother Anderson" (unpublished manuscript), ibid., folder 91, p. 23. Dillon believed that Black Hawk was based on a Native American leader known for his resistance to American military forces in Illinois, Wisconsin, and Iowa and that the images used in New Orleans churches had been imported from the Chicago area. If this is the case, his exclusivity to Louisiana in the Spiritual Church is ironic. Perhaps it was designed to avoid any of the anti-American sentiments that might be implied by venerating him in an area where his history was well known. For a brief history of Black Hawk, see www.wisconsinhistory.org/dictionary/index.asp?action=view&term_id=2030&keyword=black+hawk.

38. Interview with Corrine Williams, LWP, folder 591, p. 133.

39. "Saint Black Hawk . . . Indian Worshipped by Spiritualists," ibid., pp. 140–43. Mother Dora may be the only Spiritual Church mother to mention this dog.

40. Ibid.

41. Ibid. Dora also said that Anderson was visited by a spirit called White Eagle, who was not useful in the South because Anderson had already given Black Hawk reign over this territory.

42. Interview with Mother L. C. Crosier, ibid., pp. 73–76. On Anderson's tumultuous relationships with students, see "Father Thomas on Black Hawk," ibid., p. 135, as well as interviews

with Dora Tyson, ibid., p. 89; Father Thomas, by McKinney, ibid., pp. 98, 101–6; and James Cook, ibid., p. 125.

43. *Louisiana Weekly*, 5 December 1936, ibid., pp. 95–97; "Funeral of Mother Leafy Anderson," ibid., p. 111; interview with James Cook, ibid., pp. 125–26. The closeness of the Anderson model to other Christian denominations is demonstrated by associations with them in both life and death. LWP researchers interviewed a Baptist preacher who admitted to being an associate of Anderson's, and participants at her funeral noted the presence of Christian ministers, who onlookers believed were present to attract members of Anderson's congregation into their own churches. In addition, many of the Spiritual Churches in New Orleans became part of an interstate federation called the Spiritual Churches of the Southwest, which seemingly standardized—or some might say stagnated—the practices and doctrine of the Spiritual Churches into a form closely resembling other Protestant Christian denominations.

44. Catherine Dillon notes, ibid., folder 91, p. 38; charter for Mother Anderson's church, ibid., folder 591, pp. 40, 44; "Insert, description of Eli (Elias) Williams," ibid., p. 49. Co-workers reported working as washers, cooks, servants, and so on.

45. Interview with Dora Tyson, ibid., folder 591, pp. 89–90. This is also reminiscent of the statements about Marie Laveau and her group leaving offerings for the poor in Congo Square and Laveau providing assistance to those in economic need.

46. Arrest record on Mother Anderson, ibid., p. 10; "Funeral of Mother Leafy Anderson," ibid., 109–11; interview with Ms. Alice, ibid., p. 114; interview with James Cook, ibid., pp. 122, 124.

Chapter Three

1. "Voodoo in St. Roch Cemetery," Tallant Papers, reel 8, pp. 359–60.

2. Ibid.

3. Ibid.

4. Newbell Niles Puckett, *Folk Beliefs of the Southern Negro* (New York: Negro Universities Press, 1926), p. 178.

5. Ibid., p. 167.

6. Yvonne P. Chireau, *Black Magic: Religion and the African American Conjuring Tradition* (Berkeley: University of California Press, 2003), p. 15. Chireau contends that the most "salient functional value for blacks had to do with . . . racial opposition," specifically in conflicts with owners during the antebellum period.

7. Puckett, *Folk Beliefs of the Southern Negro*, p. 168.

8. Ibid., p. 196.

9. Ibid., pp. 239, 244, 256, 265.

10. Ibid., p. 310.

11. Ibid., pp. 192, 206.

12. Ibid., pp. 190–92, 206–7, 214, 275.

13. Tallant Papers, reel 6, pp. 12–14, 17, 18.

14. Hurston, "Hoodoo in America," p. 318.

15. Ibid., pp. 318–19.

16. Chireau, *Black Magic*, p. 123. Some earlier scholars writing in a period characterized by racial segregation may have bought into this perception. The writings of later scholars like Chireau may simply have been too narrowly construed. Chireau notes the importance of context to the practice of conjure throughout the United States, especially as Blacks moved to urban milieus. It is easy to read discussion of conjure among diverse African American communities as contributing to this idea of conjure, similar to but not synonymous with New Orleans Voodoo, as a kind of racial knowledge. Chireau suggests, however, that the similarities in conjure traditions in distinct African American communities resulted from shared histories of slavery, oppression, and African cultural antecedents.

17. Rosemary Levy Zumwalt, *American Folklore Scholarship: A Dialogue of Dissent* (Bloomington: Indiana University Press, 1988), pp. 5–7, 14.

18. Ibid., p. 21.

19. Ibid., p. 100.

20. Ibid., pp. 131–32, quoting Richard M. Dorson's *American Folklore* (1977).

21. Norman R. Yetman, "An Introduction to the WPA Slave Narratives," memory.loc.gov /ammem/snhtml/.

22. Harry Middleton Hyatt, *Hoodoo—Conjuration—Witchcraft—Rootwork,* Memoirs of the Alma Egan Hyatt Foundation, 5 vols. (Hannibal, MO: Western, 1970), 1:ii, xvi (hereafter *Hoodoo*).

23. Ibid., 3:xiv.

24. Ibid., 1:xxix.

25. Chireau, *Black Magic*, p. 7.

26. Ibid., p. 19.

27. Ibid., pp. 25, 33, 53.

28. Jeffrey E. Anderson, *Conjure in African American Society* (Baton Rouge: Louisiana State University Press, 2007), pp. 51, 74.

29. Ibid., p. 4. Even in his discussion of the co-opting of conjure by southern whites in order to distinguish the southern culture from its northern counterpart in the face of the homogenizing effects of corporatism, national advertising, and consumerism, he describes its use by whites, along with other folk beliefs, to accentuate the distinctiveness of southern identity by juxtaposing images of the "aristocratic planters and their happy but dependent 'servants,'" thereby perpetuating the view of whites as outsiders in the practice of Voodoo and limiting any discussion of actual interracial participation.

30. Ibid., pp. 76–78. Anderson writes, "Surprisingly, a number of Hyatt's information argued that whites were also strong believers in hoodoo" (78).

31. Hyatt, *Hoodoo*, 2:1409, 1459, 1669, 1676.

32. Palmié, "Conventionalization, Distortion and Plagiarism," pp. 315–44.

33. *New Orleans Item*, 4 October 1908, Tallant Papers, reel 8.

34. *Sunday Item-Tribune*, 30 October 1929, Metropolitan Section. See also "Negro Superstitions and Folk-Thoughts Traced to White Men," *New Orleans Item*, 12 November 1926. In this latter interview, with Newbell Niles Puckett on his research in New Orleans, Puckett claims that

"Negro race pride is forcing many more or less illiterate negroes to give up, or at least to subdue and refuse to pass on, the old beliefs for fear of ridicule from the more developed members of their race."

35. Interview, by Hazel Breaux and Robert McKinney, and interview with Gloria Jones, by McKinney, Tallant Papers, reel 8, pp. 643–45 and 734–35.

36. *New Orleans States,* 31 October 1913; *New Orleans Times-Democrat,* 30 September 1913; and *New Orleans Item,* 1913, Tallant Papers, reel 8, pp. 111, 113, and 114–15.

37. *New Orleans Item,* 13 April 1924, ibid., pp. 197–99. The author writes: "In New Orleans the voodoo men still do a considerable business in charms. Their houses are in all the Negro sections, but their names are never whispered loudly enough for a white man to hear" (199).

38. Ibid., 13 February 1928, ibid., p. 232.

39. Hurston, "Hoodoo in America," p. 380.

40. Hyatt, *Hoodoo,* 1:800.

41. Ibid., 1:801.

42. Ibid., 1:801, 884–85, 1905.

43. Ibid., 1:801, 1902.

44. Ibid., 1:1352.

45. Ibid., 1:1300.

46. Ibid., 1:1301–2.

47. "The Jeff Horn Spiritual Catholic Church," Tallant Papers, reel 8, pp. 560–66.

48. "Voodooism Still Thrives in New Orleans," *New Orleans Item-Tribune,* 22 April 1928, magazine section, 5, and *New Orleans Times,* 28 June 1872, Tallant Papers, reel 8, pp. 248–55 and 4–5.

49. Hyatt, *Hoodoo,* 2:1781–90, 1909.

50. Tallant Papers, reel 7, p. 203.

51. Hyatt, *Hoodoo,* 2:768.

52. *New Orleans Times-Picayune,* 14 May 1927, Tallant Papers, reel 8, p. 224.

53. *New Orleans Morning Tribune,* 14 May 1927, ibid., p. 223.

54. "The Ideal Drug Store," ibid., reel 7, p. 261.

55. Hyatt, *Hoodoo,* 1:777–78. Either "Madam Helen" was a common moniker among female workers or Helen was very well known, and it is unclear whether this Madam Helen and the previously mentioned worker by the same name are in fact the same woman.

56. Ibid.; "Mrs. Johnson, the Fortune Teller of Batture," by Hazel Breaux and Cecil Wright, Tallant Papers, reel 7, pp. 365–71. Mrs. Johnson kept separate waiting rooms for whites and Blacks. Her physical description does not include a racial designation, though because she was interviewed by Breaux and Wright, both presumably white, we might assume that this woman was white as well.

57. "Rev. Alice Mancuso, (WHITE)," ibid., reel 9, pp. 339–40.

58. "The Daniel Helping Hand Spiritual Church," ibid., reel 8, pp. 493–95.

59. "Phases of Mediumship," ibid., reel 9, pp. 264–67.

60. "Sacred Heart Spiritualist Church," ibid., reel 8, pp. 513–14.

61. "Emperor Haile Selassi Nu-Way Ethiopia Mystic Light Baptist and Spiritual and Kingdom Church," ibid., pp. 580–85.

62. "Popular Gris-Gris Among present Day Hoodoo Queens," ibid., pp. 338–48.

63. Hyatt, *Hoodoo*, 2:1681–82.

64. For examples, see ibid., 2:1408, 1684, 1768, and 3:1907, as well as Tallant Papers, reel 6, p. 36.

65. Tallant Papers, reel 9, p. 295.

66. Ibid., p. 244.

67. "Mother Catherine's Funeral," ibid., p. 224.

68. Tallant Papers, reel 9, p. 293.

69. "Mother Rita—Successor to Mother Catherine," ibid., pp. 237–41.

70. Hurston, "Hoodoo in America," p. 396.

71. Ibid., pp. 408–10, quotations on 408 and 409.

72. Ibid., p. 410.

73. Ibid., pp. 408–10, quotation on 409.

74. "Orleans 'Voodoo Doctor Fails to Fix,' Is Jailed," *Louisiana Weekly*, 9 February 1929, Tallant Papers, reel 8, p. 256.

75. Interview, 15 August 1940, ibid., reel 8; "Dr. James Alexander—Indian Jim," ibid., pp. 381–82 (where it is reported that Jim had a white wife and that white women were arrested at his home); "The Vodou Superstitions," *New Orleans Daily Picayune*, 1 March 1891; "The Voudou Party," ibid., 30 May 1889. Articles describing the raid on Dr. Jim Alexander's Voodoo dance in 1889 all mention that thirteen of the women in attendance were white, two of whom were only seventeen years old. "The Voodoo Doctor," ibid., 20 August 1890.

76. "Last of the Voodoos," *Harper's Weekly*, Tallant Papers, reel 7, pp. 182–87.

77. "Lafcadio Hearn: Consort of a Negress," *Daily News*, 6 August 1906, ibid., reel 8, pp. 67–69.

78. Ibid.

79. Tallant Papers, reel 6, pp. 58–61.

80. Ibid., reel 8, pp. 567–68, 66–67.

81. Ibid., reel 7, p. 278.

82. "When the Thunder is Over Mother Kate Francis Will March Right Through Hebbin's Doors," ibid., reel 9, pp. 178–89.

83. "Mother Kate Francis Has Returned Already," ibid., p. 190. Mother Kate's followers undoubtedly targeted Corpus Christi because of the importance of Catholicism to the culture of New Orleans's Afro-Creole community.

84. Hurston, "Hoodoo in America," pp. 357, 362, 368, 380, 387, 390.

85. Hirsch and Logsdon, *Creole New Orleans*, pp. 190–91.

86. Ibid., p. 265.

87. Arthe Agnes Anthony, "The Negro Creole Community in New Orleans, 1880–1920: An Oral History" (PhD diss., University of California, Irvine, 1978), pp. 34, 46, 47, 93, 108, 139, speaks to the continuity of color as an issue in intraracial relations of the Black community and concentration of the African American population that identifies as Creole in the Fourth, Fifth, Sixth, and Seventh Wards north of Canal Street. For association between Creoles and the Seventh Ward, see p. 143. The *New Orleans Item-Tribune* of 5 August 1928 situates Marie Laveau's house in

the "quadroon quarter" of the city and specifies that it was the residents below Canal Street who held her in dread even after her death.

88. "Death of the Queen of the Voudous Just Before St. John's Eve," *New Orleans Democrat*, 17 June 1881, Tallant Papers, reel 8, p. 188.

89. Ibid.

90. Hilda Phelps Hammond, "Behind the Veil of Voodooism in America," *New Orleans Times-Picayune*, 5 October 1930, Tallant Papers, reel 8, pp. 260–66.

91. Ibid.

92. *New Orleans Item*, 21 January 1927, Tallant Papers, p. 220; *New Orleans Item-Tribune*, 8 February 1925, ibid., pp. 204–10.

93. "Voudous—Superstition Which is Passing," *New Orleans American*, 7 November 1915, ibid., reel 8, pp. 140–48.

94. Hyatt, *Hoodoo*, 2:1282.

95. Tallant Papers, reel 8, pp. 805–7.

96. J. Anderson, *Conjure in African American Society*, pp. 2–5. Anderson notes that even Americans in the post–Civil War South who sought to separate themselves from African Americans via Jim Crow simultaneously defined their identity as southerners in part by referencing African American folk traditions like conjure. Similarly, scholars in whiteness studies have long contended that whiteness is defined in reference to Blackness.

Chapter Four

1. "Mind Reader," in Hyatt, *Hoodoo*, 2:1822.

2. "Nahnee—Boss of Algiers," ibid., 2:1360–61. Another of Nahnee's rites, for a woman who wanted to "rule" a man, involved extracting dirt from the left foot, using the left hand, and from under fingernails of that hand, and feeding it to a man consistently in his food and coffee. Nahnee also had a similar ritual that required a man to wash with a towel first used by the woman who wanted to control him, and still another that required the woman to tie a cloth around her waist.

3. "Madam Lindsey," ibid., 2:1502–3. Madam Lindsey also performed a rite to make a person agreeable and to decrease the likelihood of "fussin'" or fighting by burning a cream-colored candle and sandalwood before a picture of Saint Jude while reciting the prayer purchased with the picture, presumably from a store that specialized in Catholic ritual supplies.

4. See www.catholic.org/saints/stindex.php?lst=R.

5. Hyatt, *Hoodoo*, 1:884–87.

6. Ibid. While the woman said that she had begun to attend church daily and that she had converted to Catholicism following this incident, she also said that she had not been baptized nor confirmed as a Catholic. Thus, through rituals making use of candles in colors based on the intended purpose of the rite and calling of a Catholic saint that fell somewhere between Voodoo and a kind of folk Catholicism, she had come to view herself as a member of the church. For another worker who used Saint Rita to return husbands, see "House Parties in New Orleans and Algiers During the Great Depression," ibid., 5:2124–25.

7. Hagiography is an idolizing or idealizing biography. In Christian context specifically, hagiographies recounted saints' lives and especially their miracles, frequently explaining how or why they had become patrons of particular causes for members of the church.

8. "Boy-Girl or Girl-Boy," ibid., 2:1681.

9. Hyatt, *Hoodoo*, 1:874.

10. Ibid., 1:880.

11. Ibid.; "Mind Reader," ibid., 2:1819. The worker called Mind Reader believed that Rita was a saint dedicated to children and claimed that she was one of the youngest saints in heaven.

12. Hyatt, *Hoodoo*, 1:884.

13. "Boy-Girl or Girl-Boy," ibid., 2:1680–81. Boy-Girl said that Saint Rita had had a miraculous head injury of some kind that changed into a star after her death.

14. "A Woman Named Ida," ibid., 2:1654.

15. Hyatt, *Hoodoo*, 1:880–87; "Rosa a Hoodoo Woman," ibid., 3:2077. Much as some workers extrapolated Saint Rita's benefit from her story, others extrapolated her story from her paintings and statuary. Rosa, a worker from New Orleans, believed that the injury depicted on St. Rita's head had been inflicted by her abusive, drunken husband, whose cruelty she said had turned Rita against men and "all boy babies."

16. "Beer for St. Peter—Cigar and Whiskey for St. Anthony," ibid., 2:1229.

17. Hyatt, *Hoodoo*, 1:881.

18. "'Doctor' Caffrey," ibid., 2:1463.

19. Interview with Lala Hopkins by Breaux and McKinney, Tallant Papers, reel 8, p. 350.

20. Interview with Lala Hopkins on Marie Comtesse, ibid., p. 805. The statement reads: "He didn't do no work but Ah nebber seen him much. Yeah, he worked wid her sometimes." I take this to mean that Louis did not have a day job but worked with his wife, though the phrasing is awkward and confusing.

21. "When the Thunder is Over Mother Kate Francis Will March Right Through Hebbin's Doors," ibid., reel 9, p. 178.

22. Ibid.

23. Ibid.

24. "Barefooted and Gold Crowned Mother Kate Lies in State," November 1939, ibid., reel 7, p. 235.

25. Ibid.

26. "When the Thunder is Over Mother Kate Francis Will March Right Through Hebbin's Doors," ibid., reel 9, p. 182.

27. Ibid.

28. "Mother Kate Francis has Returned Already—Co-workers Agree," ibid., p. 194. Mother Bowers maintained that Father Daniel had purchased a brand-new Chevrolet just a few months after opening his church.

29. "Rev. Alice Mancuso (WHITE)," ibid., p. 339.

30. "Dey Tried to Run Me Outa Louisiana," in Hyatt, *Hoodoo*, 2:1584. Rites resembling the traditional love potion were employed by workers on occasion. For example, a professional from Memphis who claimed to have spent time in Louisiana had a rite whose effects resembled those

of a traditional love potion, in other words, a formula that could attract men in general rather than a specific man. She prescribed salt and sugar placed in a small bag with olive oil for a client to "Bathe down wit" to attract numerous men. A number of rites only required the worker or client to know the subject in passing, if at all, so that they might also be construed as functioning like love potions.

31. "Nahnee—Boss of Algiers," ibid., 2:1355–57.

32. Ibid., 2:1363. Among these was a rite that required a female client wishing to attract a man to use three different perfumes, love powder, and the bow from a man's hat. The use of a man's hat bow to manipulate him in any number of ways was one of the gender-specific formula components common among workers in the early twentieth century. For a similar rite, see "A Woman and Her Three Saints," ibid., 2:1403; for a rite to keep someone dreaming of you by pinning their photograph under your bed, see ibid.; for a rite using a woman's hair and hawthorne perfume, see "Dey Tried to Run Me Outa Louisiana," ibid., 2:1585; for a rite to draw a man's mind by wearing his underclothes, see "A Woman and Her Three Saints," ibid., 2:1404; and for a rite to get a woman to follow one using a hand made of blue linen, blue apparently representing true love, and containing a woman's hair, all in a red flannel bag, see "Candle Diviner of New Orleans," ibid., 3:1970.

33. "Private Shrine of a Young Girl," ibid., 3:2226.

34. "Gifted Medium," ibid., 2:965.

35. "Undercover Man," ibid., 2:1672; "Dey Tried to Run Me Outa Louisiana," ibid., 2:1579.

36. "Mind Reader," ibid., 2:1823. The Mind Reader also had a rite to hold a mate in which the client wore the bow from the hat of the man next to her skin on the left side of her body. A seventeen-year-old girl used a rite in which she ground underarm and pubic hair into the man's coffee beans and then dripped and sweetened it to keep him attached to a client. She also had a rite to make a man love a woman in which she cooked him a steak with some of the woman's pubic hair. "Private Shrine of a Young Girl," ibid., 3:2223.

37. "Gifted Medium," ibid., 2:958.

38. "Dark Glasses—Dark Lady—Dark Deeds," ibid., 2:1060–61.

39. "Custodian of a Shrine" ibid., 2:1139; "Madam Lindsey," ibid., 2:1507; "Dey Tried to Run Me Outa Louisiana," ibid., 2:1579 (burying socks in a Vaseline jar fed with urine under the stairs to keep a man); "Mind Reader," ibid., 2:1823 (burying a sock under the stairs with nine pins and needles to keep a mate around); "Private Shrine of Young Girl," ibid., 3:2226 (burying socks or underwear dressed with the subject's hair to attract the subject or keep him or her from thinking of anyone else).

40. "Nahnee—Boss of Algiers," ibid., 2:1357, 1360, 1362–64; "Algiers Atmosphere About Her," ibid., 3:1905, 1912 (burying a bottle containing the subject's urine or taking the subject's waist and leg measurements by making knots in a cloth and burying that in a can under the stairs to keep the subject from leaving; Hyatt supposed that only lower-body measurements were taken, since a similar rite using the length of the body would kill the subject); "Candle Diviner of New Orleans," ibid., 3:1969–70 (burying dirt from a foot track under a door to keep someone close); "This Skeleton Was Not . . . ," ibid., 5:2277 (using a crucifix and the client's name to cross himself in order to stop the subject from returning to a former home).

41. "Black Cat Lucky Bone Maker Advises Author," ibid., 3:2263–64.

42. Ibid., p. 2264.

43. "Undercover Man," ibid., 2:1672.

44. "How to Use Johnny Conqueror Root," Tallant Papers, reel 8, pp. 298–300.

45. Ibid.

46. In "Nahnee—Boss of Algiers," in Hyatt, Hoodoo, 2:1404–5, Nahnee describes a rite that allowed her to control the mood of a subject by manipulating the subject's handwriting in a letter they had written with either vinegar or sugar. While the pronouns she uses specify a female client working on a male subject, the formula may not have been gender specific. For a rite for inducing general attention or obedience, see "The Doctor Walks Backwards," ibid., 3:2146–47.

47. "Candle Diviner of New Orleans," ibid., 3:1971 (keeping a man who has become attracted to another woman and is about to leave).

48. "Dark Glasses—Dark Lady—Dark Deeds," ibid., 2:1065. This worker also offered a rite that would keep either a man or woman at home using socks or stockings. Ibid., p. 1069. For a rite with an apple as the main ingredient that not only brings a man back to a woman but controls his anger, see "Candle Diviner of New Orleans," ibid., 3:1982; and for a rite that brings a man home and stops him from thinking of others, see "House Parties in New Orleans During the Great Depression," ibid., 3:2125.

49. "Custodian of a Shrine," ibid., 2:1156.

50. See "Beer for St. Peter—Cigar and Whiskey for St. Anthony," ibid., 2:1231–32 (sprinkling brown sugar clandestinely in a spouse's comb). For keeping a man agreeable, see "This Skeleton Was Not . . . ," ibid., 5:2275.

51. "First Informant in New Orleans," ibid., 2:1631, 1635. For a rite that specifically stops a woman from suing for divorce, which involved a man's wearing his underclothes inside out and creating a hand out of certain boiled herbs, see "Havana Man," ibid., 2:1781. For a similar rite prescribed for use by a woman on a man, requiring a woman to walk the burned remnants of a man's shoe sole through his house, throw the sole over his house, and bury it under his stairs, see "This Skeleton Was Not . . . ," ibid., vol. 5. See also "Ah Don' Talk Plain," ibid., 3:2118, for a rite to make someone "crazy" or keep a man or woman "under your feet," depending on whether socks or stockings are employed. The same informant had a red-bean rite that would keep "someone" out of the house for six days.

52. "Mildred Fortune Interview," Tallant Papers, reel 9, pp. 155–59.

53. "Beer for St. Peter—Cigar and Whiskey for St. Anthony," in Hyatt, Hoodoo, 2:1224. Rites that stop at keeping a man, specifically a husband, at home are relatively common. See also "Man to the Manner Born," ibid., 2:1765, for a rite using dirt from the bottom of a man's feet, a dirty sock, and the last of his used bathwater sprinkled outside the client's door to accomplish something similar.

54. "Nahnee—Boss of Algiers," ibid., 2:1372. This formula was almost always given to a woman for use on a man, and similar formulas to stop men from drinking were relatively common. See also "Mind Reader," ibid., 2:1827; "Candle Diviner of New Orleans," ibid., 3:2076; "House Parties in New Orleans During the Great Depression," ibid., 3:2128; and "This Skeleton Was Not . . . ," ibid., 5:2274.

55. "Madam Lindsey," ibid., 2:1504–5. A much simpler version of this rite merely requires

that the woman put a quarter the man has given her into a handkerchief and wear it in her shoe. See "Dey Tried to Run Me Outa Louisiana," ibid., 2:1579.

56. "House Parties in New Orleans and Algiers During the Great Depression," ibid., 3:2121–22.

57. Ibid., 3:2124.

58. "Dey Tried to Run Me Outa Louisiana," ibid., 2:1579. See also "Havana Man," ibid., 2:1788, for a more generalized rite prescribed for a woman who wanted to get money or any favor from a man: boiling and wearing a red onion and several other ingredients. A Memphis worker, interviewed in Tennessee but formerly operating in New Orleans, also had a number of rites for getting a man to give money to a woman. Among them was a formula that required a woman to use a needle to write what she wanted on red candles, which the informant indicated were used for luck and to make someone love you. The client would burn the candles beginning late the night before or early in the morning of the man's payday.

59. "A Woman Named Ida," ibid., 2:1664–65.

60. "Private Shrine of Young Girl," ibid., 3:2224.

61. "Black Cat Lucky Bone Maker Advises Author," ibid., 3:2261.

62. Ibid., 3:2262.

63. "Custodian of a Shrine," ibid., 2:1151–52. Nahnee had a similar rite that required the client to put the sleeping man's left hand into a pan of water or wrap it in a towel moistened with a combination of water and the woman's urine. See "Nahnee—the Boss of Algiers," ibid., 2:1404. In contrast, Madam Lindsey used a rite in which the client put the man's shoes under his bed to keep him asleep and put his hand into a basin of water while he slept to get him to answer questions without waking him. See "Madam Lindsey," ibid., 2:1508. The Havana Man used a sleep rite that required the woman to boil her man's underwear and sprinkle and rub the water used for boiling on him. See "Havana Man," ibid., 2:1783–84. See also "Mind Reader," ibid., 2:1824; and "Candle Diviner of New Orleans," ibid., 3:1970.

64. "Rosa a Hoodoo Woman," ibid., 3:2070.

65. "Emperor Haile Selassi Nu-Way Mystic Light Baptist and Spiritual and Kingdom Church," Tallant Papers, reel 9, pp. 128–32.

66. "Cuffie Cuffs Carrie Cash," *New Orleans Item*, 22 March 1938, ibid., reel 8, p. 290.

67. "Rosa a Hoodoo Woman," in Hyatt, *Hoodoo*, 3:2079–80.

68. "Madam O. Lindsey," ibid., 2:1632–33.

69. Ibid., 2:1635; "Dat's Accordin' Tuh Science: Science is Great," ibid., 3:2305. This rite stops a woman from having intercourse with another man by applying her discharge to a handkerchief washed in a mixture of the man's urine and water and kept in a vial or container.

70. "Man to the Manner Born," ibid., 2:1765.

71. "Beer for St. Peter—Cigar and Whiskey for St. Anthony," ibid., 2:1234.

72. "A Woman Named Ida," ibid., 2:1658. For a similar rite using slightly different materials, see "Rosa a Hoodoo Woman," ibid., 3:2074.

73. "Undercover Man," ibid., 2:1670.

74. Ibid.; "Mind Reader," ibid., 2:1827. For a similar rite using underwear and graveyard dirt, see "Candle Diviner of New Orleans," ibid., 3:1976.

75. "The 'Unkus' Man," ibid., 2:1302.

76. "Man to the Manner Born," ibid., 2:1771.

77. Leslie J. Reagan, *When Abortion Was a Crime: Women, Medicine, and Law in the United States, 1867–1973* (Berkeley: University of California Press, 1998), pp. 7–8.

78. "This Skeleton Was Not . . . ," in Hyatt, *Hoodoo*, 5:2276.

79. "Information Furnished by Mrs. Robertson," Tallant Papers, reel 7, p. 29.

80. "Dark Lady—Dark Glasses—Dark Deeds," in Hyatt, *Hoodoo*, 2:1074.

81. "Nahnee—Boss of Algiers," ibid., 2:1372. For other scrubs and material applied to the body to draw trade for hustlin' women, including one using the woman's own urine and sugar, see "A Woman and Her Three Saints," ibid., 2:1414. For a rite that involved pouring bathwater and urine in front of a "spo'tin'" house to achieve similar , see "Madam Lindsey," ibid., 2:1507. "Havana Man" ibid., 2:1789, also describes a wash made from the remnants of a bath used after sex, white pearl buttons, and garlic.

82. "Boy-Girl or Girl-Boy," ibid., 2:1686. She also had rites for keeping stolen money from a customer robbed by a sex worker that involved creating a scrub made from sugar, incense, and milk.

83. "White Candle—White Man, Red Candle—Dark Man, Black Candle—Enemy Man," ibid., 1:801.

84. "Wen the Thunder is Over Mother Kate Francis will March Right Through Hebbin's Doors," Tallant Papers, reel 6, pp. 182–83.

Chapter Five

1. "Marie Comtesse," Tallant Papers, reel 8, pp. 803, 805–7.

2. "Mother Kate Francis," LWP, folder 39.

3. The term *worker* is not to be confused with the term *co-worker* used by Spiritualists, though they are probably not unrelated.

4. William Leach, *Land of Desire: Merchants, Power, and the Rise of a New American Culture* (New York: Pantheon Books, 1993), pp. xiii, 3, 7–9.

5. Hyatt, *Hoodoo*, 4:i.

6. Ibid., 5:iii, 1903.

7. U.S. Bureau of the Census, *Fifteenth Census of the United States: 1930 Unemployment Bulletin, Louisiana, Unemployment Returns by Classes* (Washington, DC: GPO, 1930), pp. 1–22.

8. Hyatt, *Hoodoo*, 3:2295.

9. Ibid., 1:805–8. Most often candles were burned by workers in order to call upon the aid and power of the saints, but candle rites were also employed to influence individuals, usually by burning a candle over a piece of paper on which the name of the intended object of the rite was written.

10. Ibid., 1:787, 832.

11. Ibid., 2:1072, 1143.

12. Ibid., 2:1508.

13. Ibid., 2:1062, 1143, 1231, 1369, 1402, 1467, 1505, 1656, 1769, 1782, 1382; 3:2121, 2127, 2296.

14. Ibid., 1:878; 2:1682, 1368–69; 3:2297.

15. Ibid., 2:1141, 1146.

16. Ibid., 2:1146.

17. Ibid., 2:1381.

18. Ibid., 3:2226.

19. Ibid., 1:862, 863, 864, 869, 873, 878; 2:949, 1374, 1820.

20. Ibid., 2:1770.

21. Ibid., 2:1666–67.

22. Ibid., 2:1277, 1628.

23. Ibid., 1:814.

24. Ibid., 1:874; 2:1666–67, 1652 (Saint Peter).

25. Ibid., 3:2276, 1772, 1680.

26. Jackson Lears, *Fables of Abundance: A Cultural History of Advertising in America* (New York: Basic Books 1994), pp. 44–45. There is a long tradition of Protestant denunciations of gambling in the United States, and the resemblance between stock-market speculation and gambling was a major theme in late nineteenth-century critiques of capitalism.

27. Hyatt, *Hoodoo*, 2:1506. Similarly, an informant identified as the Black Cat Lucky Bone Maker said that because of the possible negative consequences of performing the rite oneself, the making of a black cat bone required the worker to have someone else kill the animal. The Black Cat Lucky Bone Maker thus implied that while he would profit or help a client profit by using the bone, he was unwilling to incur the negative spiritual consequences of extracting it.

28. Ibid., 3:2265.

29. Ibid., 3:1909.

30. Arjun Appadurai, ed., *The Social Life of Things: Commodities in Cultural Perspective* (New York: Cambridge University Press, 1988).

31. Hyatt, *Hoodoo*, 1:794–95.

32. Arnold Hirsch, "Simply a Matter of Black and White: The Transformation of Race and Politics in Twentieth-Century New Orleans," in Hirsch and Logsdon, *Creole New Orleans*, pp. 262–319.

33. Viviana A. Zelizer, "The Social Meaning of Money: 'Special Monies,'" *American Journal of Sociology* 95, no. 2 (September 1989): 359.

34. Leach, *Land of Desire*, p. 6.

35. Hyatt, *Hoodoo*, 1:876; 2:957.

36. Ibid., 2:1374, 1652.

37. Margaret Jane Radin, *Contested Commodities: The Trouble with Trade in Sex, Children, Body Parts, and Other Things* (Cambridge, MA: Harvard University Press, 2001), p. 6.

38. Hyatt, *Hoodoo*, 2:1684.

39. Leach, *Land of Desire*, p. 11.

40. Hyatt, *Hoodoo*, 2:1655.

41. Ibid., 2:1755, 1825, 1635–38. A similar hand was made of John the Conqueror root, devil's shoestrings (another root employed by workers), lodestone, and a silver dime, but rather than pouring whiskey on it, the client was to soak it in the chamber lye, or urine, of the client's wife.

42. Ibid., 2:1755.

43. Ibid., 2:1769. In at least one instance, money in and of itself generated luck for gambling and thus more money: "If yo' wants tuh be lucky an' if yo' wants tuh gamble, git chew a piece of white lodestone an; git chew three silvah dimes. An' don't let chure wife or none of yore friends put dere han's on it, an' don' shoot dat fo' no money, don' fo'git an' spend it, but keep it wit chure silvah money."

44. Ibid., 3:1912, 1073, 1377.

45. Zelizer, "Social Meaning of Money," pp. 346–47.

46. Hyatt, Hoodoo, 2:1063.

47. Ibid., 2:1503–4.

48. Ibid., 1:865, 867. Such boxes are generally used for donations to the church or for collections for charitable causes.

49. Ibid., 2:1140, 1155.

50. Zelizer, "Social Meaning of Money," p. 351.

51. Brian Brazeal, "Blood, Money and Fame: Nagô Magic in the Bahian Backlands" (PhD diss., University of Chicago, 2007); Beatriz Gois Dantas, Nagô Grandma and White Papa: Candomblé and the Creation of Afro-Brazilian Identity (Chapel Hill: University of North Carolina Press, 2009); Karen McCarthey Brown, Mama Lola: A Vodou Priestess in Brooklyn (1991; reprint, Berkeley: University of California Press, 2001).

52. See, for example, "Beats 2 Alleged Hoodoo Women Victim of Spell," New Orleans Times-Democrat, 30 September 1913; and "Italian Woman Uses Broomstick To Break Up Voodoo Powder's Charm," New Orleans Item, 1913.

53. Reagan, When Abortion Was a Crime, pp. 3, 10.

54. "Negro 'Wonder Worker' and Woman 'Doctor' Try to Cure Dr. Newhauser," New Orleans Times-Democrat, 29 January 1913.

55. "Dr. Rockford Lewis Failed . . . Gloom Seems Certain for Voodoosim," interview by McKinney, Tallant Papers, reel 8, pp. 433–36; "Innocence Plea in Voodoo Case," New Orleans Item, 15 September 1938.

56. "Dr. Cat, Peddler of 'Everlasting Life,' Called Swindler," New Orleans Item, 2 July 1914.

57. See charges levied against the mother and daughter Rosalie and Casimani D'Amico, the latter of whom, at fifteen years of age, was the only practitioner in the surveyed cases prosecuted in juvenile court. New Orleans Item and New Orleans Times-Democrat, 30 September 1913.

58. City Ordinances, Book 11, Series C.S. (11714–13464), Ordinance 13347 C.S., Tallant Papers, reel 7, pp. 17–22.

59. See chapter 2.

60. Earl Wright, "Rockford Lewis Victim in Gun Mishap," Louisiana Weekly, 27 August 1960.

61. Father Thomas, interview by McKinney, LWP, folder 591, p. 101.

62. Mother Keller, interview by McKinney, ibid., pp. 82–84 (McKinney described Keller as a "staunch enemy of Mother Leafy Anderson"); interview with Captain Williams, of the Detectives Bureau, ibid., p. 128.

63. Father Thomas, interview by McKinney, ibid., pp. 99, 101, 119–20, 125.

64. "Emperor Haile Selassi Nu-Way Ethiopia Mystic Light Baptist and Spiritual and Kingdom Church," Tallant Papers, reel 9, pp. 128–32.

65. "St. Paul Spiritualist Temple No. 1," ibid., pp. 136–39.

66. Father Thomas, interview by McKinney, LWP, folder 591.

Chapter Six

Note to chapter title: Hyatt, *Hoodoo*, 2:1589.

1. Interview with Lala Hopkins, 10 March 1937, Tallant Papers, reel 8, pp. 349–53.

2. Sanborn Fire Insurance Maps for New Orleans, 1940; interview with Lala Hopkins, March 1937, Tallant Papers, reel 8. Lala's home was located at 2020 Orleans Street, which some years later would become the site of the Lafayette Housing development. This later shift in the neighborhood may add credence to Louisiana Writers' Project researchers' negative assessment of her dwelling and suggest that the rest of this neighborhood was not so affluent either.

3. Interviews with Lala Hopkins, 10 March 1937, Tallant Papers, reel 8, pp. 349–53, and April 1937, ibid., p. 803.

4. Hyatt, *Hoodoo*, 2:1279.

5. "Voodoo Doctor's Equipment," Tallant Papers, reel 8.

6. Zora Neale Hurston, *Mules and Men* (1969; reprint, New York: Negro Universities Press, 1990).

7. "Hoodoo Price List," Tallant Papers, reel 8.

8. "Voodooism Still Thrives in New Orleans," *New Orleans Item-Tribune*, 22 April 1928, magazine section, p. 5.

9. "'Love Philtre' Fake Lands 'Uncle' in Jail," *New Orleans Morning Tribune*, 16 April 1925.

10. Leach, *Land of Desire*, p. 124.

11. Hyatt, *Hoodoo*, 2:1672.

12. Ibid., 2:1286–87.

13. Interview with Alexander Augustin, Tallant Papers, reel 8, p. 754.

14. Ibid.

15. *New Orleans Times-Democrat*, 20 October 1902.

16. Assessments, Orleans Parish, 1md/3ad, blk 478. The value of the property, owned by Robert Mogul, was assessed at twelve hundred dollars, which included the cost of land and of the improvements erected on the property.

17. Hyatt, *Hoodoo*, 2:1642–50.

18. Assessments, Orleans Parish, 2md/7ad, blk 266; Sanborn Fire Insurance Maps for New Orleans, 1940, vol. 2.

19. Interview with Professor Hall, Tallant Papers, reel 8.

20. Ibid.

21. Assessments, Orleans Parish, 2md/7ad, blk 418. It is possible that J. R. Hall was an alias

and that he may have owned some property, though for his claim to be true, he would have had to purchase property under a number of aliases, some of them women's names.

22. U.S. Bureau of the Census, *Sixteenth Census of the United States, 1940: Population and Housing Statistics for Census Tracts* (Washington, DC: GPO, 1941), vol. 3. Of the 12.2 percent, 719 were listed as Negro and only 12 as other.

23. In the *New Orleans Item*, 6 February 1934, Lewis noted: "I didn't go no further than the fourth reader, on account of when I got to the fifth reader they put me back." Presumably the readers were numbered according to grade level.

24. "Interview with Dr. Rockford Lewis Failed . . . Gloom Seems Certain for Voodooism," LWP, folder 44 (pt. 2 of 2).

25. *New Orleans Item*, 6 February 1934, p. 2.

26. Hyatt, *Hoodoo*, 2:1672, 1687.

27. Lears, *Fables of Abundance*, p. 42.

28. Assessments, Orleans Parish, 3md/9th ward, blk 118; Sanborn Fire Insurance Maps for New Orleans, 1940; interview with A. Rockford Lewis, Tallant Papers, reel 8, pp. 303–4.

29. Earl Wright, "Rockford Lewis Victim in Gun Mishap," *Louisiana Weekly*, 27 August 1960.

30. Interview with Lala Hopkins, 10 March 1937, Tallant Papers, reel 8, pp. 349–53.

31. Wright, "Rockford Lewis Victim in Gun Mishap."

32. Jacobs and Kaslow, *Spiritual Churches of New Orleans*, pp. 1–3. Some scholars believe that Anderson transplanted her church model from Chicago, but a number of sociologists maintained that the movement in Chicago originated in the Crescent City.

33. Catherine Dillon manuscript, LWP, folder 91 (folder 1 of 3, pt. 2 of 2), pp. 21, 39–40.

34. Ibid., p. 22.

35. Notes on charter for Mother Anderson's church, ibid., folder 591, p. 1.

36. Charter for Mother Anderson's church, ibid., pp. 2–6.

37. Will of Catherine Jenkins, Tallant Papers, reel 9.

38. Ibid.

39. Sanborn Fire Insurance Maps for New Orleans, 1909, vol. 2; Assessments, Orleans Parish, 1937.

40. Sanborn Fire Insurance Maps for New Orleans, 1940, vol. 1, #18, blk 621; Assessments, Orleans Parish, 1937.

41. While the value of homes on any given block in the city ranged widely, often the largest and most valuable edifices were situated on the corners, especially where they marked large thoroughfares.

42. Sanborn Fire Insurance Maps for New Orleans, 1940, vol. 5, #491, blk 430; Assessments, Orleans Parish, 1937; *New Orleans City Directory, 1936*.

43. Tallant Papers, reel 8, pp. 512–14.

44. Walz v. Tax Commission of the City of New York, 135 U.S. 664 (1970).

45. Hyatt, *Hoodoo*, 2:770.

46. Ibid., 2:954.

47. Sanborn Fire Insurance Maps for New Orleans, 1940; Assessments, Orleans Parish, 1937.

48. Interview with Joseph Lyons, Tallant Papers, reel 9, pp. 128–32.

49. Ibid.

50. Ibid.

51. Ibid.

52. Sanborn Fire Insurance Maps for New Orleans, 1940; Assessments, Orleans Parish, 1937. Frances Cooper was listed at this address a year after the interview with Lyons, suggesting that Lyons had moved on and that his church was not very stable. *New Orleans City Directory, 1938*.

53. To Sullivan's point, however, this adaptation to the norms of organized religion required an economic investment to create the structure and infrastructure around their practices necessary for obtaining this legitimacy, placing an economic burden on some who sought to exercise freedom of religion in the United States.

54. Arrest record on Mother Anderson, LWP, folder 591, pp. 9–10.

55. Sanborn Fire Insurance Maps for New Orleans, 1940; Assessments, Orleans Parish, 1936–37.

56. C. Long, *Spiritual Merchants*, 148–49.

57. "Sherlock Holmes Goes Voodoo Hunting," Tallant Papers, reel 8.

58. Interview with Lala Hopkins, ibid.

59. C. Long, *Spiritual Merchants*. Long has said that the Cracker Jack Drug Store was owned by George A. Thomas and his wife. Though they were not directly listed, it is possible that they owned the Diana Realty then or at some previous or later date.

Epilogue

1. "The Voodoo Gods Say That They Have Struck Down a Mighty Man" and "Gris-gris is Still on William Stander," *Louisiana Weekly*, 9 and 27 January 1940, LWP, folder 44.

BIBLIOGRAPHY

Primary Sources

Manuscript Collections

Christian, Marcus, Collection. Louisiana and Special Collections Department, Earl K. Long Library, University of New Orleans.

Louisiana Writers' Project. Works Progress Administration, Federal Writers' Project. Cammie G. Henry Research Center, Eugene P. Watson Memorial Library, Northwestern State University, Natchitoches, Louisiana.

Tallant, Robert, Papers, 1938–1957. Louisiana Division, New Orleans Public Library.

Government Documents

Assessments, Orleans Parish. Bureau of Governmental Research, City Archives, New Orleans Public Library.

Sanborn Fire Insurance Maps for New Orleans, 1885–1940.

Newspapers

Louisiana Weekly (1929–40)
New Orleans Daily Picayune (1881–95)
New Orleans Democrat (1881)
New Orleans Item (1904–47)
New Orleans States (1913)
New Orleans Times-Democrat (1902–30)
New Orleans Times-Picayune (1914–38)

Published Primary Sources

Hyatt, Harry Middleton. *Hoodoo—Conjuration—Witchcraft—Rootwork*. Memoirs of the Alma Egan Hyatt Foundation. 5 vols. Hannibal, MO: Western, 1970.

New Orleans (Orleans Parish, LA) City Directory. Dallas: R. L. Polk, 1920–. New Orleans Public Library.

Secondary Sources

Anderson, Benedict. *Imagined Communities: Reflections on the Origin and Spread of Nationalism*. London: Verso, 1983.

Anderson, Jeffrey E. *Conjure in African American Society*. Baton Rouge: Louisiana State University Press, 2007.

Anderson, R. Bentley. *Black, White, and Catholic: New Orleans Interracialism, 1947–1956*. Nashville: Vanderbilt University Press, 2005.

Anthony, Arthe Agnes. "The Negro Creole Community in New Orleans, 1880–1920: An Oral History." PhD diss., University of California, Irvine, 1978.

Appadurai, Arjun, ed. *The Social Life of Things: Commodities in Cultural Perspective*. New York: Cambridge University Press, 1986.

Arnesen, Eric. *Waterfront Workers of New Orleans: Race, Class, and Politics, 1863–1923*. New York: Oxford University Press, 1991.

Asad, Talal. *Genealogies of Religion: Discipline and Reasons of Power in Christianity and Islam*. Baltimore: Johns Hopkins University Press, 1993.

Asbury, Herbert. *The French Quarter: An Informal History of the New Orleans Underworld*. New York: Knopf, 1936.

Baer, Hans A. *The Black Spiritual Movement: A Religious Response to Racism*. Knoxville: University of Tennessee Press, 1984.

Bell, Caryn Cossé. *Revolution, Romanticism, and the Afro-Creole Protest Tradition in Louisiana, 1718–1868*. Baton Rouge: Louisiana State University Press, 1997.

Bennett, James B. *Religion and the Rise of Jim Crow in New Orleans*. Princeton, NJ: Princeton University Press, 2005.

Borges, Dain. "Healing Mischief: Witchcraft in Brazilian Law and Literature, 1890–1922." In *Crime and Punishment in Latin America*, edited by Ricardo D. Salvatore, Carlos Aguirre, and Gilbert M. Joseph. Durham, NC: Duke University Press, 2001.

Brazeal, Brian. "Blood, Money and Fame: Nagô Magic in the Bahian Backlands." PhD diss., University of Chicago, 2007.

Brown, David H. *Santeria Enthroned: Art, Ritual, and Innovation in an Afro-Cuban Religion*. Chicago: University of Chicago Press, 2003.

Brown, Karen McCarthey. *Mama Lola: A Vodou Priestess in Brooklyn.* 1991. Reprint. Berkeley: University of California Press, 2001.

Chireau, Yvonne P. *Black Magic: Religion and the African American Conjuring Tradition.* Berkeley: University of California Press, 2003.

Comaroff, Jean, and John L. Comaroff. "Occult Economies and the Violence of Abstraction: Notes from the South African Postcolony." *American Ethnologist* 26, no. 2 (May 1999): 279–303.

Dantas, Beatriz Gois. *Nagô Grandma and White Papa: Candomblé and the Creation of Afro-Brazilian Identity.* Chapel Hill: University of North Carolina Press, 2009.

Desdunes, Rodolphe Lucien. *Our People and Our History: A Tribute to the Creole People of Color in Memory of the Great Men They Have Given Us and of the Good Works They Have Accomplished.* Translated and edited by Sister Dorothea Olga McCants. Baton Rouge: Louisiana State University Press, 1973.

Desmangles, Leslie G. *Faces of the Gods: Vodou and Roman Catholicism in Haiti.* Chapel Hill: University of North Carolina Press, 1992.

Doukas, Dimitra. *Worked Over: The Corporate Sabotage of an American Community.* Ithaca, NY: Cornell University Press, 2003.

Dubois, Laurent. *Avengers of the New World: The Story of the Haitian Revolution.* Cambridge, MA: Belknap Press of Harvard University Press, 2004.

———. *A Colony of Citizens: Revolution and Slave Emancipation in the French Caribbean, 1787–1804.* Chapel Hill: University of North Carolina Press, 2004.

Dundes, Alan. *Mother Wit from the Laughing Barrel: Readings in the Interpretation of Afro-American Folklore.* Jackson: University Press of Mississippi, 1990.

Evans, Curtis. *The Burden of Black Religion.* New York: Oxford University Press, 2008.

Fandrich, Ina J. *The Mysterious Voodoo Queen, Marie Laveaux: A Study of Powerful Female Leadership in Nineteenth Century New Orleans.* New York: Routledge, 2005.

Fick, Carolyn E. *The Making of Haiti: The Saint Domingue Revolution from Below.* Knoxville: University of Tennessee Press, 1990.

Geggus, David. "Marronage, Voodoo, and the Saint Domingue Slave Revolt of 1791." *Proceedings of the Annual Meeting of the French Colonial Historical Society* 15 (1992): 22–35.

Genovese, Eugene D. *Roll, Jordan, Roll: The World the Slaves Made.* New York: Pantheon Books, 1974.

Guillory, Monique. "Some Enchanted Evening on the Auction Block: The Cultural Legacy of the New Orleans Quadroon Balls." PhD diss., New York University, 1999.

Hahn, Steven. *A Nation Under Our Feet: Black Political Struggles in the Rural South, From Slavery to the Great Migration.* Cambridge, MA: Belknap Press of Harvard University Press, 2003.

Harding, Rachel E. *A Refuge in Thunder: Candomblé and Alternative Spaces of Blackness.* Bloomington: Indiana University Press, 2000.

Hirsch, Arnold. "Simply a Matter of Black and White: The Transformation of Race and Politics in Twentieth-Century New Orleans." In Hirsch and Logsdon, 262–319.

Hirsch, Arnold, and Joseph Logsdon, eds. *Creole New Orleans: Race and Americanization.* Baton Rouge: Louisiana State University Press, 1992.

Holbraad, Martin. "Religious 'Speculation': The Rise of Ifá Cults and Consumption in Post-Soviet Cuba." *Journal of Latin American Studies* 36, no. 4 (November 2004): 643–63.

Holloway, Joseph. *Africanisms in American Culture.* Bloomington: Indiana University Press, 1990.

Holt, Thomas C. *The Problem of Freedom: Race, Labor, and Politics in Jamaica and Britain, 1832–1938.* Baltimore: Johns Hopkins University Press, 1992.

Hurston, Zora Neale. "Hoodoo in America." *Journal of American Folklore* 44, no. 174 (October–December 1931): 317–417.

———. *Mules and Men.* 1969. Reprint. New York: Harper Perennial, 1990.

Jacobs, Claude F., and Andrew J. Kaslow. *The Spiritual Churches of New Orleans: Origins, Beliefs, and Rituals of an African American Religion.* Knoxville: University of Tennessee Press, 2001.

Johnson, Jerah. *Congo Square in New Orleans.* New Orleans: Louisiana Landmarks Society, 1995.

Kein, Sybil, ed. *Creole: The History and Legacy of Louisiana's Free People of Color.* Baton Rouge: Louisiana State University Press, 2000.

Laguerre, Michel S. *Voodoo and Politics in Haiti.* New York: St. Martin's, 1989.

Leach, William. *Land of Desire: Merchants, Power, and the Rise of a New American Culture.* New York: Pantheon Books, 1993.

Lears, Jackson. *Fables of Abundance: A Cultural History of Advertising in America.* New York: Basic Books, 1994.

Long, Alecia. *The Great Southern Babylon: Sex, Race, and Respectability in New Orleans, 1865–1920.* Baton Rouge: Louisiana State University Press, 2004.

Long, Carolyn Morrow. *A New Orleans Voudou Priestess: The Legend and Reality of Marie Laveau.* Gainesville: University Press of Florida, 2006.

———. *Spiritual Merchants: Religion, Magic and Commerce.* Knoxville: University of Tennessee Press, 2001.

Matory, James Lorand. *Black Atlantic Religion: Tradition, Transnationalism, and Matriarchy in the Afro-Brazilian Candomblé.* Princeton, NJ: Princeton University Press, 2005.

Metraux, Alfred. *Voodoo in Haiti.* Translated by Hugo Charteris. New York: Shocken Books, 1972.

Palmié, Stephan. "Conventionalization, Distortion and Plagiarism in the Historiography of Afro-Caribbean Religion in New Orleans." In *Creoles and Cajuns,* edited by W. Binder. Frankfurt: Peter Lang, 1998.

———. "Fascinans or Tremendum? Permutations of the State, the Body, and the Divine in Late-Twentieth-Century Havana." *New West Indian Guide / Nieuwe West-Indische Gids* 78, nos. 3–4 (2004): 229–68.

———. "Which Center, Whose Margin? Notes Towards an Archaeology of U.S. Supreme Court Case 91-948." In *Inside and Outside the Law,* edited by O. Harris, 184–209. London: Routledge, 1993.

———. *Wizards and Scientists: Explorations in Afro-Cuban Modernity and Tradition.* Durham, NC: Duke University Press, 2002.

Pedraza, Teresita. "'This Too Shall Pass': The Resistance and Endurance of Religion in Cuba." *Cuban Studies* 28 (1998): 16–39.

Porteous, Laura. "The Gri-Gri Case: A Criminal Trial in Louisiana during the Spanish Regime, 1773." *Louisiana Historical Quarterly* 17 (1934): 48–63.

Puckett, Newbell Niles. *Folk Beliefs of the Southern Negro.* New York: Negro Universities Press, 1926.

Raboteau, Albert J. *Slave Religion: The "Invisible Institution" in the Antebellum South.* New York: Oxford University Press, 1978.

Radin, Margaret Jane. *Contested Commodities: The Trouble with Trade in Sex, Children, Body Parts, and Other Things.* Cambridge, MA: Harvard University Press, 1996.

Reagan, Leslie J. *When Abortion Was a Crime: Women, Medicine, and Law in the United States, 1867–1973.* Berkeley: University of California Press, 1998.

Reed, Germaine A. "Race Legislation in Louisiana, 1864–1920." *Louisiana History: The Journal of the Louisiana Historical Association* 6, no. 4 (Autumn 1965): 379–92.

Renda, Mary A. *Taking Haiti: Military Occupation and the Culture of U.S. Imperialism, 1915–1940.* Chapel Hill: University of North Carolina Press, 2001.

Sahlins, Marshall. *Culture and Practical Reason.* Chicago: University of Chicago Press, 1976.

Saxon, Lyle, ed. *Gumbo Ya-Ya: A Collection of Louisiana Folk Tales.* Boston: Riverside, 1945.

Scott, Rebecca J. *Degrees of Freedom: Louisiana and Cuba after Slavery.* Cambridge, MA: Belknap Press of Harvard University Press, 2005.

Smith, Jonathan Z. *Relating Religion: Essays in the Study of Religion.* Chicago: University of Chicago Press, 2004.

Smith, Theophus H. *Conjuring Culture: Biblical Formations of Black America.* New York: Oxford University Press, 1994.

Souther, Mark J. *New Orleans on Parade: Tourism and the Transformation of the Crescent City.* Baton Rouge: Louisiana State University Press, 2006.

Stanonis, Anthony J. *Creating the Big Easy: New Orleans and the Emergence of Modern Tourism, 1918–1945.* Athens: University of Georgia Press, 2006.

Sullivan, Winnifred Faller. *The Impossibility of Religious Freedom.* Princeton, NJ: Princeton University Press, 2005.

Tallant, Robert. *Voodoo in New Orleans*. New York: Macmillan, 1946.

Touchstone, Blake. "Voodoo in New Orleans." *Louisiana History: The Journal of the Louisiana Historical Association* 13, no. 4 (Autumn 1972): 371–86.

Tregle, Joseph G., Jr. "Creoles and Americans." In Hirsch and Logsdon, *Creole New Orleans*.

Wall, Bennet H., ed. *Louisiana: A History*. Wheeling, IL: Harlan Davidson, 2002.

Ward, Martha. *Voodoo Queen: The Spirited Lives of Marie Laveau*. Jackson: University Press of Mississippi, 2004.

Webb, Julie Yvonne. "Louisiana Voodoo and Superstition Related to Health." *HSMHA Health Reports* 86, no. 4 (April 1971): 291–301.

Wilmore, Gayraud S. *Black Religion and Black Radicalism: An Interpretation of the Religious History of Afro-American People*. Maryknoll, NY: Orbis Books, 1998.

Wirtz, Kristina. "Santeria in Cuban National Consciousness." *Journal of Latin American Anthropology* 9, no. 2 (2004): 409–38.

Worthy, Barbara Ann. *Blacks in New Orleans from the Great Depression to the Civil Rights Movement, 1930–1960*. New Orleans: Southern University at New Orleans, Center for African and African American Studies, 1994.

Yaeger, Patricia. *The Geography of Identity*. Ann Arbor: University of Michigan Press, 1996.

Zelizer, Viviana A. "The Social Meaning of Money: 'Special Monies.'" *American Journal of Sociology* 95, no. 2 (September 1989): 342–77.

Zumwalt, Rosemary Levy. *American Folklore Scholarship: A Dialogue of Dissent*. Bloomington: Indiana University Press, 1988.

INDEX